Another Development

Another Development

Participation, Empowerment and Well-being in Rural India

Runa Sarkar
Anup Sinha

Routledge
Taylor & Francis Group

LONDON AND NEW YORK

First published 2015
by Routledge

2 Park Square, Milton Park, Abingdon, Oxfordshire OX14 4RN
711 Third Avenue, New York, NY 10017

Routledge is an imprint of the Taylor & Francis Group, an informa business

First issued in paperback 2017

Typeset by
Shine Graphics
A-8/249 East Gokalpuri, Amar Colony
Delhi 110 094

British Library Cataloguing-in-Publication Data
A catalogue record of this book is available from the British Library

ISBN 978-1-138-82241-2 (hbk)
ISBN 978-0-8153-7318-6 (pbk)

Contents

Plates   vii
Maps   ix
Tables and Figures   x
Abbreviations   xi
Glossary   xiv
Preface   xix
Acknowledgements   xxiii

1. Development as Transformation   1
2. Development as Intervention   16

I. Water and Well-being

3. Channelling Prosperity and Progress   41
4. The Power of Politics: Self-reliance Denied   61
5. Stillness and Change: Lives and Landscapes   80

II. Empowerment and Entrepreneurship

6. Control and Creation: The Worlds of Two Women   105
7. Between the Moneylender and the Deep Blue Sea:
    Stories from Fishing Communities in Kerala   127
8. Packaging Heritage to Unpack Ambitions:
    Himalayan Homestays   147

III. People and Participation

9. Natural Resource Management: The Limits
    to Conservation   173
10. Creating Big Organisations with Small Farmers   192

11. Choosing to Change   214

12. Women, Water and Green Energy   236

13. Sometime in the Future, in Someplace Else:
     Another Development   257

Bibliography   277
About the Authors   284
Index   285

Plates

3.1   Covered Drainage System in the Streets of Nidhal 'Village'   48

3.2   Meeting the VWC at the Community Hall of the
Cooperative Building, Nidhal   49

3.3   The Ramoshi Settlement at Nidhal: A Stark Contrast
to the Nirmal Gram   58

4.1   Tree Plantations at Bhalki Village   65

4.2   The Watershed Project Ensures Assured Water Supply   66

5.1   Meeting the Beneficiaries at Piparna   87

5.2   Stall-feeding of Sirohi Goats at Piparna   89

5.3   Meticulously Constructed Watershed Structures
in the Rocky Terrain of Padla   94

6.1   Milk-packaging Machine at Jyoti's Gau Amrit
Processing Unit: The Promise of Overtaking Amul   110

6.2   Jyoti with Representatives from her Federation of SHGs   116

6.3   Weaving of *Galeys* at Yansenpa's Residence   119

7.1   Fishing Boats: How Far Will They Have to Go
for the Next Catch?   130

7.2   Matsya Samrudhi: A Government Initiative to
Add Value to Fishing Produce   139

7.3   Cage Fishing as a Supplement to Livelihood Activities   142

8.1   Code of Conduct for Ecotourists   151

8.2   A Well-prepared Bed and Clean Monogrammed Linen
for Ecotourists   154

8.3   Traditional Lepcha House, Lingee–Payong:
One of the Tourist Attractions   166

9.1   Cattle Wealth, Insured to Smoothen Income Flows   177

9.2   A Signature Move towards Empowerment   179

9.3   Do They See Another Future? The Eyes Say it All.   183

10.1   Vasundhara Processing and Packaging Unit   198
10.2   Cashew Trees with Watershed Bunding Structures   207
10.3   Standing Committee Meeting of all Cooperative
       Representatives at Karjan   209

11.1   The New Government Grain Procurement Centre
       at Kapartunga   220
11.2   List of Farm Implements and their Rental Rates
       at the Krishi Yantra Bank   223
11.3   Tailoring Enterprise at Barpani   228

12.1   The Future Operators of the Hydel Power Plant
       at Vetamamidi   242
12.2   Turbine Room under the Control Room
       at the Hydel Power Station   243

Maps

3.1 Satara District in Maharashtra 42

4.1 Bardhaman District in West Bengal 62

5.1 Udaipur District in Rajasthan 81

6.1 Solan District in Himachal Pradesh 107
6.2 Lower Subansiri District in Arunachal Pradesh 118

7.1 Alappuzha District in Kerala 128

8.1 East and South Sikkim Districts 150

9.1 Chittoor District in Andhra Pradesh 174

10.1 Valsad District in Gujarat 193

11.1 Jashpur and Raigarh Districts in Chhattisgarh 215

12.1 East Godavari District in Andhra Pradesh 239

Tables and Figures

Tables

4.1 Targeted and Actual Outcomes of the Watershed Project
at Bhalki   67

10.1 Schematic of the Structure of VAPCOL   197

12.1 Revenue Generated from MHPP at Vetamamidi
and its Distribution   246

Figures

2.1 An Exploratory Framework for Analysis   20

6.1 The Activity Net of Jyoti's SHGs   115

Abbreviations

AGM	Assistant General Manager
AKUCS	Arun Kutir Udyog Cooperative Society
APTRANSCO	Andhra Pradesh Power Transmission Company
APTRIPCO	Andhra Pradesh Tribal Power Company Limited
BDO	Block Development Officer
BJP	Bharatiya Janata Party
BJUC	Bhalki Jalbivajika Unnayan Committee
BPL	below poverty line
BSF	Border Security Force
BSNL	Bharat Sanchar Nigam Limited
CAPA	Community Action for Poverty Alleviation
CAPART	Council for Advancement of People's Action and Rural Technology
CBOs	community-based organisations
CBP	Capacity Building Phase
CPI(M)	Communist Party of India (Marxist)
CPR	Common Property Resources
CSR	corporate social responsibility
DC	District Collector
DDM	District Development Manager
DHRUVA	Dharampur Utthan Vahini
DONER	Department of North East Region (DONER). All the States in the North Eastern Region are Special Category States whose Development Plans are centrally financed on the basis of 90 per cent grant and 10 per cent loan.
DRDA	District Rural Development Authority
DWMA	District Water Management Authority
ECOSS	Ecotourism and Conservation Society of Sikkim
EMI	equal monthly installment
FES	Foundation for Ecological Security
FIP	Final Implementation Phase

GSGSK	Gandhi Smaraka Grama Seva Kendram
GTZ	German Technical Cooperation
GVM	Gram Vikas Mandal
HDI	Human Development Index
HUL	Hindustan Unilever Limited
ICDS	Integrated Child Development Services
IGWDP	Indo-German Watershed Development Programme
IIMC	Indian Institute of Management Calcutta
ITDA	Integrated Tribal Development Agency
JFM	joint forest management
JLG	Joint Liability Group
JMKS	Jagriti Mahila Kisan Samiti
KCC	Kisan Credit Card
KEEP	Khedi Eco-tourism and Eco-development Promotion Society
KfW	German Development Bank
KVIC	Khadi and Village Industries Commission
LTDC	Lingee Tourism Development Cell
MASS	Mitra Association for Social Service
MGNREGA	Mahatma Gandhi National Rural Employment Guarantee Act
MHPPs	mini hydel power plants
MLA	Member of the Legislative Assembly
MNREs	Ministry of Non-conventional and Renewable Energy sources
MoU	memorandum of understanding
MSS	Mekhala Sasraya Samithi
NABARD	National Bank for Agriculture and Rural Development
NEDCAP	Non-conventional Energy Development Corporation of Andhra Pradesh
NGO	non-governmental organisation
NRAA	National Rainfed Area Authority
NREGA	National Rural Employment Guarantee Act
NRV	non-resident villager
NTFP	non-timber forest products
OBCs	Other Backward Classes

PFA	Programme Facilitation Agency
PHC	primary health centre
PIA	Programme Implementation Agency
PMU	Project Management Unit
PMGSY	Pradhan Mantri Gram Sadak Yojana
PPPs	public-private partnerships
PRA	Participatory Rural Appraisal
PRI	Panchayati Raj Institution
PWD	Public Works Department
RBI	Reserve Bank of India
RIDF	Rural Infrastructure Development Fund
RSS	Raigarh Sahyog Samiti
SC	Scheduled Caste
SFURTI	Scheme of Fund for Regeneration of Traditional Industries
SHG	self-help group
SHPI	Self Help Promoting Institute
SP	Sarpanch Pati
ST	Scheduled Tribe
TDP	Tribal Development Programme
TRICOR	Andhra Pradesh Scheduled Tribes Cooperative Finance Corporation Limited
UNDP	United Nations Development Programme
UNESCO	United Nations Educational, Scientific and Cultural Organization
UPNRM	Umbrella Project for Natural Resource Management
VAPCOL	Valsad Agricultural Producers Company Limited
VDC	Village Development Committee
VDP	Village Development Programme
VMC	Village Management Committee
VWC	Village Watershed Committee
WASMO	Water and Sanitation Management Organisation
WOTR	Water Organisation Trust
YIP	Yield Improvement Programme
YSS	Yojana Sasray Samiti

Glossary

aakaal	Bad times, through drought and famines
aarthikdaan	Monetary donation
acre, hectare, bigha (measures of land)	In West Bengal, the bigha was standardised under British colonial rule at 1,600 square yards (0.1338 hectare or 0.3306 acre); this is often interpreted as being 1/3 acre (it is precisely 40/121 acre). In metric units, a bigha is hence 1,333 square metres (1 acre = 0.4 hectare). However, the bigha measure varies widely across India.
adivasi	Tribals
amla	Type of fruit
anganwadi	Crèche for taking care of infants and children
angrezi	English
Apatani	A scheduled tribe in Arunachal Pradesh
arbi	A kind of tuber
asabhya	Uncivilised
Ayojana Samiti	Organising association
ayurvedic	Traditional form of herbal medicine
azolla	A nutritional supplement for cows
baalwaan	Crèche for taking care of infants
badhaigiri	Carpentry
bandhej	Type of tie-dye practiced mainly in Rajasthan and Gujarat
banjar	Wasteland
bari	House
Bhagaban	God
bhaluk	Bear (animal)
bicholiyas	Moneylenders and business community
chana	Gram, a leguminous grain

charagah	Grazing commons
charagah samitis	Committees to look after common grazing land
charaibandi	Ban on grazing of animals
Chenchu	A scheduled tribe in Andhra Pradesh
chiraunji	A variety of Indian spice
chullas	Clay ovens
CM Sahab ka Doodh	Milk for the Chief Minister
Daktarbabu	A medical practitioner
dalals	Middlemen
Dashami	A festival date
Dev bhumi	Land of the Gods
Diwali	A festival of lights
Doodh Ganga	Name of a scheme to promote milk production
dupatta	Long multipurpose scarf, as part of a woman's clothing
Dussehra	A festival
Erugula	A scheduled tribe in Andhra Pradesh
fauji	Of the armed forces
galeys	A traditional skirt worn by women in Arunachal Pradesh
ganja	Cannabis or marijuana
GauAmrit	Ambrosia from the cow
ghar ke mukhia	Head of the household
ghee	Clarified butter
ghunghat	Veil or headscarf to cover one's head and face
Gram Swachata Abhiyan	Village cleanliness drive
Gram Unnayan Daptar	Village development department
Gram Vikas Mandals	Village development councils
Gram Vikas Samiti	Village development committee
gram	Village
haats	Village markets
haldi	Turmeric
handia	A country liquor, usually made from rice
Holi	A festival of colours

Indira Awas Yojana	A government scheme for low-cost housing
Jan Samasya Nivaran Shivir	Public problems resolution committee
jangalkatabandi	Ban on felling forest trees
Kaji para	Refers to a part of a village inhabited by Muslims
kantha	A light quilt or covering
kapor porey	Wears clothes
karimeem	A fish famous in Kerala, known for its taste
karyakartas	Workers
khaatichaas	Buttermilk
kharif	The main crop harvested in autumn
kheti	Farms
kirana	Small neighbourhood shop selling a variety of goods
kisan	Farmer
Koidara	A Scheduled Tribe in Andhra Pradesh
Kokna	A Scheduled Tribe in Gujarat
Kolcha	A Scheduled Tribe in Gujarat
krishi yantra	Agricultural implements
Kurkure	A kind of popular branded savoury snack
lac	The scarlet resinous secretion of an insect
lakeer ka fakeer	Slave to the written rule
Lepchas	A Scheduled Tribe in Sikkim
machan	A platform
mahajans	Traditional moneylenders
Mahila Mandal	Women's association
mahua	A local intoxicating drink made from the fruit of the mahua tree
mazdoori	Wages
mazdoors	Workers
meetaneen	Midwives
mela	A fair or carnival
mugh	A kind of lentil or daal
nagli	An inferior cereal rich in fibres
nashabandi	Ban on intoxicants

nigoo	An inferior cereal rich in fibres
nirmal gaon	Clean village
nullahs	Large gutters, could be carrying waste
paanlote	Watershed
pan thelakiya	Paan (betel leaf) shop
Panchayat	Constitutionally elected body at the village level
paneer	Cottage cheese
patta	Landownership document
peena	To drink
peetna	To beat (physically)
pradhan	Chief
pucca	Houses made from bricks and cement
raajmistry	A mason
rabi	Winter crop
ragi	Millet
Ramoshis	A Scheduled Tribe in Maharashtra
ramro laagchho	I am enjoying it
ratanjyot	Kind of edible fruit
sabha	Council
sachiv	Secretary
Sahbhagi Vikas Yojana	Cooperative Development Plan
sahukars	Moneylenders
sakhimandals	Friends associations, essentially a form of a self-help group
samiti	Committee or council
samudayik bhavan	Community hall
samudayik jagrukta	Overall consciousness
santulit paryavaran	balanced environment
sapota	Type of fruit
sarpanchpati	Husband of the head of the village
sarpanch	Head of the village panchayat
Satipatis	A clan of people who decline any form of governmental assistance
seba dharma	The religion of service
Section 25 Company	A non-profit organisation, registered under the Companies Act 1956. The company is formed as a limited company

	for promoting commerce, art, science, religion, charity or any other useful object; it can earn profits and expand its operations, but it cannot pay any dividends to its members.
sethsahukars	Moneylenders and business community
shashakgan	Rulers or administrators
Shiv Ratri	A festival
shramdaan	Voluntary unpaid labour
Sirohi	A breed of goat
sitafal	A kind of edible fruit
subabul	A tree that grows in dry and arid areas
Sugali	A Scheduled Tribe in Andhra Pradesh
Suraj mukhi sanstha	A self-help group named Sunflower
tehsil/taluka	Administrative unit comprising more than one village
tarun mandals	Youth forums
therakan	The traditional usurious moneylender in Kerala
urad	A kind of lentil or daal
vadapaos	A traditional fast food popular in western India
Vyasan Mukti	Freedom from addiction
wadi	Small fruit orchard
wadiwalas	Owners of wadis
Warli	A Scheduled Tribe in Gujarat
weltanschauung	World view
Yannadi	A Scheduled Tribe in Andhra Pradesh
yog shivir	A camp for yoga
Yojana	Plan

Preface

India is well known for its diversity, across people and across geographies. Embedded in this diversity are inequalities that separate a world of the 'haves' from a world of the 'have-nots'. Efforts to bring the latter into the world of the 'haves' are being made continuously by designing a variety of development projects: some innovative, some quite mundane. These projects are supposed to offer the 'have-nots' opportunities to reach, and be included in, the world of the 'haves'. Often, we as academics get involved with the design, implementation or evaluation of these projects. What really is the impact of such projects? Do they really offer pathways to exit poverty, deprivation or economic insecurity? What implications do these projects have on the people around them, or on the natural environment? Are the stories coming out of these projects consistent with India's growth story in a globalised world? With greater emphasis on corporate social responsibility (CSR) by the corporate world, such projects are only expected to increase. Is there an ideal design for such projects? Is there a magic formula that could include India's poor into the world of the rich? These were some of the questions that were on our minds when we commenced our study on micro-interventions which has led to this book.

We found that, in general, the micro-interventions varied from place to place but all were essentially aimed at one village or a block of villages to empower the people to use market mechanisms to improve their lot. It is also becoming quite common for large private corporations to promote micro-interventions that increase economic activities. For instance, the interventions of ITC and Hindustan Unilever Limited (HUL) are designed as integral parts of their business strategy, and are quite well known in this regard. This was different from the large public works programmes during the initial decades of planning in India. However, it is not to deny the complete eclipse of big ticket projects across the entire nation. The Mahatma Gandhi National Rural Employment Guarantee Act (MGNREGA) is one such scheme that guarantees 100 days of employment at a specified wage.

We wanted to study these interventions not as a set of projects that failed or succeeded in terms of some quantitative targets of asset creation or incomes, but rather as a process that entailed people's participation and affected their aspirations and their apprehensions. What did these processes and their outcomes imply for economic development and the bigger process of transformation? We looked at some of the micro stories of villages and people, and narrate them to a wide and diverse set of readers through this book.

We found that the National Bank for Agriculture and Rural Development (NABARD) was one organisation that had operations (and were involved in development activities) in every single district of India. This, we believed, would give us the widest variety of stories, and the most extensive locations, to choose from. The funds for the project were obtained through a research grant from the Indian Institute of Management Calcutta (IIMC). When we approached NABARD they immediately agreed to help us in identifying locations, accessing information, as well as in connecting to the programme implementation agency (usually a non-governmental organisation or NGO) and through them to the participants and beneficiaries.

The purpose was *not to evaluate* NABARD's projects. Indeed, NABARD's involvement varied from project to project. NABARD seldom implements such projects on its own. It is essentially a facilitator that catalyses many of these projects by bringing together an idea, an implementing agency, banks, and people. Many of NABARD's projects are also not unique in the sense that similar projects are carried out by government agencies, private corporations and NGOs in other parts of India.

To ensure that we were not missing out on any significantly different schemes of intervention that aim to diversify rural livelihoods and incomes, we did one field study of a project where NABARD was not involved at all. This additional field study, essentially for the sake of control, was undertaken (but not reported as a case in this book) in the Padamati-1 Watershed in Jaipalguri district of West Bengal. The watershed was financed by the government of West Bengal. The design was similar to the ones we studied. The participation of the local people, through self-help groups (SHGs), was an essential component. The increased availability of water would be used as a focal point to promote new economic activities, such as becoming a seed village, and improve the productivity of existing ones. Finally, at the completion of the project, the subsequent management of the assets created and the sustaining of opportunities identified would be the responsibility of the beneficiaries themselves. We are also aware of studies that talk about such interventions to promote and create rural livelihood opportunities at the aggregate level. For instance, the *India Rural Development Report 2012–2013* (IDFC 2013) documents the features of similar kinds of projects across India, aggregated at the state level.

The details of the projects we studied obviously varied from context to context. The grants-to-loans proportion of the funding pattern also varied, as did the livelihood opportunities identified. We saw such opportunities vary from rearing cattle, to horticulture, from seed breeding to plantation forestry. Since our focus was on people-based issues of well-being, empowerment and participation, these variations did not make any material difference to our study. Studying more interventions, with or without the involvement of NABARD, would definitely add to the depth and richness of our descriptions, but would be unlikely to change the conclusions reached.

There were some things of significance that we could not do. First, we did not touch upon the complex history and culture of each region we visited. A deeper study of the context of the interventions was not made. For instance, we did not probe into how local power structures emerged in these villages. The vastness of India was evident in the rich heterogeneity of people and places. Development experiences were also different in different locations, as have been the outcomes of those experiences. Second, in some places the market mechanism had brought rural people into the ambit of the expansion of modern industry, and many struggles and resistances around land and the environment had resulted. These encounters of big industry with small people, which are significant stories in themselves, were not the focus of our book. Instead, we looked at smaller things and less organised people.

We have masked the names of all individuals we talked to, to protect their identity. However, names of places and the implementing agencies are real. Wherever we went we made it clear to people that we were writing a book about development and took their permission to use what they told us. We also told them that we would not reveal their identity. We have avoided naming NABARD officials too who might have been posted in that location at that period of time.

What struck us was the efficiency with which officers of NABARD responded to our needs, and the extent of their knowledge. The officers collectively carry a wealth of experience that no other development agency in India is likely to possess. Information about ground conditions and expertise about the local dynamics and problems of project management would be expected from an organisation with such extensive roots in rural India. But the depth of knowledge and the commitment of the staff in the fields were totally unexpected. Finally, what we realised in our travels across India, wherever we went, and whosoever we talked to (the villagers and the NGO personnel), was that everyone knew the district development manager (DDM) of NABARD who, without fail, commanded considerable respect. This respect was undoubtedly founded on the learning and the knowledgeableness of the DDM, but above everything else it was based on the honesty and integrity of the NABARD personnel. On numerous occasions, we heard many villagers wish that government officials would be more like the NABARD people!

The case studies were undertaken during 2010 and 2011. The stories from the field are narrated in Chapters 3 to 12 in this book. Chapters 1 and 2 provide a framework for and theoretical underpinning of the study. In Chapter 13 we discuss some of our conclusions. During the field visits both of us had occasion to travel and spend long days with people whom we would, in the normal course of our middle-class academic existence, have never met. The experiencing of the vastness of India was both enriching and enlightening. We found different kinds of people in different places, but there were similarities too — the sheer energy to live and to dream about a future that was better, was something that touched us deeply. We have no pretensions that our narratives will influence policies and processes. However, both of us fervently hope that some readers will be stimulated to think more about the bottom of society's pyramid — not as a place where one could possibly sell more goods and services, but rather as a space where a million dreams are born, yet very few ever get fulfilled.

Acknowledgements

The idea of writing this book goes back to 2009 when we, along with another colleague, Bhaskar Chakraborty, discussed the possibility of studying micro-interventions in rural India, with the objective of understanding the human side of development, not always revealed by economists' quantitative analyses. We decided to take the help of the National Bank for Agriculture and Rural Development (NABARD) in this regard. However, we approached our own institution for funding the research so as to retain academic independence. We are thankful to the Indian Institute of Management Calcutta (IIMC) for providing us a research grant. Two other colleagues, Biswatosh Saha and Partha Sarathi Das Gupta, helped us on several occasions during the research proposal and refereeing stages. Later, they also patiently dealt with our numerous requests to extend the project's deadline. Comments from an anonymous referee when the proposal was being reviewed helped us considerably to focus on the project details and forced us to structure our thoughts and think a little deeper. We are grateful to the referee. Bhaskar Chakraborty actively participated during the conception, design and initial phases of the research project. Although he was unable to continue with the project, we deeply acknowledge his contributions. Several of the ideas coming forth in this book may have emanated from the rich discussions the three of us had.

After the project was approved by IIMC and we approached NABARD, the then chairman, U. Sarangi, the managing director, K. G. Karmakar, and the executive director, S. K. Mitra, promised to extend all the help we would need. Subsequently, the then chairman, P. Bakshi, continued to provide support and encouragement. C. K. Gopalakrishnan, D. Deshpande and S. Gupta at the head office helped us identify a set of suitable projects. Their help was invaluable in making the field visits possible. In the field, the district development managers (DDMs) and other senior officers of the regional office provided crucial logistic support and often acted as our interpreters. We would especially like to thank P. Mondal, R. Pramanik, A. Lama, R. S. Reddy, U. Garg, A. Ratnoo, V. Mohanan, M. P. Pahadsingh, B. K. Singhal, M. Sarkar, Vai Phai, D. Ravindra, G. K. Salvekar,

S. Sharma, K. S. S. Somayajulu, S. Padmanabhan, and N. C. Bhowal of NABARD. We are also thankful to the current chairman, H. K. Bhanwala, and B. S. Suran.

Besides, representatives of the project implementation agencies and the villagers themselves patiently spent an enormous amount of time with us. They are who the book is about and it would not have been possible without their involvement.

Throughout the project, P. Mohanaiah of NABARD was an invaluable source of strength and support. He provided advice and helped solve many of our problems with patience and good humour. The project would have never been completed without his unstinted support. Indeed, in the course of the project, he became a personal friend.

We would also like to acknowledge the assistance provided by our colleague Biju Paul Abraham, who helped us in Kerala, interpreting for us and taking notes on our behalf. He also looked after some of our administrative responsibilities at IIMC while we were away on field visits. Raghabendra Chattopadhyay and Amitava Bose acted as sounding boards for many of our ideas as they were taking shape. The former also read through some of our initial drafts and provided critical comments. Aditi Jhunjhunwala and Anusree Kejriwal provided painstaking research assistance at the initial stages of the project. The MBA elective classes of 2012–13 and 2013–14 on Economics of Sustainable Development at IIMC served as a test audience for our case studies. Some of their questions and comments helped us hone the ideas presented in this book. We are grateful to them.

An anonymous publisher's referee gave us incisive comments on the first draft, which helped us revise the manuscript. We are appreciative of this feedback. We would like to thank the editorial team at Routledge, New Delhi, for steering the book towards completion.

This book has been a long time in the making and we may have missed acknowledging some of the people who helped us along the way. The omissions are inadvertent. We remain solely responsible for any remaining inadequacies and errors in the book.

Finally, we would like to thank our families who bore with us through our long absences and absent-mindedness, with the eternal hope that one day the book would see the light of day.

1

Development as Transformation

Human beings have always tried to change the world. In the contemporary world we inhabit, the task that engages human attention and effort the most is the project of development. We relentlessly seek to change the conditions of material living, producing knowledge, new goods, and new services to consume. In the process we also change the way we relate to one another in society. Scholars and thinkers have always grappled with questions of change and the meaning of development. A deeper engagement has been attempted to understand development as a historical process of *transformation* of society.

What is Development?

The term development is used in the social sciences to mean a variety of different things to different scholars (Bardhan 1988; Escobar 1997; Ferguson 1994; Gidden 1971; Grillo and Stirrat 1997; Johnson 2009; Lewis 1988; Moore 1966; Polanyi 1944; Sen 1988, 1999; Waters 1999). It is not surprising that we have an astonishing range of theories and approaches to development. Most economists use the term to focus on changes in material living conditions and the opportunity to consume more from an ever-expanding set of goods and services produced by society. Sociologists use the term in a wider sense to include changes in social institutions such as family or class, qualitative aspects of living such as liberties and rights, and belief systems. Anthropologists are interested in looking at the processes of change in society, and how people relate to one another in terms of social relations and culture.

Apart from the distinctions in focus, there are deeper philosophical differences too. If development is about transformation then are there any universal ends that are to be attained? In other words, does transformation imply an improvement in a set of accepted goals of development? Is there a teleology of change as progress, in the sense that there are well accepted ultimate goals, and well-defined ways of achieving those goals? There are many scholars (Foucault 1980; Lyotard 1984; Skinner 1985) who deny the existence of a universal pattern of change leading to transformation that can be described as development. If that is indeed so, development is about contextual change, without any predetermined ends. Therefore, development is essentially unpredictable in nature. From the wide range of lenses through which development may be viewed, it is evident that different schools of thought exist that inform the debates and discussions about development.

Even if one views development primarily as changes in material living conditions, there are broader issues of concern as to what is to be achieved, and how. There is, to begin with, a very narrow view of development where an increase in the availability of goods and services is sufficient for the desired change. This view constitutes an exclusive concern with aggregate economic growth. However, growth is likely to have physical limits if it is entirely dependent on land-based agriculture. Industry, on the other hand, using science-based technology, has the potential to produce a far greater quantum and variety of goods and services. Hence, one might then argue that development is not only growth, but growth through industrialisation, brought about by a structural break from the dependence on agriculture. It is in this sense that the history of the industrial revolution in Western Europe is taken as the genesis of a great transformation that laid the foundation of modern economic growth.

While an ever-growing basket of goods and services may be adequate for economic growth for society as a whole, how would it translate into bread and butter propositions for people residing in that society? How are the benefits of growth to be distributed among the populace? Would not the universal access to this basket of goods and services be of some social value? Hence, questions of equality and fairness of the distributional consequences of growth have received extensive attention.

Finally, it is possible to view development as change towards some predetermined goals that are not merely material and measurable, but non-material too such as certain liberties and rights (Rawls 1971). The goal outcomes are characterised by notions of fairness and justice. In such a situation what would the criteria be for judging two alternative outcomes for two societies at the same point of time, or two states of affairs of the same society at two different points of time? Ethical judgements about growth and distributional changes are inevitable. These judgements can be extended to cover future generations too. The ethical concerns are not merely about people living in a society at the present, but may also extend to people who would populate society in the future. In other words, are the development process and the desired outcomes sustainable over a reasonable period of time, extending into the foreseeable future (Dasgupta 2001)?

Thus, even starting from a purely material view of development, one can quite easily widen the notion to a set of material and non-material goals achievable as social outcomes with certain desirable features of fairness and sustainability. From the individual to the social, the private to the public, from the micro picture of a single institution to the macro canvas of a national economy, between the state and markets, all become important considerations in discussions about development. Going beyond theories of material conditions and social institutions, scholars have also focused on how the process of development changes the aspirations and ambitions of the participating people, and their own self-image (Appadurai 2004).

In each of these approaches there is no doubt that development is viewed as change. Obviously a society or a system cannot *develop* in any way by remaining exactly as it is. The change can be measured in terms of some metrics like income, consumption, a set of rights, or it could be observed in terms of new institutions, new policies, or new social customs and norms. However, the deeper question of whether to view the change as transformation, or to view it as mere alteration that could be measured and observed, remains. The word development suggests something more than mere change. It implies transformation, or changes that are at least suggestive of a transformative process.

Economic Development as Transformation

The conventional wisdom about economic development as transformation has centred round the change of a rural, traditional countryside, marked by limited local market transactions, subsistence farming, self-consumption, and primitive technologies, to a market-based industrial economy (Lewis 1954, 1979). This process would entail a transformation of feudal (pre-capitalist) economic formations to a capitalist one based on wage labour and machine-based technologies. The capitalist sector would produce for a larger market whose reach would be far beyond the territorial confines of the place of production. The modern, urban, industrial sector would draw upon the traditional, rural and agricultural sector for labour, natural resources and food. Investment in the modern sector would create the dynamic impulse for change. It would draw out the productive resources from the traditional sector. Once the transfer was complete, the traditional sector would look like the modern sector, marked by market prices being determined by the forces of demand and supply. In such visions of development, modernisation is synonymous with industry, urbanisation, profits, investments, and mass markets. Karl Marx (1998) had described all development as the progressive urbanisation of the countryside. A new, modern worldview (*weltanschauung*) would emerge, transforming society's dominant beliefs, creating new social institutions, political ideologies, and economic priorities.

This transformation process has been viewed as being either led or engineered by the state, or as an evolving process facilitated by markets and related institutions like property rights, rule of law and an enabling climate for private investment. History reveals that no attempt at development transformation has ever been entirely led by the state, or entirely triggered by the smooth autonomous functioning of markets. It has invariably been a mix of both. However, the relative role of the state as compared to that of the market does vary in different instances and different phases of transformation. Thus, when interventions which are primarily state-led encounter difficulties, or are not as successful as expected, there is a tendency to increase the emphasis on markets and related institutional support in the intervention. The converse also holds true in many other instances, when the failure of markets triggers a growing role of state interventions.

Whether this transformation can proceed without interruption, or whether the transformation can be aborted permanently into a variety of hybrid structures, has been debated by a number of scholars, and the literature on the alternative view (Amin 1976; Brewer 1980; Frank 1978; Furtado 1973; Wallerstein 1979) is arguably as rich as the literature propagating a smooth (though not necessarily linear) transformation. A basic issue marking the discussion on transformation in the social sciences, including economics, is in asserting whether there is one concept of modern capitalism brought about by the transformation from something 'not modern', or whether there is a spectrum of experiences of transition and transformation contextualised by history and fortuitous events.

A Convenient Taxonomy

Capitalism is the dominant image of all transformation in the vast literature on the advent of modernity. All transition is viewed as the materialisation of capitalism. This literature can be usefully separated into three distinct strands of arguments. The taxonomy is somewhat stylised and simplifying, but it serves a useful purpose for the field studies discussed in this book.

There are many scholars, starting with Marx (1965, 1973, 1998), to Lewis (1954) and Warren (1980), who view the transformation process as being led by the dynamic of capital accumulation and growth where the traditional pre-capitalist sector is broken down, appropriated and eclipsed by capitalism. For sure, there could be interruptions and setbacks in this transition, but according to them the ultimate triumph of capitalism or modernity would be inevitable. The existence of the traditional sector and its activities would then necessarily be a transitional and temporary phase of transformation.

There are other scholars, clubbed together as neo-Marxists (Amin 1976; Frank 1978; Wallerstein 1979), who look at the transition to capitalism being led by the economic activities in a core group of economies (the developed, affluent countries) of the world that draw upon the resources of the periphery (the underdeveloped, poor countries) for accumulation and growth. The relationship is one where the periphery can only be affected by the growth of the core through a complex set of market relations. The periphery is not capitalist but represents some variety of pre-capitalism that is subject to change through the dynamic of the relationship with the core. However, the ability of the core to transform the periphery is limited by the depth and strength of its own dynamics of accumulation. The underdevelopment of the periphery is precisely a consequence of the development of the core. The ability for autonomous transformation by the periphery, according to these scholars, is absent. However, the penetration of capitalism into the geography of the periphery is not a theoretical impossibility but some kind of empirically observed limit to capital's ability to grow. Hence, the lack of transformative development arises out of the basic dependence of the periphery on the expansion of the core. If the core has limits to growth, the presence of this dependence will continue indefinitely. The two distinct systems of capitalism and pre-capitalism coexist in a superior-subordinate relationship. The pre-capitalism of the periphery cannot become capitalism on its own strength.

The third strand of the debate on transformation (Chatterjee 2008; Sanyal 2007; Taylor 1979) relates to the impossibility of the world economy, especially the postcolonial economies, to transform into capitalism as is imagined in its ideal form. This impossibility arises not because of the dependence of the pre-capitalistic economic formations with capital, but because of the structure of capitalism itself, which inherently contains its other, non-capital (and not pre-capital) within itself. Hence transformation is a theoretical impossibility. Capital creates non-capital and it also destroys it in different contexts and different geographies. There is only one system, and it is far from the ideal construct of capitalism. It contains capitalistic as well as non-capitalistic features and activities in its fold. While quantitative changes and alterations may be observed, transformation never will be.

The Inevitability of Transformation

Lewis (1954) had suggested that underdevelopment as observed in terms of a traditional society, with limited market penetration and primitive production technologies, was characterised by surplus labour which could be drawn away from the sector without affecting the subsistence production of food. The surplus may not be observed in terms of open unemployment. They were disguised as employed persons, but who were actually sharing the productive work that could be done by a much lower number of workers. If there was an industrial sector that used capital and modern technologies, and used the economic surplus (profits) to invest in capacity creation, then the process would never be constrained by the lack of cheap and adequate labour. The dynamic of investment would create a demand for labour and the demand could be met out of an elastic supply of the surplus workers from the traditional sector at a low and constant wage rate.

Once the surplus labour was used up, the traditional sector would be marked by shortages, and the rule of the market forces of demand and supply would hold sway. A small but dynamic modern sector would suffice to transform the traditional sector into a part of the modern economy.

Lewis did not make clear how the embryonic form of the dynamic modern sector came into being, nor did he elaborate on the varieties of non-modern activities that constitute the traditional sector and the story of their ultimate eclipse. If there were a modern sector, however tiny, the traditional sector would be sucked into the transformation process. The final result would be the creation of a full-fledged market economy and capitalist enterprises (private or publicly owned) using wage labour and producing for mass markets. Transformation would cease, though changes in technologies, production and consumption patterns would be obviously possible. Lewis was quite aware of the things that could go wrong and the many interruptions that could occur in the process of transformation to what he described as a developed economy. However, many of these difficulties and problems could be sorted out by a state planner or policymaker who could design interventions for eliminating them altogether, or at least reducing the seriousness of the difficulties in holding back the transformation. To Lewis it was a one-off transformation to modernity. Between the enabling state and the forces of the market the transition was possible and desirable.

Marx, though writing many decades before Lewis, had analysed the transition to capitalism on a much wider plane and as a historical process. He proposed a general method to analyse how societies changed and transformed over time. He suggested that the way society produced material goods and organised social living could be described as the mode of production of a particular society, or for many societies at a particular historical juncture. The mode of production could be thought of as comprising the forces of production and the relations of production. The forces of production encompass the state of technology or knowledge, the mode of organisation of production and the degree of development of the most important element in the forces of production — namely human beings. Relations of production imply the social condition under which production takes place, the ways by which the products of human labour are appropriated, the principles of distribution of the social product, the ideology and modes of thought and, above all, the *weltanschauung* within which society operates at any moment of time (Baran and Hobsbawm 1961).

There is, according to Marx, an ever present tension between the forces of production and the relations of production. The forces of production tend to continuously gain in depth and scope with new knowledge and new human abilities changing in a dynamic manner. The relations of production on the other hand tend to be sticky, slow to change and conservative. The organisation of social living tends to favour some classes and discriminate against others. Hence vested interests arise, and those who stand to gain from the existing arrangements tend to oppose the changes required to accommodate new forces of production. The possibility of new opportunities and gains (including gaining greater freedom) becomes clear to a new social class. The dominant class with privileges and power comes to oppose the new interests that emerge from the possibilities of new forces of production. The clash of interests can, and often does, become violent.

Outcomes of this conflict between classes, between the old and the new, between the privileged and the upstart, are not always predictable. Depending on the historical circumstance, the process of change can unfold in a variety of ways. There could be violent upheavals from below or relatively peaceful transformations from above. There could be protracted periods of stagnation and the power of the ruling class could block or slow down the development of new economic and social organisations with new rules of the game. For Marx, however, the ultimate triumph of the forces of production had been validated in human history. Whatever may have been the interruptions, in the long run it has tended to overcome all hurdles in the process of transformation.

Capitalism and the way it emerged from feudalism in Western Europe was a historical example of the transformation, with capitalism providing a more progressive, dynamic and complete alternative to the traditional forms of feudalism (pre-capitalism) and its organisation of society. Given his method of analysis, Marx went on to show the inherent problems of capitalism as a system, and how it contained the seeds of its own destruction, to be eventually replaced by a new system and a new dominant social class.

Despite the possibility of slow, interrupted or blocked development, the ultimate triumph of a new system was inevitable. This inevitability, according to Marx, was the result of the ability of human beings to will and work towards change. It was human agency that was ultimately indomitable and invincible in its ability to change the world.

The Hybridisation of Delayed Transformation

Following Marx's analysis of capitalism's emergence from pre-capitalism, especially in Western Europe, a number of Marxist scholars have studied the phenomenon of underdevelopment. Countries that are typically underdeveloped as compared to the developed countries have two common features. The first feature was that these countries had been colonies of the developed economies in the past. The second was the prevalence of material poverty and the noticeable presence of a variety of pre-capitalist, archaic economic organisations and activities. The persistence of traditional economic organisations and activities much after the advent of modern capitalism in parts of the world led many scholars to doubt whether Marx's prediction that the dynamics of capital accumulation would batter down the Chinese wall of pre-capitalist traditional production processes was accurate or not.

Contributors to this literature on understanding underdevelopment as a process have offered a variety of explanations. Frank (1978) and Amin (1976) have argued that the old set of market relations that the developed economies (the centre or core) established with the underdeveloped economies (the periphery), to transfer economic surplus to enable capital accumulation in the developed economies, continued to be present even after the colonies were granted political independence. Repatriation of profits by foreign enterprises was a common method through which the transfer took place. The trade relationship (though seemingly free and voluntary) was unequal and was the other route through which a net transfer of resources took place to facilitate capital accumulation in the core. The historical process of the old imperialism continued, albeit the economic relationships in the postcolonial era were more sophisticated and seemingly more voluntary and mutually acceptable. Wallerstein (1979) developed this argument into describing a world system of unevenly distributed hierarchy of political power and economic wealth. The economies that had a stronger presence of capitalist enterprises using wage labour and modern technologies also had states that were politically more powerful with superior global influence.

According to these authors there was one system of capitalism in the world but characterised by uneven development. The inner logic of accumulation would imply that the parts that are underdeveloped cannot expect to achieve a structure of developed capitalism on their own since underdevelopment was part of the same process that created development in the core. They were two sides of the same coin. There have been debates about whether the unevenness was a symptom of underdeveloped capitalism or whether the observed hierarchy of structures and activities was actually an articulation of different modes of production (capitalist and pre-capitalist) coexisting simultaneously. They were logically connected as a structural unit. It follows from the analysis that the coexistence of the capitalist pre-capitalist structural tie was geographically divided according to the territorial spaces of nation states. Even within a nation state, modern and traditional organisations of production could be simultaneously observed.

The obvious question about the relative dominance of the capitalist mode of production remains. Why does capitalism not begin to dominate and appropriate the traditional sector? Why does the structure not change? Why does the metaphoric 'Chinese wall' not crumble? There are a number of carefully nuanced arguments provided in the literature that propose to explain the persistence of the structures that are far removed from the ideal type of capitalism modelled on the economies of Western Europe, particularly Britain. We will quickly touch upon four such arguments that highlight the difficulties associated with the structural change to capitalism.

The first argument revolves around the domination of merchant capital over industrial capital (Kay 1975). Trading activities enable the transfer of surplus to the core and also enable the opening up of the periphery as a market for the products of industrial capital. The criticality of this relationship creates the resistance to the break-up of this nexus without which a complete structural change would not be possible. The second set of arguments revolves around the degree of penetration of industrial capital into the pre-capitalist structures. Like the old empire–colony relationship, the structure of industrial capital penetrates and transforms pre-capitalism only to the extent that it is useful and serves a specific purpose for helping accumulation and growth (Taylor 1979). The essential nature of the structural coexistence of the two systems is evident when one finds that postcolonial experiences with development (without the old imperial nexus) has not been able to do away with the structure of coexistence of the modern with the traditional. A related but distinct argument relates to the importance of the traditional sector as a reservoir of cheap labour and natural resources (Meillassoux 1983). This is the pool into which industrial capital dips as and when required. Modern industrial capital needs the traditional sector using archaic methods of production to serve the overarching needs of capital accumulation.

The final argument revolves around the political importance of the state and its arms of governance. The modern and the traditional are different, yet they are observed to coexist. Modernity or industrial capital, with all its apparatus of governing societies, either does not want to transform or fails to transform the traditional pre-capitalism. The state becomes active in creating what some authors have called a 'constructed hegemony' (Chatterjee 2008) built on both persuasion as well as coercion. The modern state's ability to engineer what Gramsci (1971) called a passive revolution is critical in this context. The state continually negotiates with pre-capitalism (in its variety of forms and structures) to ensure continuity and also to appropriate or neutralise any resistance and opposition to the power of capital and its institutions. Overt and extensive use of coercive power by the state is difficult in the age of democracy and open political institutions.

What do all these arguments imply for the transition to modern capitalism? Clearly they do not provide any theoretical reason why the need of pre-capitalism to survive and coexist will not disappear. The love–hate relationship of modernity and tradition, industrial capital and pre-capitalist modes of production is not stable as a system. The term used by some scholars (Gramsci 1971) to refer to this situation of persistence of coexistence is 'blocked dialectic' — a hurdle, as it were, from moving the thesis and its antithesis to a full-fledged synthesis depicting the new system or new mode of production. A heterogeneous mix of capital and pre-capital may be observed. The underlying relationship of mutual dependence can be discerned, and the transition, while possible, could be indefinitely delayed. The importance of human agency remains evident in the constant oppositions and resistances to the hegemony of capital, and the constant construction and re-construction of persuasion and coercion.

Struggles against capitalism have taken the form of protecting human lives and livelihoods against the disruption of new technologies and new processes of using social labour. More recently, such struggles have centred round environmental assets and access to common property resources like fields and forests (Healy et al. 2013). According to some scholars the struggle is not only about capital confronting labour, but also about capital confronting nature (O'Connor 1998; Sheppard et al. 2009).

The Impossibility of Transformation

There has been a relatively recent work by Sanyal (2007), who has argued that there is no possibility of underdeveloped capitalism to transform into full-fledged modern capitalism, or the blocked dialectic of transition to become unblocked. His analysis of the dynamics of capitalist accumulation is based on the distinction he makes between capitalism as a system and a capitalistic enterprise using wage labour and producing for extensive markets. Capitalism is made up of an accumulation economy (the set of capitalistic enterprises with its apparatus of influence and power) and what Sanyal describes as a need economy. The former has the characteristics of modern capitalism while the latter has the character of a traditional pre-capitalist sector marked by small scale of operations in family, or self-owned and operated enterprises, with a reliance on local resources and labour-using technologies. The markets for these activities are marked by ease of entry and exit, and are not well regulated, often operating in the grey zone of legality as far as existing labour legislation and safety rules are concerned. The people involved in this sector are of course vulnerable to fluctuating economic fortunes, fluctuations over which they have no control.

What Sanyal focuses on is the relationship between the accumulation economy and the need economy. The accumulation economy appropriates activities in the need economy and dispossesses people of assets and sources of livelihoods — a phenomenon he refers to as primitive accumulation. To achieve this, force is used on occasions, on other occasions the persuasion of politically negotiated settlements suffice. On the other hand, in different contexts, the traditional pre-capitalist sector is produced as an effect of accumulation, in the form of redundant individuals with obsolete skills and unstable incomes and livelihoods. The accumulation economy in its urge to create order from chaos, law from lawlessness and useful product from raw materials necessarily creates 'wastes' and 'wasted individuals' (Bauman 2004). However, on considerations of social legitimacy, there is a need to recycle the waste and prevent complete decay and disappearance. It is the role of governance to provide the excluded and the redundant with opportunities to survive.

Since the dynamic of the accumulation economy and the need economy is to create as well as negate each other in an integral fashion, Sanyal refuses to use the prefix 'pre' and instead chooses to use the prefix 'non' to describe the system outside the accumulation economy. Non-capital is the other of capital. This categorisation implies a couple of things that are significant as far as the question of transition and capitalist transformation is concerned. Going beyond the historicism of the earlier contributors to this literature, he argues that transformation of capitalism to the ideal state can only be imaginary. There is no theoretical possibility of the transformation, because the capital and non-capital complex, with its differences and heterogeneity, *is* capitalism. It is here to stay. Hence the question of human agency to transform or to block the transformation to modernity becomes irrelevant.

The need economy is the manifestation of non-capital marked by a variety of activities that are not motivated by the accumulation of capital. Increasingly, these parts of the global economy require interventions by international organisations like the World Bank or United Nations Development Programme (UNDP), arms of national governments and other formal financial institutions like banks, or even institutions of civil society like non-governmental organisations (NGOs). These interventions essentially aim to manage and contain the socially adverse consequences of poverty, dispossession and displacement. The effort to contain the effects of deprivation within the confines of the need economy takes centre stage. The strategy underlying these interventions is characterised by certain features that, while attempting to ensure a minimum standard of living, also ensure the strengthening of the market relationship between the need economy and the accumulation economy. Instead of the direct provision of basic goods for the poor, the strategy of accumulation provides productive assets for individuals, or a group of individuals, so that they can access markets to earn a livelihood. A portfolio of activities is made available, and some skills are imparted for taking up new activities. The reason is to provide sustainable income flows for the rehabilitation of the dispossessed.

The hegemony of capital in the postcolonial world is consistent with heterogeneity and differences in its structural architecture. The essential relationship is between the need economy and the accumulation economy, where the latter draws accumulation from the former, not through profit transfers but through a direct mix of coercion and persuasion. This is the process of primitive accumulation that creates dispossession of assets and livelihoods. At the same time, capital creates opportunities for the need economy to contribute to growth and for the inhabitants to participate in markets. This provides a double advantage. New and sustainable livelihoods offer a support system to poor people making them contribute to social wealth. These people are the ones who are excluded from the accumulation economy, or have been discarded by it as obsolete and unemployable. It also offers, at the same time, an opportunity for local markets to be integrated with wider national and global markets that offer an outlet for its products to the accumulation economy, opening up the access to the proverbial gold at the bottom of the pyramid. Here development and capital accumulation are distinct processes. Development provides the legitimacy for capital accumulation by creating and renewing the need economy. Poverty and underdevelopment are seen as the 'outcome of the arising of capital rather than a residual of the pre-capitalist past' (Sanyal 2007: 255).

A similar postmodern understanding of modernity as a manifestation of capital with a propensity to create incessant wastes of human lives and livelihoods is due to Bauman (2004). According to him, the obsession with including people in the ways of the modern world, as well as the exclusive tendency of removing and setting aside the wastes of humanity that arise from the process of accumulation and the creation of order, stem from the same root, which can be described as:

> [T]he global spread of the modern way of life, which by now has reached the furthest limits of the planet (emphasis added). It has cancelled the division between the "centre" and "periphery", or more correctly between "modern"

(or "developed") and "pre-modern" (or "underdeveloped" or "backward") forms of life. (ibid.: 69)

The modern process of order-building is not merely a postcolonial phenomenon. Economic change takes place everywhere and so everywhere human waste of the dispossessed is produced and turned out in ever rising numbers. It is in this sense that, according to Bauman (2013), the planet is full.

The assertion that capitalism coexists systematically with non-capital obviously negates the view of history as the story of great transformations. It takes a more contextual view of history in terms of the narratives of local change. What the assertion keeps in the dark is how this self-perpetuating structure of capitalism came about in the first place. In denying the possibilities of history this view of the world seems to deny any role of human agency to act upon, transform or even imagine change from the here and now of existence.

Observing Change

Within this fullness and interconnectedness of the planet, it is possible to examine actual experiences of change. These changes could be within a village or in the relationships between a village and a town. The change could also be observed in the linkages between a rural sector and an urban sector or between the periphery and the core nations. Is it possible to discern from these patterns of changes whether transformation is the inevitable outcome of development, or is it impossible? Or are there factors that impede transformation leading to the emergence of hybrid structures?

For this purpose we have used the recent experience of India as the canvas to see whether the changes taking place validate any of the theoretical positions discussed above. We have examined changes at the basic level of the village and studied specific development interventions. It is to this discussion that we now turn.

2

Development as Intervention

India's 'Tryst with Destiny': Shifting Focus

Independent India's experience of economic development led by state planning was mixed. The Nehruvian era of the 1950s and 1960s marked the critical role of five year plans in economic growth and development. There were many industries created and institutions established. Despite the large new public sector enterprises and public investments in infrastructure, growth rates were low, poverty and deprivation refused to go away, and unemployment and lack of education became well known features of Indian society. The large agricultural sector was marked by low productivity and dependence on monsoons despite the Green Revolution that brought the use of high-yielding seeds and chemical fertilisers. The overall performance was poor, certainly in relation to the expectations created surrounding India's 'tryst with destiny' (Joshi and Little 1994; Mohan 2008). Moreover, many countries that had followed different development strategies had moved ahead, not only in terms of incomes, but also in terms of social opportunities and attainments in education and health. These countries, such as South Korea, Singapore or Thailand, had depended more on markets for economic growth. On the other hand, by the end of the 1980s, the countries that had depended heavily on state-led growth, like the Soviet Union and the economies of East Europe, had run into difficulties, or, like China, had moved away from state-led to market-driven strategies.

By the end of the 1980s there were political uncertainties, economic crises and a popular dissatisfaction with government and the public sector. By this time, too, many new captains of industry had emerged who were more confident to lead the economic transformation in India without the claustrophobic apparatus of government control that was referred to as the license raj.

The well known economic reforms that began in 1991, reflecting the resurgence of faith in markets, began to shift India's development strategy to a more market-friendly approach. In this approach, markets would play equally important roles in the industrial as well as the agricultural sector. It was becoming evident that industrial investments were inadequate or unable to transform the backward rural sector during the decades of state-led planning. It was now believed that the market would have to provide solutions to the problem of poverty, which industrial growth had not been able to address.

As a reaction to the disappointing results of top-down approaches in devising effective policies (Lipton 1977; Streeten and Lipton 1968), a new approach, where the livelihoods of people became the focal point of rural development, gained popularity from the 1990s (Narayan and Glinskaya 2007; Narayan et al. 2000; Scoones 1998). The policy challenge was to transform a poor petty production economy into a productive, technologically prosperous advanced economy (Das 2011; Frankel 1971; Furtado 1973). Direct interventions to reduce poverty were not something new. They had been tried since the 5th Five Year Plan in the 1970s. However, the nature of the interventions changed since the introduction of market-based reforms in 1991, evident from the 9th Five Year Plan. A noticeable feature of the change was a reduced emphasis on grants and an increased focus on credit markets, financial inclusion and loans for microenterprises (Harris–White and Subramanian 1999).

Economic policies were crafted so as to facilitate the functioning of markets. The 'friendliness' of the market-friendly approach was in the form of government support provided to markets. There were three essential elements of this support. The first was to create and improve access to markets, such as the labour market, credit market and product market. To maximise access to markets the government had to ensure that infrastructure — both physical and financial — was adequate. This was the second important role of the government in the development strategy. The third requirement was to create human capabilities through primary education and basic health and hygiene so that people could avail of market opportunities as they arose in the process of development. The provision of primary education and basic health in areas marked by acute deprivation, however, could not be left to the market as private profitability in these activities was absent yet social returns were indisputably high (Dreze and Sen 1995, 2002).

Over and above the design of an intervention, there must be processes in place to enable its implementation. The impact would be little if the people involved were not convinced about the purpose of the interventions. In such a situation, their involvement and participation would be low. Even if the people were convinced, they would have to be empowered so as to take independent decisions about the process through which the project was to be implemented. They would have to take ownership such that benefits could continue even after the project was completed. A higher form of empowerment would be when people could take decisions about their future beyond the immediate boundaries of the micro-intervention. While the *India Rural Development Report* (IDFC 2013) looks at similar issues, it does so at the level of the state, but we decided to delve deeper into the projects themselves.

What implication did this change in development strategy have for the larger question of development as transformation, as discussed in the previous chapter? Would alterations in the material conditions of living in rural India accelerate possibilities for structural change, or would they merely represent quantitative increments without much strength or depth, simply adding to the growth statistic? It is in the context of these broad questions that we set out to study some development interventions or projects in rural settings across India.

Towards an Exploratory Framework

First, we wanted to understand the process of implementation. Implementation would usually revolve around a complex set of ideas, activities and people. It would include the concept and design of the project, the resources that would be required, the people and organisations that had to be brought together, the dynamics of the delivery system, and actual outcomes. We viewed the network of resources, people and intervening organisations that got together to implement the project as a temporary organisation and explored how that functioned. Moreover, people's participation being a key element of the intervention process, we also sought to understand what brought them together and the extent of their involvement. Above all, we tried to discern whether the process facilitated the emergence of a nascent

treating the process of development as elitist and 'top down'. Chambers noted the ideal kind of participation as:

> The essence . . . is change and reversals — of role, relationship and learning. Outsiders do not dominate and lecture; they facilitate, sit down, listen and learn. Outsiders do not transfer technology; they share methods, which local people can use for their own appraisal, planning, action monitoring and evaluation. Outsiders do not impose their reality; they encourage and enable local people to express their own. (1997: 103)

In practice, however, participation could be of various types (Chambers 2011; Midgley 2011). On one extreme there may be situations where participation takes the form of tokenism and the involvement of people is merely nominal. On the other extreme there may be situations where participation is transformative and people take decisions about the project that can have far-reaching effects on their lives and on the life of the community. The domain of participation may vary too. Participation in a one-off village meeting is obviously different from participation in the entire duration of the development project. In a similar way, participation in representative politics may be substantially different from serving in a managing committee overseeing a specific project. The intrinsic value of participation as a member of a community, or being a citizen may be seen in terms of contributing to the self-realisation of an individual. Bebbington states that

> a person's assets, such as land, are not merely means with which he or she makes a living: they also give meaning to that person's world. Assets are not simply resources that people use in building livelihoods; they are assets that give him the capability to be and act. Assets should not be understood only as things that allow survival, adaptation and poverty alleviation, they are also the basis of agent's power to act and to reproduce, challenge or change the rules that govern the control, use and transformation of resources. (1999: 2022)

However, the instrumental value of participation in a development project necessarily has social implications; as such participation leads to the realisation of collective goals. The act of participation may create new goals or raise new questions. Effective participation enables people to discern new interests and opportunities, and discover new confidence to take on new projects.

Participatory development may have problems of its own. Apart from tokenism and nominal participation, there may be a propensity to treat the community involved in the development project as homogeneous. The NGO often assumes that a random representation of the community suffices for meaningful participation. The assumption of homogeneity is misleading given the diversity of caste, class, religions, and occupations, but convenient for the uninformed or insensitive bureaucracy. In such a situation, the relatively powerful and articulate elite of the community acquires a larger role in the temporary organisation.

Interventions: The Livelihoods Approach

The term livelihood, essentially interdisciplinary in nature, is used from different perspectives. It is about how people live and earn their living. It is a flexible term which can be described in the context of locales like rural-urban or farm and non-farm. It refers to occupations like farming, raising livestock and fishing. It has something to do with social differentiations like gender and age. Sustainability or resilience is another characterisation of livelihood. Finally, livelihoods may be thought of as pathways to a desired style of living with definite directions in which changes are supposed to take place.

> But in reality people combine different activities in a complex bricolage or portfolio of activities. Outcomes of course vary, and how different strategies affect livelihood pathways or trajectories is an important concern for livelihood analysis. The dynamic, longitudinal analysis emphasizes such terms as coping, adaptation, improvement, diversification and transformation. Analyses at the individual level can in turn aggregate up to complex livelihood strategies and pathways at household, village or even district levels. (Scoones 2010: 160)

In most poor rural economies livelihood is a complex mix of agriculture, farm labour, wage employment, and microenterprise (Datta and Sharma 2009) — a portfolio of activities with different levels of importance attached that change over time. The livelihoods approach found wide acceptance in official policy discourse after the World Summit for Social Development in 1995 held at Copenhagen

(Mohanty 1995). The set of activities for a particular project is created through a process of negotiated learning between the locals (whose livelihoods are to be diversified) and outsiders.

One kind of livelihood diversification arises out of a pure survivalist strategy, where non-farm activity is a vital form of subsistence. Agricultural income from marginal land or income from being a farm labourer may not suffice for survival. The search for alternative sources of income from common property, such as a forest or a lake, opportunities in microenterprise, or work in the unskilled services sector may become important. The households may remain trapped in a low-income overcrowded informal sector. However, some nascent opportunity for becoming a small but reasonably successful entrepreneur would remain open, where some capital is needed to transform a self-employment start-up arising out of poverty into a microenterprise with four or five wage workers. The second kind of diversification is possible when a household's activity feeds into a larger enterprise of capital accumulation. Activities like horticulture or contract farming may be an outsourced part of the supply chain of a larger enterprise. Here, too, the assurance of income and market access may be attractive, but the incomes earned in many instances may be well below the minimum wage available in the formal sector. It is important to understand the implications of this process.

Outcomes and Impacts

Augmented incomes are the minimal expectations from a development intervention. The success of the livelihoods approach depends on the increase in average incomes of the participants, or at least on the reduced variability of income flows. The provision of alternative earning opportunities during lean seasons of the beneficiary's primary activity, through improved risk management measures, or the creation of additional productive assets, yields a supplementary income flow. However, these do not suffice for an initiative to be called sustainable. For instance, if the opportunity for increased income is tied to the initial distribution of assets, then the intervention reinforces and contributes to greater inequality amongst the beneficiaries. A rise in inequality cannot be viewed as adding to the prospects of sustainability. Amongst other things, the increase in inequality contributes to social discontent. The extent of the increase in average incomes itself is also of significance. Marginal increases (or reduced variability) in income is beneficial in the sense that it serves as an alternative to a social 'safety net' for the household. However, if the average does not increase sufficiently and the rise is only incremental, the vulnerability of the household to economic shocks may not be entirely removed. A larger (non-incremental) change that can radically alter the lives of the beneficiaries is indicative of a deeper transformation.

One of the many ways of augmenting livelihoods in villages is the use of natural capital to create new livelihoods. Thus, an intervention often involves improving access to and management of environmental resources with the help of beneficiaries, or generating more natural capital as private assets such as planting trees for timber or promoting horticulture. This leads to improved sustainability as the overall stock of ecological assets grows, both through better natural resource management practices and through an increase in natural capital base. Moreover, a popular mechanism for better management of the environment is privatising the commons, which could cut both ways; while individual ownership may lead to better protection of the privatised commons, in a land-scarce poor society it may also result in an unsustainable increase in pressure on the ecosystem services from remaining common natural assets. Exclusive promotion of the instrumental value of the environment may lead to overexploitation of natural capital. A consequence of this may be that the environment itself becomes a hurdle for transformation.

One measure of success of an intervention is whether it can stimulate human agency of the beneficiaries through which they are able to view the world in a different light and pursue new goals or challenge existing rules from their experience of development. The degree of transformation is dependent on the extent to which the intervention is able to empower the people involved so that they can voice their needs, shoulder responsibility and play an active role in the decision-making process of the community.

Sustainability

A sustainable rural livelihood

> comprises the capabilities, assets (including both material and social resources) and activities for a means of living. A livelihood is sustainable

when it can cope with and recover from stresses and shocks, maintain or enhance its capabilities and assets, and provide sustainable livelihood opportunities for the next generation; and which contributes net benefits to other livelihoods at the local and global levels and in the short and long term. (Chambers and Conway 1992: 6)

Sustainability links inputs (like capital or people's participation) and outputs (livelihood strategies) in a wider framework of well-being within and across generations. It also highlights outcomes like income and wealth creation, augmentation of natural resources and changed aspirations. It is an approach whereby the community and local ecological services are meshed together to provide a means to a living without depleting the natural resource base. This may be emulated by future generations too. The issue of sustainability reflects not only the quest for managing the natural resource base but also fundamentally reflects the ability of people in a community to deeply engage with and imagine a future world. It is an essential manifestation of human agency.

There are many concerns related to the sustainability of development interventions, such as the conservation of the local environment, management of common property resources and the opportunity to migrate away from the rural sector. The new generation, with more education and possibly better nutritional attainment and health, may wish to go out into the urban areas looking for modern industrial or service sector jobs. These jobs may be growing, but are there enough? Will a migration into the modern sector result in a shortage of labour in the farmlands in the future? One important implication of sustainability is that interventions not only create positive outcomes on a one-off basis, but also result in a continuous stream of benefits into the future. The distribution of such benefits is determined by the prevailing ideas of social justice and ensuing rights and entitlements.

From the Framework to the Field

Very broadly, development projects (micro-interventions) in India are implemented in three ways. One way is when the government (central or state or panchayat) identifies a project and has line departments (government officials) implement it. The second way is when the government offers an NGO the opportunity to implement a project identified by it. In each of these there would be a mix of loans and grants. The third way is when NABARD either takes a government-designed project or, like a laboratory, experiments with some projects designed by it. In both cases it offers the project to an agency (usually one or more NGOs) to deliver. Once again, these projects have a mix of grants and loans. The loans are not necessarily from NABARD, but facilitated by them via connecting to Rural Banks and Cooperative Banks, or even a Lead Commercial Bank in a district.

Of the many institutions set up in the country to promote economic development, NABARD is unique in the sense that though it is primarily a financial institution it also plays the role of a development agency. The latter role is small compared to NABARD's role as the apex institution for rural and cooperative banks. NABARD, unlike any other development agency, has a District Development Manager posted in every district of India at the rank of Assistant General Manager. The manager supervises a large portfolio of diverse projects. She also assesses the ground-level credit need for agricultural and related operations.

The mission of NABARD is 'promoting sustainable and equitable agriculture and rural development through effective credit support related services, institution building and other innovative initiatives' (NABARD 2014). It has been a leader in experimenting with innovative intervention mechanisms that combine income and wealth creation with environmental conservation and social engineering. It has in its portfolio a wide variety of projects that relate to self-help groups (SHGs) and microfinance, rural infrastructure building, watershed creation and management, and people-based, comprehensive livelihood projects. The large variety of projects, and their sheer numbers along with the impressive spread across all states of India, makes NABARD a depository of significant amounts of experience, knowledge and data.

The specific projects that we studied were selected in consultation with NABARD. Given its experience and expertise, we sought its assistance to identify representative projects that would be worth studying in detail based on their complexity and challenging nature. The criteria for selection included: (*a*) the multiplicity of objectives, that is, the outcome of the project affected the participants across multiple dimensions such as income and wealth, livelihoods, natural and social capital; (*b*) the diversity of projects, their terrains, geographies and the ethnicities of participants. To select from an impressively large set of live projects, we spent three days with departmental heads at the NABARD head office. We requested them to identify for our purposes around 20 projects that would cover the expanse of India as far as possible and cover the variety of projects they are involved in. We asked them to provide us a mix of projects — new and old, successful and unsuccessful (according to their judgement), simple, and those with thorny problems — without telling us what was what. From this set of 20, we chose about 11. For these, the degree of NABARD's involvement varied from project to project. We adopted convenience sampling which, we thought, would be pretty representative of projects across India, where an all-India institution was involved. On an average, we spent about 10 person days at each project site, after obtaining a clear understanding of project background and financials from the data provided to us. NABARD's District Development Managers were vital in serving as a bridge between us and the participants. NABARD facilitated our research in terms of providing access to data, and crucial support in the field. Funding for the project came from Indian Institute of Management Calcutta (IIMC).

A Word on Method

We started our investigations with the notion that there is no absolute measure of success or failure of a project. Instead we expected that there would be differences in how projects evolve, their impact on people's lives and livelihoods and their transformative implications. A grounded theory approach (Glaser and Strauss 1967) was adopted, and our narratives emerged as a result of participative listening, interacting with a diverse set of stakeholders at all levels, ranging from the change agents to the non-beneficiaries, most often in focused group interviews. We also reviewed data collected by many of the NGOs who were involved in the interventions, as well as routine progress reports with NABARD. We viewed these projects beyond the perspective of conventional economics where the focus is more on quantitative outcomes. Our primary focus was on understanding how participants change and *emerge* from the project, and how the project in turn affects their present and future. Our approach was necessarily flexible, as we were experiencing a diverse set of interventions in different socio-economic and cultural settings.

When one is trying to ask questions such as 'what', 'how' or 'why' rather than 'how many' or 'how much', qualitative research is the recommended strategy (Eisenhardt and Graebner 2007; Yin 2003). Since our research questions were more in line with trying to explore the development process, it lent itself to a qualitative exploration. Further, Eisenhardt and Grabener (2007) and Graebner (2009) suggest that in situations where current theoretical developments provide conflicting accounts, an in-depth qualitative enquiry is a useful research strategy. Thus, because there could be alternative paths of development, our enquiry sought to throw some light on empirical implications of development interventions through in-depth multiple case analyses.

The strength of multiple cases lies in their capability to permit replication logic (Yin 2003). By allowing the cases to be treated as a series of experiments, replication ensures that the insights gained are not idiosyncratic to a single case but are consistently replicated across multiple cases. This leads to a robust approach to validating alternative theoretical propositions (Eisenhardt and Graebner 2007).

A clearer understanding of these experiences of development could provide valuable evidence and lessons for people involved with the nitty-gritty of managing a project. It would also help us in discerning how these micro-interventions fit into the big picture of macroeconomic development, and whether they lead to transformation or not. This book is a record of our observations and learning from the field, a short preview of which follows.

Notes from a Changing Rural Landscape

The narratives from the villages we visited, comprising Chapters 3 to 12, are presented in three distinct sections. The first section, 'Water and Well-being', discusses the implementation of watershed projects in three different parts of India. The importance of water as a resource is being increasingly felt and interventions focus on the natural means of water management and groundwater recharging. The second section, 'Empowerment and Entrepreneurship', narrates the instances of how individuals, with a bit of support, can create livelihoods not

Part I

Water and Well-being

Water, as everybody knows, is part of nature's life support system. It is needed not only for drinking and fulfilling daily needs, but also for growing crops and raising livestock. Yet the availability of water is often taken for granted and a sudden drought or flood reminds us of how vulnerable we are to the vagaries of nature. In a country that is primarily dependant on the monsoons for its water needs, it is important to design mechanisms to recharge the groundwater or develop processes to store water so that it is available round the year. A watershed is nature's way of managing water resources so as to ensure that naturally available water is not wasted, but used for recharge. However, over the years, several natural watersheds have been destroyed through unsustainable farming practices, clearing forests and shrubs for habitation, and altering the natural topography to create farm lands. Hence, there is a need to restore and rebuild watersheds to halt the alarming depletion of groundwater levels.

A watershed is a natural hydrological unit where water from a primary source, such as a river or a stream, gets distributed over an area of land through smaller streams and channels, creating pools of surface water depending on the topography of the region. Usually there is a slight incline from the source of the water to the final sink where it drains into. The upper headland is called the 'ridge' and the lower part of the drainage system is called the 'valley'. In the process of the ridge to valley movement of the water, some of it also gets trapped in subsoil layers of small stones and clay. Some of the water seeps in further downwards to recharge the water table of the region. The area of a watershed could vary widely from a few hectares to thousands of hectares.

The hydrological cycle essentially recycles the same water. Hence, any overuse or destruction of the natural channels of flowing water would alter the surface drainage and the groundwater drainage. The water table could get depleted and altered flows could lead to water run-offs into areas where the water cannot be productively used. Hence, it is important to ensure that the watershed is optimally used and maintained. Sometimes the drainage system also gets altered through erosion and natural decay.

Rain-fed agriculture accounts for over 60 per cent of net sown area, 100 per cent of forests, and supports 66 per cent of cattle of the country (NRRA 2013). Ensuring a functional watershed (suitably repaired, altered and maintained) is very important in such areas. The importance arises from two basic reasons. The first is the conservation of water and ensuring maximum recycling and recharging. The importance of water as a common natural resource cannot be overemphasised. The second reason is that the improved availability of water ensures a wider range of livelihood opportunities for people living in the watershed area. A larger variety of crops, horticulture and other cash crops, livestock rearing and fodder availability, and reforestation are a few examples of economically beneficial outcomes. The potential benefits of a better managed watershed are available to the local population and hence their participation is considered critical in ensuring that the benefits are indeed harnessed to the well-being of the region as a whole, providing additional incomes and assets.

The perceived need for better management of water resources and the importance of supplementary livelihood opportunities helped launch the Indo-German Watershed Development Programme (IGWDP) in 1992 as a collaborative venture between the government of Germany and the Government of India, with the National Bank for Agriculture and Rural Development (NABARD) given charge of administering and managing the programme. The IGWDP was set up to develop micro watersheds in Maharashtra. NABARD and the Water Organisation Trust (WOTR) would give technical training and managerial support, over and above monitoring the overall progress of the programme. The German Technical Cooperation (GTZ) and the German Development Bank (KfW) would provide the finance, both for the Capacity Building Phase (CBP) and the Full Implementation Phase (FIP) of the IGWDP, through the Government of India, NABARD and WOTR.

Watershed development would entail the identification of a geographical area where a watershed could be developed, followed by specific soil and land treatment to ensure maximum use of available water along the inclination. Once the water availability was maximised along with the desired direction of flow and associated storage capacities were built, the attention would be focused on how to leverage the water for better (or newer) crops. It would also include afforestation

and horticulture, livestock rearing, and pasture and fodder development. A host of farm and non-farm activities could be supported by
better utilisation of water. However, they would require new skills for
the individual as well as the community. These skills would have to
be imparted through adequate training and the building up of capacity
to avail of new opportunities. Finally, over and above skills, financial
resources in the form of microcredit would be required to support a
whole new set of economic activities.

The identification of an area where a watershed could be developed would not necessarily match with the administrative zone like a
taluka or a panchayat since the watershed area would be determined
as an ecological unit rather than an administrative one. The watershed
project would treat every hectare of land to improve the soil quality and water drainage. If part of the land was forestland, the forest
authorities would have to be involved and Joint Forest Management
(JFM) processes designed so that the people's involvement would
remain and there would be no conflict between them and the forest
authorities. The treatment would be done on the basis of survey
numbers, so that every farmer would be involved and identified as
a potential beneficiary. The gram sabha, the body representing the
entire village, would then accept and ratify the project. Once this was
done, the people of the area had to demonstrate their commitment
by undertaking *shramdaan* (voluntary unpaid labour) for the project.
They would also have to give assurances like promising to stay away
from liquor, banning free grazing in the commons, banning felling of
trees, and eschewing water-intensive crops.

The people of the village would then form the Village Watershed
Committee (VWC) and work with the programme implementing
agency (PIA), which was usually a non-governmental organisation
(NGO), to create the civil works such as bunds and check dams and
check weirs. Concerned government agencies would provide the
technical know-how and extension services if and when sought. The
initial work would be done on a small area and then, on successful
completion, the full project would be implemented. Training would
be also imparted during CBP for people to understand the structure of the watershed and its management. Skill training would be
imparted to ensure that people are able to maximise the use of improved water availability through a diversification of their livelihood

busy season was over. Others had gone to work in different cities of Maharashtra like Pune or Mumbai. A few had joined the armed forces or the civil services. One person, Shashidhar Shinde, who had joined the civil services, was determined to change the way of life of his fellow villagers.

Shinde kept returning to his village, trying to organise a group of people who would carry forward his dream of change. He was also quick to see the opportunity of networking with people who had migrated out of the village, and had reasonably stable jobs elsewhere. He was instrumental in creating an active database of the migrants and reaching out to them for help, guidance and, above all, some financial contribution for developing the village. He also realised that to engage people who had roots in the village, but had moved on, it was necessary to make them feel proud of their village. The Gadgebaba Gram Swachata Abhiyan of the Government of Maharashtra, a competition for the cleanest village, provided him with a ready opportunity to showcase Nidhal across the state. For this purpose, he put together a small band of people, 'karyakartas', as he calls them, who would start cleaning up the village. Nidhal won the prize, carrying an award of Rs 1.250 million in 2000–1, after which there was no looking back for collective action in Nidhal. The village participated in the Community Action for Poverty Alleviation Programme in 2002–3 and the villagers constructed nine check dams at a total cost of Rs 1.10 million, of which 36 per cent was raised through local contributions. The residents found new confidence in their own abilities to organise and work together. The migrants became proud and conscious of their roots. Some of them even considered coming back to live in the village.

The vagaries of the monsoons ultimately caught up with the villagers. A couple of years of poor rainfall (the return of *aakaal*, or drought, as the villagers put it) made some of them realise that revisiting the aborted watershed project was the only durable solution to the scarcity of water. The small band of people who had become close to Shinde took up the task of convincing the rest of the villagers that they should petition NABARD to revive the watershed project, and also that they themselves would be able to implement it. All they required was some exposure to such a project, adequate participation by the villagers, and a bit of technical training to take care of the civil works involved.

They succeeded in getting the village charged up and in convincing NABARD (with some persuasion) to revive the project. A Village Watershed Committee (VWC) was formed and a field supervisor for looking after the technicalities of dam construction was employed. He was the only 'outsider'.

NABARD asked for four days of *shramdaan* (voluntary unpaid labour) as a demonstration of the villagers' ability to mobilise collective effort. This was organised quickly, within a period of a fortnight, and the four days of work that was set as the target, was actually accomplished in a little over three days. By June 2004, the Nidhal Watershed Project was resumed with a total financial sanction of Rs 10.9 million. The project measures would take up about 79.5 per cent of the expenses, project management around 14.5 per cent and the remaining 6 per cent would be used for creating a Women's Development Fund, and a small fund for maintenance.

The total geographical area of the Nidhal watershed is around 2,001 hectares. Of this, 1,560 hectares is private cultivable land. The amount of private but uncultivable land is only 182 hectares and forest land is 223 hectares. Around 12 hectares of revenue land and 24 hectares of non-agricultural land make up the rest of the area. The project was supposed to have been completed by 31 October 2010. When we visited the watershed in May 2011 the project was not yet complete, but according to the VWC more than 90 per cent of the work had been done. The PIA is the VWC, registered as Panlot Khestra Vikas Snastha-Nidhal, with 19 members, of which four are female. A women's committee called the Nirmal Sanyukta Mahila Samittee-Nidhal has been registered for taking up the maintenance of the completed watershed.

Making People Participate: Shinde's Role

Shashidhar Shinde played a critical role in mobilising groups to pool their resources and work together. According to him, his initial motivation came from comments made by his school headmaster during a felicitation ceremony held in Shinde's honour. The issue of the lack of a proper school building, due to which the school was downgraded from higher secondary to secondary level, was raised. During Shinde's school days, classes had to be held at the local temple. Shinde, who had learnt to appreciate the value of a good education, resolved to seek contributions from the community for constructing a school building.

His first move in this direction was to create a network of non-resident villagers (NRVs) who had migrated out. He first connected with the NRVs through a letter around 1983, and then held a meeting for the entire community at Nidhal during Diwali that year to collect contributions. There were almost 750 such NRVs, of whom around 680 attended the meeting, as did most villagers. The annual contributions were set at Rs 51 per village household and Rs 100 per NRV. With the total contribution exceeding Rs 100,000 annually, building construction commenced but proceeded slowly, taking over a decade. During this time, this process of contributing towards community assets took root in people's minds. They became more community oriented and their trust levels improved. Their next decision was to construct a temple. This was completed in three years using the same fund flow mechanism.

A natural division of labour emerged within the community, with a core group of people taking over the organisation and supervision of such construction activities. This core group was being referred to as Shinde's karyakartas by the villagers, though we understood neither the precise status nor the process of their selection. We observed that the village had several youth clubs whose walls were adorned with Shinde's statements and pictures, and inferred that these village youth perhaps played the role of hands-on facilitators. Shinde realised the need for karyakartas when he first started to mobilise the NRVs to help in the construction of the school. He realised that the middle-aged NRV had familial responsibilities and other commitments which, despite their best intentions, left them with little time to devote to village development activities. He felt the need to build a cadre of development workers who would be willing to make some personal sacrifice for the upliftment of their village. While there was a dearth of karyakartas in the beginning, as their efforts began to yield fruit, the number of karyakartas had grown to the point where they were difficult to manage. In addition there were *tarun mandals* (youth forums) mentored by Shinde for different hamlets, and a registered federation of these youth forums. Youth were automatically made members of the *tarun mandal* after clearing their secondary exams and they were involved in constructive activities through which they are supposed to develop their personality and leadership skills.

Success with construction of physical assets motivated NRVs to introduce new cropping practices in the village, such as grape and pomegranate cultivation, since both could grow in areas with low rainfall. When these experiments failed, the villagers realised that the root of the solution to improved agricultural productivity or success in growing new crops was the availability of groundwater. Some of the NRVs had heard of the IGWDP watershed initiative in Maharashtra, administered by NABARD, and a team of villagers approached the NABARD local office to consider implementing a watershed project at Nidhal. However, the project was abandoned, as already discussed in the preceding section. In Shinde's opinion, this was because of the inability (or unwillingness) of the non-governmental organisation (NGO) to engage with the natural leaders and karyakartas of the village (including Shinde).

Around 2000, Shinde, as part of the rural development department of Maharashtra, was involved in formulating a policy on health and sanitation, and the *nirmal gaon* (clean village) campaign was launched. Knowing the state of sanitation in other villages in the state, Shinde was fairly confident that his village had a fair chance of winning an award. A gram sabha was organised to inform the villagers about the campaign and seek their support. Shinde's karyakartas physically locked people out of their homes to get them to attend the meeting. It was decided to participate in the campaign with the objective of winning at least one of the many prizes instituted by the department. The process of changing people's sanitation habits, eliminating open drains, ensuring garbage is disposed of properly took over a year, but the efforts paid off as the village received numerous cash awards amounting to Rs 1.25 million in 1999–2000 for its cleanliness.

Despite the positive tempo in the community, this period marked the beginning of a long spell of drought for the village. For six years, from 1998 onwards, tankers were used to supply drinking water to the village as there was no water available. Poor rainfall sharply reduced the agricultural output of the village. This triggered a revival in the interest around a watershed project, and a delegation from Nidhal revisited the NABARD office at Pune, only to be turned back as it was against the bank's policy to reopen closed projects. The NRV network now sprung into action and arranged a meeting with the NABARD official who had sanctioned the original project at Mumbai. This official was a little more open to the idea, seeing the enthusiasm of the delegation of NRVs that had approached him. A team from NABARD visited the site, identified the 150 hectares of land that would be developed in the CBP, and made the decision to reopen the project, provided that the villagers demonstrated the willingness to participate. Meanwhile, the drought continued. Finally, around 2004, NABARD's team came down to see the shramdaan from all the villagers for land development in the CBP, and sanctioned the Final Implementation Phase (FIP).

When we visited, the watershed work was nearing completion, with visible results. According to the VWC, the water table had risen by 30 ft; the recent rains might have contributed to this increase. Shinde's managerial prowess was evident in his persuading the VWC to promote drip irrigation mechanisms for farmers covering all the land from valley to ridge, to minimise water wastage. He chose this over the more obvious, but harder-to-implement, approach of banning all bore wells to preserve groundwater. Every hamlet in Nidhal was made accountable for progress in drip irrigation in their region, a scheme supported by the NRVs who had seen how successful drip irrigation was in other parts of the state. Bus connectivity between Nidhal and Mumbai had improved and the NRVs were able to visit often. Some NRVs who did not achieve success in the city had returned, while other villagers were able to leverage the existing network of NRVs to find better opportunities in the city.

The VWC hired the services of Ratan Kumar, an agricultural engineer from the same district, as field supervisor to assist with technical structures for watershed development. With his technical expertise he was able to repair and rebuild poorly built or damaged check dams from previous efforts. Interest from fixed deposits, made from the cash awards received by the village till date, was being used to maintain the existing watershed structures. He was impressed by the villagers and their levels of knowledge and eagerness to work together. According to Ratan Kumar, this social cohesion could be largely explained by the efforts made by Shinde and the vice chairman of the VWC. (He revealed that the vice chairman was Shinde's cousin.) Over a time frame of six months, Shinde and his cousin had been taking groups of 10 to 12 farmers from Nidhal to see Mumbai for as long 15 days. This exposure helped build their confidence and team spirit. They visited different government offices to learn of the different facilities they could avail. Shinde was also instrumental in introducing pomegranate in the village, based on observing the economics of pomegranate in Ahmadnagar where he was posted for a while. In addition, he facilitated farmers' access to the pomegranate market. Ratan Kumar claimed that a 2 hectares plot of pomegranate could fetch revenue of up to Rs 700,000 annually. He had an interesting analogy — he considered pomegranate as the fruit that filled the wallet of the watershed project.

Outcomes: Assets and Livelihood Opportunities

As we entered Nidhal, what struck us was the cleanliness and 'urban nature' of the entire village. There were cemented paths all around and no open drains were visible — wherever we looked we could see well constructed buildings — with a large privately owned nursing home facing the cooperative building that we entered (see Plate 3.1).

Plate 3.1: Covered Drainage System in the Streets of Nidhal 'Village'

Source: All photographs in this volume have been taken by the authors, unless otherwise specified.

The setting of the meeting with the villagers was rather formal, with plenty of chairs arranged in an orderly manner, and we were pleasantly surprised to see a larger fraction of women in the audience than we had seen elsewhere (see Plate 3.2). This, they claimed, was because many of the menfolk were away attending a marriage in a nearby village. We, along with all the attendees, were served Pepsi, which was also a surprise, as we had expected tea. The field engineer of the watershed, Ratan Kumar, conducted the meeting. We were impressed by the patient hearing that this group of people gave him. Among the people sitting in the front row, four represented the VWC. The village sarpanch, a lady, was there too (see Box 3.1).

Later, we spoke to six beneficiaries of the watershed who were not VWC members. Some of them had land at higher altitudes and others had land in the valley, with landholding size varying from 3 to 12 acres. They discussed how they switched from the traditional cereal crops of jowar and bajra in rain-fed land to high value fruits such as guava, *sapota* and *sitafal* for cash income using drip irrigation. Forward linkages with markets were in place, and farmers had a choice where

Plate 3.2: Meeting the VWC at the Community Hall of the Cooperative Building, Nidhal

Box 3.1: The Making of a Sarpanch

Sarpanch of the village, a lady named Madhuri Bai, had come to Nidhal 21 years ago as a newly-wed bride from a nearby village in Satara district where the fields were green and water was not a problem. She found the village dry and dirty. She had accompanied her husband, a clerk in the army, to an earlier posting in Jallandhar. When her husband shifted to Nashik she came back to stay in the village and decided to contribute towards its development. Her two sons are studying. The younger one is in class 12 and studies in the town of Nashik where he stays with his father. The elder son studies engineering in a college in Lonavla. The sarpanch, who has just a secondary education, runs a beauty parlour and also tends the family plot of 10 acres. She campaigned for the panchayat seat because it was reserved for a scheduled caste (SC) woman. Her husband did not mind since the children had grown up, but could not campaign for his wife as he was a government employee. Moreover, her husband's sister-in-law was also in the fray, leading to some friction in the family, but this was sorted out eventually. This was the second time that she had contested, even though she won in 2005, she did not take up the post of sarpanch as her children were too young.

The beauty parlour was a good place for networking and she was able to campaign successfully among the womenfolk of the village. The sarpanch had a lot of suggestions and plans she was working on with the panchayat — a new road, a new bridge and a crematorium. She did not seem afraid to handle banks and other government departments, and was grateful for the support and inspiration that Shinde provided the panchayat. Madhuri Bai was part of the VWC in 2004, but stepped down as a member after she was elected as sarpanch of the village panchayat in 2005, although she did not take up the post at that time.

to sell their produce depending on the prevailing price in each market. This information they received from local traders (*dalals*) over the phone. Surplus crop was sold at Mumbai where prices were on a per kilogram basis. They also had cattle which yielded additional income through the sale of milk, for which the milk chains are well established. The group we talked to owned about five cows each, on an average, which yielded 7 litres to 8 litres of milk a day which sold for Rs 16 per litre. They claimed that after the watershed development their disposable incomes had more than doubled, and this was only the tip of the iceberg, as they had just started to get a positive stream of income from their fruit orchards. Some of them were experimenting with new crops or processes. Gopi had diversified into growing figs in addition to pomegranates. Sunil (officially recorded as a below poverty line or BPL farmer) planned a fully organic fruit orchard on 0.25 acres of his land such that he could sell fruit round the year. After the watershed programme, Sunil returned from Pune (where he used to ply rickshaws) to tend to his land. They talked about another group of farmers who were experimenting with growing produce in a net-house, which they got at a subsidised rate from the government by pooling their lands together. The same group had now applied for assistance to the national horticulture board for growing fruit trees collectively. They narrated to us the story of Sanjiv, a cloth merchant, who was also a member of the VWC, who had visited Singapore and Thailand recently as a reward from his suppliers for outstanding retail sales. In addition to a roaring retail business in cloth and ready-made garments, Sanjiv owned over 20 coconut trees and an orchard of over 1,000 pomegranate trees. We also got to know of another farmer with 10 acres of land who had taken an individual loan of Rs 400,000 to purchase a tractor. Rental income from the tractor was estimated by his peers to be about Rs 300,000 a year. Even with employing a driver at Rs 6,000 per month, he had already repaid 75 per cent of his loan.

So far, as part of the watershed programme, 150,000 saplings had been planted, and over 800 hectares of land brought under drip irrigation. This resulted in a 25-fold increase in irrigated area. Crops were grown around the year, including water-intensive sugar cane using drip irrigation. The village cooperative, set up after watershed activities commenced, had a processing unit for pomegranate, green peas and potatoes along with several greenhouses. It was claimed that gross annual earnings from selling processed pomegranate exceeded Rs 10 million in 2010.

The villagers informed us that to retain Nidhal's reputation as a model village, every individual planted at least one tree each year, so as to ensure that 4,000 trees were planted in the village annually. This was being supported by the government, through a grant of Rs 400,000 for three years. They also conducted melas on *santulit paryavaran* (balanced environment) to spread awareness on 4 March every year. Through the 'Swajaladhara Yojana', Nidhal now had metered drinking water round the clock, marking a quantum jump in living conditions in the village. The village was also a recipient of a Rs 500,000 grant from the chief minister's fund in recognition of its overall progress. The problem of alcoholism was once quite common. They claimed that the *paanlote* (watershed) project had encouraged people to stop supplying liquor as there were alternative opportunities for livelihood available.

Vishal, who was the leading liquor producer in the village, had switched to growing peanuts and cucumber. Although liquor production and sale was monetarily more beneficial, he realised the negative impact this was having on the households that consumed liquor. This realisation, according to him, came from persistent conversations with Shinde. Vishal also joined the Vyasan Mukti movement, and though the village was not completely alcohol free, about 80 per cent families no longer consumed liquor. Many recounted memories of an incident when the faces of drunken mazdoors were blackened, and they were paraded on the village streets before being handed over to the police.

Like Sunil, the farmers we spoke to averred that all 60 BPL families in the village were now better off, though the tag BPL had stayed on — *naam ke liye rahe gaye*. The villagers claimed that from being a notorious village with 'the greatest number of non-performing assets in the past' (probably referring to defaults), Nidhal had evolved into a place where moneylenders and bankers were eager to provide credit.

Self-help Groups (SHGs) and the Involvement of Women

In Nidhal we found the SHG movement to be quite strong and active. Women seemed confident about taking loans and trying out different income-earning livelihood schemes. There were around 70 SHGs in the village of which 10 were made up of women from BPL families. These SHGs were given a grant of Rs 50,000 each from the panchayat to start their activities. Every woman in the village was a member of some SHG or the other. Every SHG, in turn, had a bank account. Hence, there was 100 per cent financial inclusion. The 34 SHGs in the watershed area, comprising 581 members, had a collective savings of Rs 1.97 million. In one or two of the relatively richer SHGs, the monthly contribution was claimed to be Rs 3,000. This came as a surprise to us as we were used to hearing of monthly contributions of the order of Rs 50 to Rs 100 a month in the other villages we had visited. The collective savings were large enough to service the unforeseen economic needs of the villagers. Thus, the SHGs with a bigger pool of loanable funds had successfully replaced the *sahukar*s (moneylenders) as the source for distress borrowing.

All the ladies we met were educated and literate. All their children were going to school or college, often in other cities in Maharashtra. Many of them had their own shops making pickles and *vada pao*s, or tailoring and embroidering clothes. The women we spoke to appeared to be independent, unafraid to take their own business decisions and felt no compulsion to consult their husbands for this purpose. A lady had taken a loan of Rs 50,000 from her SHG and was buying furniture from Satara (the relatively nearby district town) and utensils from Pune to sell in Nidhal. Another lady was running her own cloth store with help from a few other women. In the village, more than 80 per cent of the womenfolk claimed to be literate. The ones who were illiterate (mostly middle-aged or old) were encouraged to participate in the Maharashtra government's adult education programme.

The ladies had had opportunities for training in a variety of skills, as part of the CBP of the watershed project. The range of training varied from running a beauty parlour, dress design and tailoring, candle making, dairy development, waste water usage to rainwater harvesting. Many SHG members were actually reverse migrants, who had spent some years in Mumbai, but had returned to the village and were instrumental in training some local women. The solidarity among women was noticeable. All the women came together every 15 days and cleaned the village. They were proud of the award they had received for cleanliness, and did not want that image to be tarnished. The women claimed that all the households had two-wheelers, and there were as many as 20–30 cars in the village. All had mobiles and TV connections. Most families cooked using gas cylinders though a few had *chulla*s. Many had hot water geyser connections too. They were not too concerned about conserving the natural environment, though they were aware of the ban on cutting trees in the village and its neighbourhood.

According to these women we talked to, caste or economic means (above or below the poverty line) were not important issues. They did not care much about party politics. They wanted to ensure that the development of the village was independent of the complications of party politics. They also wanted that party politicians not interfere with the development process in Nidhal. Health was not an important concern. They thought the region was not much polluted and hence environment-related health hazards were low. They all relied on the Primary Health Centre (PHC) as the first line of defence. Otherwise the availability of private health care was adequate. Pusegaon, 9 km away, was the place where complicated cases were taken to. As far as school education was concerned the villagers had been able to build a school out of their own initiative and funds.

On talking about the future of their next generation and the importance of education, almost all the women we interviewed were aware of the instrumental value of education in obtaining employment and making a living. Some were clearly aware of the empowering role of education and its value in self-realisation. For instance, one lady was emphatically supportive of her little girl's ambition to get into the state civil service or even aspire to become an officer of the Indian Civil Service. There was no problem if the next generation went off to far away cities for higher education or employment, but it was important that they kept contact with the village and their roots, and helped in the development of the village as far as possible.

Looking into the Future

As many as 80 families who had migrated from Nidhal to towns and cities before the construction of the watershed had now returned to the village. People had realised that migrating to cities for a job was not always advisable as the number of jobs were few and jobseekers many. Also, the villagers had realised that the quality of life in a village was better than living in a slum in a city. However, enrolment in the armed forces was encouraged and several young men regularly left the village for that purpose. Captain Balaram Shinde, treasurer of the watershed committee, who had been in the Indian army, proudly proclaimed that while he had seen fertile farmlands in Punjab and West Bengal, the agricultural practices in Nidhal were superior.

The VWC members confirmed to us that they had created a maintenance fund and made regular contributions towards it. The maintenance fund, currently at Rs 224,000, was to ensure that when NABARD disengaged, there were enough resources for the VWC to continue with the upkeep of the watershed structures. Moreover, the VWC was currently acting as a social and technical support service provider for watershed development in a neighbouring village, Kolewadi, which would result in some income for the VWC. It intended to take up more such consulting opportunities in the future. Future challenges for the watershed committee included ensuring that people continued to value the importance of water, even in years of normal rainfall.

The VWC had identified around 135 families, who, because of their poverty, were vulnerable to even minor fluctuations in their incomes. As a result of this vulnerability, they were likely to be more concerned with their current incomes rather than the long-term conservation of water. Doubts remained about the effectiveness of the VWC's slogan of *mango mat, khud karo* ('do not ask, do it yourself') for this group of people, as there were concerns that this group could never become self-reliant. We noted that the relatively more affluent people usually did not put in physical labour, but were happy to donate money. In fact, shramdaan and *aarthik daan* (monetary donation) were treated as pure substitutes by the well-to-do. It was considered to be an important way of redistributing wealth.

With over 260 families (out of a total of 582 families) owning over 2 hectares of land, and with only about 60 families that were landless, there was a rising demand for agricultural labour However, this did not translate into gains for all landless families (see Box 3.2). The well-to-do farmers were worried about the rise in daily wages. Too much activity and opportunities along with government schemes like National Rural Employment Guarantee Act (NREGA) had added to their woes. Input costs were rising too, as a result of which their margins were being squeezed. More farm mechanisation was being considered as the possible solution to the growing shortage of labour.

Looking Beyond

We also spent some time with another group of people who were backbenchers in the introductory meeting with the villagers, and who appeared a little reticent. It was not because they did not have a reasonable degree of trust in the working of the VWC. This group was of the opinion that the VWC often exaggerated the availability of water

Box 3.2: Govardhan Sutar: Untouched by Change

> Govardhan Sutar, a carpenter by trade, is in his mid-30s, although his frail frame makes him look much older. Govardhan did not possess any land and had studied only up to the seventh class. He lived with his sister as his wife had expired and they did not have any children. When he came to meet us, he was dressed in a shabby dhoti and vest. His apparel was distinctly different from the villagers around him. When we asked him about the benefits of the watershed, he expressed mixed feelings. The only tangible benefit he could identify was an improved availability of drinking water. He claimed that the watershed was good for the village and would benefit the farmers. This in turn had the potential to benefit him as he could make and repair wooden farm equipment. However, he pointed out that with increasing mechanisation this possibility was becoming bleak. So far, the demand for his services had not increased after the watershed, as people now preferred to buy ready-made furniture sourced from the city. When we enquired about his income, he estimated it to be somewhere between Rs 150 and Rs 200 a day. He was quick to point out that some of his customers paid him in kind. This was changing to a more standardised piece rate paid in cash. However, he did not perceive his total income to be rising in any significant way due to the watershed as the demand for his services was steadily declining. We enquired about whether he was availing of the benefits from the NREGA scheme, to which he responded that he was unable to do so as he did not possess a job card.

and the height of the water table. They believed that the groundwater level had not gone up in any perceptible manner in the upper (ridge) parts of the watershed. In the upper parts, two wells were now completely useless, and one check dam was dysfunctional. Reasons why they did not participate in watershed-related activities varied from not having enough time to all not needing to do it.

Alternative ways of supplementing incomes and acquiring access to productive capital were highlighted by this group. A set of five amongst them had pooled their land (35 acres) to take a loan to share (commonly own) a borewell that went 30 ft deep. Their land was not very fertile, and hence they grew fodder, and some minor commercial crops for subsistence. We found them to be extremely conscious about market price movements. The unexplained variation of prices had left these farmers dissatisfied with the market. Most of them argued that their children would be better off doing something other than farming, because despite all their efforts and innovations, the price they received was entirely beyond their control.

Was there a trace of exasperation in their voices when these farmers with land suggested that perhaps too much land was being allocated to the cultivation of fruit trees? There was a large wastage of fruits. The VWC clearly exerted some pressure — they had to all sign an agreement that they would not grow sugar cane as it used too much water. Pomegranate became the favoured variety of fruit. Now the pomegranate orchards were being hit by some skin blight, and they were worried about the losses this disease would imply. Would losses lead to lower incomes and more migration from the village again? They agreed that it would. Anyway, according to them, migration of the severely distressed still took place. According to this group, it was the unskilled but not extremely destitute migrant who had the courage to return to the village and try their hand at new opportunities and activities. The really destitute could ill afford the odds of unsuccessful reverse migration.

An important aspect of Nidhal's story of change was the lack of integration of the scheduled tribe (ST) community of Ramoshis (originally a wandering shepherd tribe that now provided the supply of wage labour for the village). The Ramoshis had a locality of their own about more than a kilometre away from the main village residential area (see Plate 3.3). The VWC informed us that the Ramoshis preferred to live near their land even though they could have opted to live in the main village. Their huts (about 50 families) were not pucca houses, and were generally in poor condition. However, we found that in the cluster of 50 huts there were at least half a dozen dish antennas for cable television. Most of the Ramoshis, it was claimed, also had cell phones. They had put in the maximum labour in the construction of the watershed. They had obtained water and electricity only after 2008. They were able to demand and get a small school building for primary classes very near the cluster of huts where they lived since the school in the centre of the village was far away for the very young children to walk to. Was this an achievement, or was it a segregation that effectively kept the Ramoshi children away from the others? The Ramoshis were either landless or had tiny landholdings averaging 0.25 acres. Their living area had one common well for the entire community, near which the new school building had come up.

This well was there before the watershed came up. Most of the men-folk worked as agricultural labourers. During the time we visited the village, the men and some women had temporarily migrated for daily work as the demand for labour was at a peak. We were told that only the infirm and very old had remained.

Plate 3.3: The Ramoshi Settlement at Nidhal: A Stark Contrast to the Nirmal Gram

On talking to some of them, one noticed the remarkable contrast to the positive energy level and optimism that most of the villagers in Nidhal exhibited. Here the inhibition to talk, the almost mechanical tendency to agree on anything the rest of the village was doing, left us in doubt about whether the Ramoshi version of 'the good life' and development was different from or congruent with the rest of the village.

Durability and Rootedness

It was the availability of water that made Nidhal a prosperous village where people seemed to have confidence in their future. The setting up of the watershed was itself an exercise in the self-realisation of a community — mustering the courage to act together. This courage came from the leadership provided by a few people in the village, particularly the civil servant who nurtured his roots and got together a set of fellow villagers. Together they were ready to face the challenge of development — not only resolve the water problem, but also fight social evils like addiction to country liquor and improve the sanitation and cleanliness of the village.

The village had seen a lot of migration for work into the armed forces or the vineyards of Nashik, or urban construction markets as far away as Pune or even Mumbai. We found a surprisingly large proportion of the VWC comprising ex-servicemen. Their attitude and approach were disciplined and they often used *fauji* language and metaphors. They kept repeating that obstacles were there only to be overcome. Finding a practical solution to real life problems was their primary objective. Clearly, the guiding spirit behind this was Shinde. His omnipresence was too much to miss. Even when he could not attend a village meeting or a festival, his words would be heard over loudspeakers fitted in his native house so that all in the village could listen and learn. Shinde's cut-outs would be used to decorate the village. His followers, who controlled the watershed committee and were generally the opinion makers in the village, viewed him as more than a great man. To them his image, one felt, was almost of messianic proportions.

The group that dominated the watershed and the affairs of the village constituted the village elite. They were all well-off relatively, in the sense that they each had 8 to 10 acres of cultivable land. They had some education — most had studied up to class eight or class 10. They seemed to be very confident and organised in what they were doing, their confidence presumably arising out of the successes that they already had had — the watershed, the numerous awards and recognitions that the village had won, and the numerous other projects that they had initiated like building a high school, a large temple and some village roads. Their ambition was clear — they wanted the village of Nidhal to gradually develop into a small town with urban facilities, public facilities like schools, colleges, hotels, hospitals (we saw a fairly large private nursing home in the village square) with paved roads and street lights. The VWC had volunteered to help other neighbouring villages with their experience of water management and the construction of Nidhal's watershed.

Beneath the apparent success of Shinde's team's organisational ability to garner the energy of the local people into doing something positive that affected their lives, some signs of power struggles were evident. It was clear the leadership of the village and the watershed committee was controlled by about a dozen people who were very close and loyal to Shinde, who had taken the early initiatives for change. Their account of their experience in the village of Nidhal appeared to be one of consensus and unity and voluntary people's participation. However, when talking to other villagers the story was not so rosy. Not all liked the power and domination of the village 'elite' close to Shinde. There were complaints about the misuse of power and many wished for an alternative leadership. The opposition was not overt. The power of the dominant group was perhaps too strong. The Ramoshi tribe and their quiet exclusion were noticeable against the energy of the vocal and active elite. Indeed the activities of the karyakartas eclipsed the role of the panchayat. This was bound to create an alternative power structure within the village which could have long-term repercussions on the democratic process.

A distinguishing feature of Nidhal was that the fruits of the watershed development were evident even before the project had been fully completed. The story had lessons on how people interested in development could actually organise themselves and muster the courage to do the project themselves, if the need so arose. Nidhal revealed the seeds of a transformative process where dynamic leadership and an imaginative use of human resources played a critical role. Yet behind the obvious successes there were evidences of rising inequalities and resentfulness against the domination of the powerful elite.

4

The Power of Politics
Self-reliance Denied

The district of Bardhaman in West Bengal is regarded as prosperous, with the people engaged in extensive agricultural activities, especially paddy cultivation (see Map 4.1). It also has a number of organised industries such as coal and steel. Bardhaman district was one of the first districts in India where the experiment of the 'Green Revolution' in terms of high-yielding varieties of seeds and chemical fertilisers was carried out in the 1960s. Bhalki is a small village in this district. The name Bhalki comes from a story that a bear (*bhaluk*) mother had raised a human boy in this place who later became the king. In memory of his bear mother, the king had erected a tomb, referred to locally as the *machan* (a platform). The forest still has some ruins from the fifteenth century. However, the village of Bhalki (located on a hillock), about 150 km from Kolkata, near the edge of a dense green sal forest (which is part of the Kanska Range), had remained arid and very poor. Water was scarce. The terrain resulted in very high run-off during the rainy season. The need to harvest water and manage it for productive use was an option available to the village provided collective action could be organised to create and install the necessary infrastructure.

The initiative, according to the villagers of Bhalki, came from two persons who worked with great patience and effort to convince the villagers to work together to build a watershed. One of them was a local political worker from the Communist Party of India (Marxist) or CPI(M), and the other was the local block development officer (BDO), a government employee. The BDO, whom the residents referred to as *Bhagaban* (God), tried to instil in them that political differences did not have a place in matters of development. He was instrumental in seeding the idea of the watershed in the minds of the villagers.

Map 4.1: Bardhaman District in West Bengal

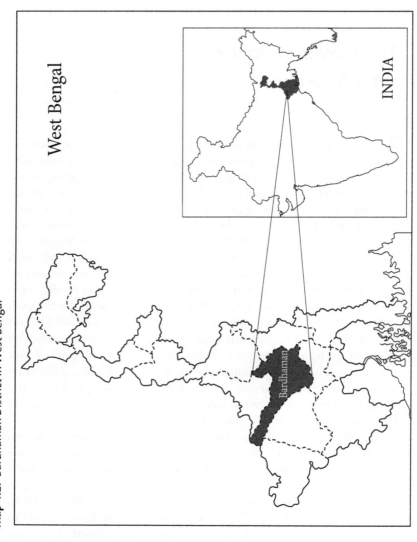

These two persons constantly mentioned the new opportunities that would arise from augmenting and managing water resources. A story the villagers keep telling, with a twinkle in their eyes, is how the two men would invite the villagers to attend awareness meetings to discuss the possibility of a watershed. The villagers were welcomed to attend the meeting on the condition that they were ready to 'leave their clothes outside'. This was a metaphor used by them to indicate that whatever political 'colours' people wore would have to be discarded when they came for the meeting. This would ensure (in an area where political polarisation is sharp and runs very deep) that ideological differences would not stand in the way of asserting the interests of the village as a community. This attitude is rare in West Bengal, especially when one of the persons championing it was himself a political functionary.

Ultimately their sustained efforts paid off, and the local people formed a non-governmental organisation (NGO) called the Bhalki Jalbivajika Unnayan Committee (BJUC) to create an institutional platform through which the National Bank for Agriculture and Rural Development (NABARD) could be approached to provide financial resources and technical know-how to build the watershed. From its inception, BJUC has been controlled by relatively well-to-do villagers belonging to the upper castes. There was little representation from tribes or minorities living in the village. The political leanings of the members of the NGO were diverse, covering the entire political spectrum. These well-to-do villagers had bought into the idea that it was possible to put the interest of the village community above their own individual political beliefs. Some of them had surplus land that could be donated to the community to build an office or plant trees. Most of the office-bearers of the NGO had independent sources of livelihoods, and hence their own economic stakes in the watershed were lower than the stakes of their relatively poorer neighbours.

A series of collective action initiatives followed in anticipation of NABARD agreeing to support the watershed. An officer of the Gram Unnayan Daptar was roped in to work with the people to form self-help groups (SHGs). The Grameen Bank piloted the setting up of a cooperative for microfinance. As these organisational changes were taking place in the village, NABARD was approached for financial resources and it agreed to give a 100 per cent grant to build the watershed.

The local political parties were indifferent to these developments, probably because the NGO did not subscribe to any specific political ideology and the village was neither big nor prosperous. NABARD, unlike in many other instances, allowed the local Village Watershed Committee (VWC) to become the de-facto Programme Implementation Agency (PIA), though the official PIA was the panchayat samiti. Local expertise and local labour was thought to be adequate to do the civil works required to construct the bunds and check dams. The watershed would entail a lot of *shramdaan* for the project to create the sense of joint ownership and responsibility. The project's design also required the involvement of women. This, in turn, necessitated the formation of women's SHGs who could help clear the terrain and plant a large number of trees as part of the afforestation programme. The watershed area covered approximately 950 hectares of which about 60 per cent of the land was privately held.

The Making of the Watershed (2002–08)

In addition to the technical civil construction and treatment of the land that is typical of any watershed, there was also a process of social re-engineering and an attempt to change the natural landscape to ensure better groundwater recharging. The process followed was actually quite bold. In anticipation of improved water availability it was decided to take *privately* owned fallow or uncultivable land (which was abundant in Bhalki village) on lease for *public* tree plantations (see Plate 4.1). Ponds were to be re-excavated for watershed development coupled with the promotion of common pisciculture. This was a little difficult at first but it was believed that once the benefits could be demonstrated, it would become easier to enter into understandings with the landowners. All planned demonstrations of benefits were to be on the worst pieces of wasteland to start with. Many of the landowners were absentees who had stayed away from the village for long periods of time. Their land was also used (without permission), with the understanding that if and when the landlord showed up, the lease would be regularised and the legitimate share of the benefits be given to the owner.

The sharing formula was as follows: from the realised proceeds of the economic activity carried out on leased land, the landowner would

Plate 4.1: Tree Plantations at Bhalki Village

get 25 per cent, the SHG which had conducted the activity would get 70 per cent, 1 per cent would go to the panchayat samiti, 2 per cent to the panchayat, and 2 per cent to the Bhalki Watershed Committee. The trees planted could be 'harvested' for fruit or for timber only after some time. Timber from the *sonajhuri* trees would take seven years. The plantations would have trees planted every year. After the completion of seven years the oldest trees could be cut down and a new set of trees planted as replacement. In the first two to three years, other schemes such as planting kitchen gardens were also initiated as supplementary livelihood opportunities. The plan was to distribute small packets of vegetable seeds to each family to plant in their own kitchen garden.

There were around 60 SHGs and 600 families totalling about 2,700 people in Bhalki. With an average size of eight to 12 members per SHG, almost all families were involved in at least one SHG. No one could be a member of more than one SHG. They were all part of the collective effort to get the watershed complete and the new natural capital installed in the village.

The Benefits

Once NABARD became involved in Bhalki, a number of other government projects descended on this erstwhile neglected area. Swajaldhara (a drinking water project) was commissioned in 2005–6. When the project cost exceeded the sanctioned amount by around Rs 200,000 due to a delay in execution, the watershed committee organised a loan from SHG funds to cover the shortfall, rather than wait for government to sanction funds to cover the deficit. In terms of other infrastructure, the prime minister's Pradhan Mantri Gram Sadak Yojana (PMGSY) scheme was used to build some connecting roads around Bhalki.

As the watershed project started showing tangible benefits, private landowners began to show interest in getting involved in the watershed activities. The water table, to begin with, was as low as 300 ft below the ground, but had risen to 160 ft at some places and was as high as 60 ft in others (see Plate 4.2). Now people had submersible pumps in their houses for water. The primary objective of the watershed

Plate 4.2: The Watershed Project Ensures Assured Water Supply

project was achieved. Further, moneylending in the traditional sense of usurious activities had declined significantly. For social exigencies people would sell their land in the past, but after the watershed, they preferred taking loans from SHG funds rather than lose their assets to scheming moneylenders. Another outcome reflecting the attitude towards collective action was apparent from the way the Mahatma Gandhi National Rural Employment Guarantee Act (MGNREGA) was executed in Bhalki as compared to other villages. The VWC had considerable influence in choosing the projects to be covered. For instance, the concrete benefits of deepening village ponds were clearly evident. Table 4.1 shows some of the targeted versus actual outcomes of the project.

Table 4.1: Targeted and Actual Outcomes of the Watershed Project at Bhalki

Asset Creation Activity	Targeted Outcome	Achieved Outcome as on 2008
Afforestation	75,000 plants	100,000 *sonajhuri* trees and around 4,000 other trees
Horticulture	3,600 plants	Around 20,000 fruit trees
Medicinal Plants	2,000 plants	Taken up by tribal SHGs, failure at marketing level
Wasteland brought under Cultivation	241 hectares	75 hectares of cultivable land brought under cultivation, uncultivable wasteland used for afforestation
Innovation	Crop Demonstration	Use of vermicompost for fruit and vegetable cultivation Maize and mustard cultivation Greenhouse technology
Bhalki *Jalavibivajika* Bank (Microfinance Institution)		378 women beneficiaries, with borrowing ranging from Rs 500 to Rs 25,000 facilitated by their SHGs

Source: All tables in this volume have been prepared by the authors.

Fault-lines Appear (2008–10)

The initial enthusiasm and commitment shown by the villagers were indeed remarkable. People had come together ignoring political differences, and in many cases, as in some of the SHGs, they had forged teams irrespective of caste and religion. The objective was to create natural assets that would give all of them additional income in the future. The watershed itself was an asset jointly owned and it would improve agricultural yields for all. There would be new income-earning opportunities from medicinal plants and fish. There was a shared purpose in all the activities and the efforts. Even the landless would stand to benefit from the income to be earned from the planted trees (jointly owned by SHGs) on leased land. The Bhalki Watershed and the Bhalki Microfinance Institution (which would provide microfinance to the SHGs) would form the major institutions that would facilitate access to finance for the villagers.

However, this feeling of togetherness and shared ambitions soon began to give way to individualistic claims to corner the maximum benefits possible. It was only after the watershed construction had been completed and the trees planted that the possibility of realising additional income became patently evident to everybody. Suddenly, there were business people from outside who were interested in obtaining timber from the village. Seed merchants were pushing new seeds and new varieties of plants with a promise to buy back the yield. During this time the absentee landlords, on whose lands trees had been planted, also surfaced in the village and became active, trying to scuttle the plans of the villagers and appropriate the entire benefit. The VWC members reported, in a couple of instances, that some trees were chopped off at night and a rumour was spread that it was the committee that was behind the mischief. The committee, however, claimed that this was the doing of the timber mafia. The allegation against the committee was that they intended to reap the full commercial returns from the trees, without doing the hard work of planting and tending to them and were actually duping the villagers.

By this time, the trees were six years old, and the common wisdom was that the best prices would be received when the trees were at least a year older. The rumour-mongers urged the villagers not to wait till the seventh year to prevent the VWC from appropriating the entire revenue from selling the trees. Slowly, this subterranean conspiracy gained momentum, and the villagers began to doubt the integrity of the VWC. Meanwhile, the politics of the state had begun to change. The influence of the CPI(M) was waning, and the panchayat of Bhalki began to take an active interest in the project for the first time. In short, a new group of stakeholders were emerging who could change the way the potential benefits would be distributed and in turn the fate of the watershed itself.

The Cracks Widen (2010–11)

We first visited Bhalki around the end of April 2010; it was hot and sultry with the sun beating down. We arrived at the 'NABARD *bari*', which houses the VWC and the Microfinance Bank. Knowing that NABARD's last tranche of grant to the watershed project was disbursed in February 2010, we were keen on understanding the outcome of the project and its future outlook rather than delving into the past.

We were informed by the VWC that if we were to visibly see the benefits from the watershed then we would have to return after the onset of the monsoons. We would then observe how the area under cultivation had gone up manifold, replacing the red desert landscape with lush green covers. The waterbodies, in some of which the re-excavation work was being carried out from VWC funds at that time, would be ready for harvesting fish. More so, this would be the first year when a mango harvest (from the trees planted as part of the watershed activities) would be sold in the nearby market of Budbud. Kanai Manna, a VWC functionary, proclaimed: 'A watershed programme can completely transform a village's economy'. Despite this positive talk, the body language of the functionaries conveyed to us a sort of helplessness, as though they were under great discomfort to maintain a positive front before us. They shared with us their interim report from December 2008 which documented the physical progress made against plans and promised to share with us the final project completion report which was under preparation then. On persistent probing we were able to discern some of the reasons behind their despondency.

We came to know that despite the watershed development project, migration away from Bhalki had not been contained. Even now, most menfolk went to other villages or nearby towns to earn a living. On a positive note, however, many people who had migrated out to urban areas now visited the village more frequently, appreciative of better connectivity, improved sanitation and the availability of water and electricity.

The fisheries department had come to Bhalki with a tried and tested idea of culturing high value prawns in freshwater ponds by lining them suitably and adding appropriate salinity. Unfortunately this experiment was a complete failure — some said the prawns contracted some epidemic (disease) while others said the saline water seeped through the lining leading to the death of all the fish. Freshwater fishing exhibited improved yields. These fish were sold in the urban markets of nearby Asansol and Durgapur.

Yet another failure was the production of organic corn. The villagers had purchased seeds to grow corn (a new plant in the village) and were able to produce 'large and juicy cobs' of corn. The seed sellers (who had also promised to buy back the harvest) kept deferring their plans to buy while the SHGs, being contractually obligated to these buyers, could not sell the corn anywhere else. This led to the corn rotting in front of their eyes. They claimed that there was a 'huge market mafia' operating in the vegetable and seed market, and it was best to avoid such uncertain experiments in the future.

In a similar vein, medicinal plant cultivation, a stated objective of the watershed project, did not work out. Many firms who had supplied seeds and promised to buy the produce, reneged on their agreement after selling the seeds. For example, in the case of aloe vera, they sold only 100 seeds with the promise to buy the leaves of the plant at Rs 1 per leaf. However, for such a deal to be economically viable for any leaf buyer, there had to be at least 300 plants, and this was not the scale that Bhalki was operating at. Later it turned out that the supplier was only a seller of seeds and had no intention of procuring the leaves. The VWC claimed that they had tried to identify a market on their own for medicinal plants, but their lack of experience and contacts contributed to their inability to deal with suave 'English-speaking' men. This implied that they could not penetrate the medicinal plant 'mafia'. Such 'spurious' plans had left them quite dejected, and had added to their frustration of not being able to achieve much more simply because they were not 'smart or networked' enough. The VWC had taken an initiative to compile a list of over 200 indigenous medicinal plants and their properties with the help of the Adivasis. This knowledge could not be converted into commercial gain because of their inability to access the market. All these instances reinforced the inhibitions the villagers had about connecting with large markets, many of them in faraway urban areas. They were also wary about trying new kinds of products.

We visited a business venture in the village which came up as a result of technical assistance and a financial grant from the horticulture department of the state government, provided to a plastics technician from the village. In the village he was however referred to as an 'engineer'. He successfully grew several exotic vegetables in greenhouses, and had some banana cultivations, all irrigated with the help of efficient water sprinklers. Linkages had been established with markets in Kolkata for sale and, having repaid his first loan, the 'engineer' was getting set to take another loan to diversify into poultry. Enthused, we asked to meet other such farmers who had benefitted from crop innovations but were disappointed to know that this was the only success story in horticulture worth demonstrating. Did the VWC not take assistance from this entrepreneur in accessing markets outside the village? We did not get an answer to this question. However, we did learn that this person was not a member of the VWC and had reaped benefits as an energetic individual who was self-confident enough to strike his own marketing deals. He was aware that without the collective action that improved water levels he would not have succeeded.

It was evident from these negative experiences that a major limiting factor was the VWC's inability to tap into the more organised market networks to leverage the gains from the watershed, which had led to anxiety about the sustainability of their efforts. This was despite them not having the worry of servicing any debt as the watershed project was financed as a 100 per cent grant from NABARD.

The Plight of the Marginalised

According to the VWC members: '*Nirakkhar meyeder chetanar abhaab*' (Illiterate women lacked consciousness). Emphasizing the role of education, they pointed out that the SHGs comprising illiterate women were habitual defaulters of loans. These women could not see beyond the immediate benefit of a small consumption loan of the order of Rs 3,000. They failed to appreciate that repaying and building up their creditworthiness could enable them to borrow much larger amounts in the future. These loans could be instrumental in changing their lives. This was especially true in the tribal settlements which formed 55 per cent of the village population. Most of the Adivasi women's groups were completely destroyed (*tachnach hoye gechhe*). To evade questions related to bad loans, these Adivasi women now were reportedly avoiding interactions with other women from successful SHGs.

We noted that the village has three distinct geographical spaces — where the Muslims lived (the *Kaji para*), where the Adivasis lived (the Bengali word used for the identification was *asabhya* or uncivilised), and where everybody else lived. The extent of segregation of the tribals was evident when the VWC members, in discussing improvements from the watershed, found it worthwhile to mention that it was now safe to venture into the tribal settlements in the evening. However, the Adivasis still burned forestland (belonging to the forest department) to smoke out wild boars and rabbits which they hunted — a traditional practice that is yet to change. They let their cows loose to graze in the forest which was a menace to rice cultivation. We found this 'us and them' distinction, the difference between those who are relatively better off and those who are backward, although both were beneficiaries of the watershed, quite astonishing. The VWC maintained that the Adivasis were yet to understand that the natural capital was theirs to use and preserve. The primary benefit of the watershed project for the tribals was that they were now connected to the rest of the world — their young men also went to other villages and towns to work and they could call for medical help from the local health centre using their mobile phones. Some evidence of the Adivasis gradually getting integrated in the village could be seen by their increasing presence (*kapor porey*, literally 'with clothes on', implying that they dressed like the rest of the villagers) in the Shiv Ratri festival and feast that took place in the Hindu settlement area. The social distance between the VWC members and the Adivasis was evident from the language used to narrate their living conditions with a tone of resentfulness mixed with an air of superiority.

The Return of Politics (2010 Onwards)

The plight of the tribal SHGs was in stark contrast to the impact of the SHG movement on the general (relatively educated) class. Many of the SHGs formed with these members had flourished — there were around 10–12 such SHGs in Bhalki with turnovers of over

Rs 200,000 each. We spoke to a small group of women, in particular Zulekha, her sister-in-law Nasreen, and two others (see Box 4.1). Their husbands all worked outside the village. These women were involved in SHGs in the first set of tree plantations, with the idea of using the proceeds from harvesting the trees for social exigencies like weddings in the family so that they could demonstrate their ability to gift something concrete to their children on their own. With the loans they intended to diversify their *kantha* (literally meaning a light quilt, but referred here as a form of embroidery seen on the quilt) work (they had been given some training on this under the aegis of NABARD, facilitated by the VWC) and expand their cattle wealth.

Box 4.1: No Light for Learning

Zulekha is a sharecropper in her mid-30s, who appeared to have the qualities of being a natural leader. We noticed Zulekha on out first visit to Bhalki, when, in the middle of a conversation of the villagers with us, she unabashedly pulled out her cell phone to take a call, decisively telling her husband (presumably) over the phone that she was busy in a meeting and would not leave till it was over. Her husband and sons were all migrant workers and she had full responsibility of taking care of work as a sharecropper as well as her own household activities. She was a pioneer among the women in setting up SHGs under the watershed scheme for tree plantations. Besides regular SHG activities, she, along with some of the other women, were involved in supervising the watershed construction activities and in reaching out to women in the Muslim and tribal communities. They had started conducting adult education classes in the verandah of the school building during the evening when the women had time to devote to learning. She had faced quite a bit of opposition from her mother-in-law and husband as her involvement meant being away from the house for most of the evening. Despite that, she had canvassed house-to-house to ensure that women attended the classes, stressing that these classes would be held late in the evening and would not interfere with their regular household chores. The classes were held regularly in the early years of the watershed, although lack of electricity meant that they had to work with oil-fired lanterns. As the funds of the VWC dwindled, the classes had to be discontinued as there was no money to replace malfunctioning lanterns and even pay for the oil. When we spoke to her last, she was searching for a way to resume classes and wondered where to access financial resources.

However, inadequate market linkages remained a problem. Over the previous six months, training opportunities had petered out too. One adverse effect of being an active SHG member associated with the watershed project was that the panchayat shunned these women when it came to administrative responsibilities generated out of other government schemes like MGNREGA.

By 2010, even simple schemes undertaken by the SHGs, like preparation of saplings, were sabotaged by the panchayat to ensure that all farmers bought saplings from other sources. This resulted in the SHG's efforts being wasted, adding to their frustration. This strife between the panchayat and the SHGs was not new, but it seemed to have intensified. The local leadership (read panchayat) was threatened by the awareness and initiative displayed by the SHGs and NGO. The women were quick to add, however, that to keep the SHGs alive there still needed to be active assistance without which they would slide back and all this progress would come to naught. This was all the more relevant now as the men went out of the village to work and were seen only for the 100 days of MGNREGA. There was a paucity of skilled labour in the village and the women had no choice but to take charge.

As NABARD had withdrawn from the project, a lot of the benefits from the past were coming undone. Within the SHGs several factions had emerged, and the collective ethos had given way to an individualistic approach for appropriation of benefits. The politically unstable condition in the village had not helped. There had been a reversal of political fortunes. The rise of the Trinamool Congress was decisive, and factionalism prevented the formation of tight groups. With the withdrawal of NABARD and the political changes, forming and maintaining SHGs were emerging as problems.

The rise in political uncertainty made the waiting period for trees to mature more risky in the watershed area. Young trees, with at least another two years to grow (mature trees are supposed to be seven to nine years old), were being sold and the land grabbed despite advise to the contrary by the VWC. Added to this was sabotage by the erstwhile *mahajan*s (moneylenders) who had been facing dwindling business with the arrival of the watershed. The VWC was of the opinion that this was hard to prevent as most of the young men of the village went away to work in other villages and nearby mills and were not around to protect their trees, which were sold willingly by confused or frightened women SHGs. It appeared that the VWC itself was marginalised — no one was paying them 2 per cent of the market share as agreed upon. The VWC members lamented that while the women SHGs had made over Rs 3 million from the proceeds of their tree plantations, the VWC was yet to receive a paisa although the panchayat had extracted its due share. Moreover, the SHGs now needed more capital funds to develop, as they needed to pay good money to these private landholders who now had elaborate contracts drawn up. Fresh land to be leased to SHGs or consortiums of SHGs would only be in terms of the new contracts, which were heavily loaded in favour of the landowners.

The VWC in Control?

As things stood, the VWC's activities did not appear to be sustainable — they had been actively looking for funds since January 2011, but without success. They had done far more than their mandate for developing the watershed, but it pained them to see their efforts crumbling. Due to poor rains in the summer, farmers had been taking short-term measures to divert water to their farms from the watershed by actually breaking some of the bunds. This was a clear indication of the dwindling authority of the VWC. As private interests were taking over, one could already see the watershed project disintegrating. The women SHGs were now forming consortiums to take large plots of land on long-term lease and cultivate timber on them, but their contracting process was completely independent of the VWC that had first shown them the way. This denied the VWC their due share of funds which were particularly needed to maintain the watershed structures. The increase in incomes of the landed beneficiaries as an indirect effect of the watershed was evident in the expenses incurred in merrymaking on Dussehra in 2011 — it was claimed that over Rs 27,000 worth of 'English' (liquor) was sold in the village on *Dashami* day alone and consumed with mutton, Kurkure, salad and fruit (in contrast to consuming local liquor and roasted forest produce in the past)! Thus, while the VWC was starved for funds, some villagers had plenty of spare income to celebrate with. The VWC cynically claimed that the incidence of drinking had gone up in the village as a result of improved inflows of money.

In one of our visits to Bhalki, we were sharing lunch with four VWC members in the autumn of 2011. Kanai was obviously an old Maoist who had once witnessed the annihilation of the well-to-do farmers; Pankaj (see Box 4.2) was a vocal supporter of the CPI(M);

Box 4.2: Receding Dreams

Pankaj Bhattacharya, a paramedical officer trained by the government, is one of the active VWC functionaries. He had no qualms sharing with us his communist leanings. He is also an amateur poet and he had recited several of his poems to us. These poems were inspired by the hard times that he had seen in his village. He is affectionately called *Daktarbabu* by the villagers. His popularity is indicated by the fact that most of the villagers consult him for their health-related problems rather than going to the primary health centre (PHC). He appreciated the improvement in quality of life for each home as a result of a higher water table, which meant that simple submersible pumps were enough to ensure adequate water for household use. However, not being a farmer himself meant that he was not too concerned about the possibility of over-extraction of groundwater. He spoke to us about how the watershed had improved the quality of life of the tribals. According to him,

> They are much better off economically and otherwise now. But bad habits are hard to change — higher incomes have merely made them switch from having *chullu* (locally made country liquor) with snails to drinking 'English' liquor with processed snacks like Kurkure. "They" have even won local tribal dancing contests at Budbud as a result of the dance training imparted by women from "our" hamlet.

A romantic at heart, Pankaj had begun with ambitious dreams about how the watershed activities would transform his village. Just as he and his VWC members had been able to transcend politics to come together for a common purpose, he had believed that the entire village would be as idealistic and put aside selfish interests to work for the common good. Alas, that was not to be.

> As greater visibility for our village meant an inflow of monetary resources through the panchayat and other development organizations, the SHGs attitudes changed. Suddenly they were competing for funds rather than cooperating with each other, and in this competitive game, political identities started to matter once again.

It was not clear to us what Pankaj was planning for the near future. He was witnessing his dreams recede and perhaps he would be left with nothing but memories of a better time in the village and his radical poetry.

Dipak was a Congress idealist who had talked about Gandhi's concept of a village republic; and Paresh had possible leanings towards the Bharatiya Janata Party (BJP), having mentioned more than once that it would be the energy of Hindus that would transform society because only they had the ethic of service to others (*seba dharma*) ingrained in them. To our surprise and apprehension, what started as a friendly discussion about the rise of the Trinamool Congress Party (no one there seemed to be involved with the Trinamool Congress at all) degenerated into a bitter quarrel with each blaming the other's politics for the failure of the watershed. It continued for some time, and at one juncture we were concerned about the possibility of physical violence and injury. It was only after we pointed out (with considerable difficulty) that they did share a common identity — they were all on the losing side — that they toned down their aggression.

Encouraged by NABARD, the watershed team had tried to spread its wings and assist other watershed initiatives in the neighbourhood. The VWC had implemented a watershed project at Dombani and were currently working with villagers at the nearby Baku village. In addition, the committee was now thinking of newer proposals to submit for funding to NABARD, one such project being that of village tourism trying to capitalise on the story behind the name of Bhalki.

Lessons that will Haunt the Future

We spoke to some members of a Joint Liability Group (JLG) — drawn from members of a number of SHGs. They mentioned how their focus had shifted from tree plantations (where land now was difficult to obtain) to vegetable cultivation which was reasonably lucrative as it could be done on smaller plots of land and, above all, could be sold in local markets. They confessed that they were together as an SHG only for the savings and loans; for other purposes they worked as individuals as there was infighting and conflicts when working as a group, however small. In discussing the condition of the schools, we realised that the women of the upper castes had reservations in sending their children to the primary school in the village as the midday meal was allegedly being cooked by a tribal woman. The adult education school started voluntarily by some of the SHGs had become defunct; it had to be stopped for lack of something as trivial as lanterns to study in the dark and lack of even torches to help illuminate the tedious walk to and from the tribal hamlet of the village.

We noted that some of the watershed structures at higher inclines were broken without a thought to the long-term implications of such diversions of rainwater. The VWC personnel expressed concern and also expressed their inability to keep repairing the structures given a paucity of funds. Further, it was evident that the VWC had been withdrawing from the watershed maintenance funds for their own recurring expenditures and in this process over Rs 200,000 had already been used up.

It appeared to us that the natural topography was just waiting to be tapped for the advantage of its residents through watershed activities. The ability of water and trees to completely alter the physical appearance of the neighbourhood and create opportunities for livelihoods was not in doubt. The villagers were quickly able to translate the natural assets into income flows by accessing the fairly well-organised market in the local Durgapur–Bardhaman belt. However, when they tried to go beyond that into markets in Kolkata, they were unable to do so. Not only that, they were rudely shocked and distressed in many instances by the losses incurred in trying to gain access. The changing landscape and related activities brought about greater visibility to the village. As one gentleman put it quite succinctly: Bhalki's daughters were getting better grooms and marriage proposals with the advent of greater water and hence greater prosperity.

The Bhalki watershed project was a good example of how political differences could be shelved for a tangible development project. Once the consensus was built, the energy generated by the local people was quite remarkable. The economic prospects looked rewarding and there was self-confidence in the ability of the local people to take the project forward. There was considerable trust reposed in NABARD, and for the initial stages it was as if nothing else mattered. Plans about the future were discussed, and the VWC's office became the hub of all activity in the village. People began to be aware of other government projects that they could target to bring into the village, once water was available and assured. However, the leadership, after the galvanising role played by one or two change agents, was appropriated by the well-to-do people in the village who also happened to be Hindus. The Muslims and Adivasis remained at the fringe, although a few Muslim women who were leading some active SHGs were feeling more empowered. The Adivasis were obviously outside the loop of change. Their experience of modernisation was in terms of going to cities and doing work as construction labour. Their traditional practices of hunting had left the VWC worried. The way the Adivasis related to nature through their activities was in sharp contrast to the vision contained in the ideology of the VWC: with little mutual appreciation and assimilation.

With the completion of NABARD's involvement in the project, the ability to keep the VWC together was becoming difficult. The VWC members were already beginning to think about their political roots. West Bengal's deep polarisation in politics and a completely fluid political atmosphere may have contributed to this frame of mind. The temporary organisation was slowly disbanding, and without the collective action of all sections of the village, the watershed and the other natural assets created would be well nigh impossible to retain. There were offers to cut down trees thus violating the sustainable felling norms to gain quick liquid cash before political and organisational uncertainties set in. The cooperative mentality that had marked the origins of the watershed was gradually disappearing without a central (non-political) agency like NABARD providing the gel to glue it together. The relative inequalities in income and wealth were showing up, the caste and community divides were coming to the fore, and individuals were seeking political support and refuge as they tried to usurp the common properties and natural assets created into individual gains. Perhaps the access to the market and new opportunities and sources of funds had nurtured a strong desire for immediate gains. This was eroding the original spirit of shramdaan and the trans-political outlook that the two change agents had weaved together in constructing what was viewed as a common good. The future had once looked discernibly different from the expectations of the past. That future appeared neither a desirable nor a feasible destination any more.

5

Stillness and Change

Lives and Landscapes

This chapter is based on our study of the Indo-German Watershed Development Programme (IGWDP) in Udaipur district of Rajasthan (see Map 5.1). The programme was the outcome of an agreement between the German Development Bank (KfW) and the National Bank for Agriculture and Rural Development (NABARD) in 2006. It aimed at improving the livelihoods of the rural poor by regenerating the degraded natural resource base of five districts of south-eastern Rajasthan. Based on a pre-project study, KfW had decided that the intervention would focus on goat rearing as a major source of livelihood. This would, in turn, require adequate fodder. Growing fodder would require land and water. The pastureland was potentially available on the slopes of the undulating terrain of the surrounding Aravalli hills. The land was arid and has been degraded through years of neglect and overgrazing. To restore the pastures, the project conceived the idea of watershed development in the region.

Over and above the development of goat husbandry, improved agricultural practices would be promoted, availability of drinking water made easier and other opportunities for livelihood diversification, such as making of artificial jewellery and traditional crafts like *bandhej* (type of tie-dye practiced mainly in Rajasthan and Gujarat), supported. Women's self-help groups (SHGs) would be formed and nurtured to create saving habits and bank linkages. There were some special efforts designed to reduce the drudgery of work that women had to undergo such as the introduction of smoke-less cooking ovens and biogas plants. Watershed activities would have a beneficial effect on small-scale irrigated farming as well.

Map 5.1: Udaipur District in Rajasthan

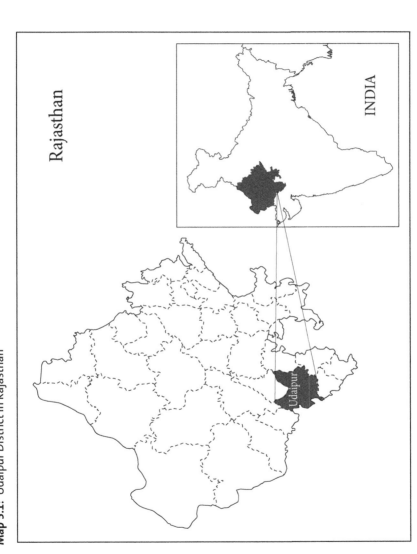

Rajasthan

Udaipur

INDIA

The objectives would be achieved through the participation of local people and the support of local institutions. Some institutions would be created to facilitate the process, while others, like the Panchayat Raj Institutions (PRIs), would be used for support and sustainability. The institutions would be of help in resource management and planning, as well as in resolving conflicts relating to land and common resources. Where forestland would be involved, a Joint Forest Management (JFM) Agreement would be used for the community and forest department to work together.

The total cost of the programme was set at €12.24 million, with the German bank contributing €11 million and the beneficiaries contributing the remainder. The project would cover areas in the Banswara, Chittorgarh, Dungarpur, Pratapgarh, and Udaipur districts of Rajasthan. The key principles of the project involved the community's ownership and participation in implementation and a pilot stage to check the feasibility of the watershed. Work would be done from ridge to valley, descending along the slope of the terrain, and survey numbers would be used to ensure the inclusion of each and every farmer. Finally, there would be a guarantee of uninterrupted flow of funds subject to satisfactory progress at every stage. Around 32 watersheds were planned in a time frame of five to seven years and covering a total area of 35,355 hectares across 133 villages with a total population of 80,391, of which about 96 per cent belonged to the Scheduled Castes (SCs) or Scheduled Tribes (STs) or Other Backward Classes (OBCs).

The project, compared to the others that we studied, was large and covered an extensive area. Each of the 32 watersheds planned would have a distinct Programme Implementation Agency (PIA), usually a non-governmental organisation (NGO). To facilitate the planning, implementation and final handing over of the watersheds, a particular organisational structure was created. Each watershed would have an initial pre-capacity building phase where the site would be identified and the formal sanctions obtained. The involvement of the community would be initiated with a gram sabha meeting where the Capacity Building Phase (CBP) plan would be prepared with inputs from the local residents and beneficiaries. To test their commitment to the project the usual *shramdaan* would be carried out and exposure visits organised to give the residents an idea of what they were trying to create. An interim phase would ensure the start of the treatment of the soil and the construction of the watershed over a small (usually 25 per cent) part of the proposed total area. Simultaneously, the training required for new livelihoods would be provided. Finally, in the Final Implementation Phase (FIP), all construction would be completed and the VWC would be handed over full responsibility of the watershed.

Project Management

The stakeholders in this project were many and varied. Apart from the villagers, the gram panchayat, the VWC, NABARD, the NGO partnering with NABARD for implementation, KfW, public officials, local banks (commercial as well as cooperative), and the specialists drawn from agricultural universities were all involved. NABARD created a temporary organisation for the duration of the project called the Programme Management Unit (PMU). The PMU comprised NABARD officials and members from each of the 32 partner organisations involved in the watersheds. Four consultants looking after forestry, animal husbandry, engineering and socio-economic aspects of the project, respectively, were also members of the PMU. The PMU had a Programme Sanctioning and Steering Committee which was a high-level committee, headed by an executive director of NABARD along with senior government officials from Rajasthan. A Programme Implementation Committee, headed by an assistant general manager (AGM) of NABARD along with three or four other members from the PMU, supervised and coordinated the implementation of the project. The Programme Implementation Committee identified, approved and sanctioned the watershed, the NGO, called the Programme Facilitating Agency (PFA), facilitated the project, the implementation was by the VWC, and independent consultants appointed by the PMU monitored the project.

The IGWDP in Rajasthan was the only place we visited where there was a formal structure of decision-making that was constructed for the specific purpose of the project. In other instances, the temporary organisations which we encountered were more informal and fluid. One reason why NABARD may have taken recourse to the PMU might have been the geographical spread of the project. The second and arguably more important reason could be the requirements of the KfW, which followed a very detailed process of monitoring.

Without the PMU, NABARD would have difficulty in supervising the progress of, and obtaining data from, 32 watersheds with distinct implementation agencies.

We learnt more about the functioning of the PMU at its quarterly review meeting where the AGM of NABARD presided and a number of PFA teams (usually two representatives) were present. Our observations about the PMU are based on this meeting, as well as the several meetings we had with the AGM of NABARD and the two PFAs of the two villages we visited, namely Foundation for Ecological Security (FES) in the village of Piparna and BAIF Development Research Foundation (BAIF) in the village of Padla.

Given the size, spread and number of participants involved, the degree of complexity of governing was substantial and small informal meetings and data flows would not suffice. To make the data on performance comparable across watersheds, a mutually agreed format would have to be adhered to. We noted that the PFAs were diverse, ranging from companies like ITC (a multi-business conglomerate), state-owned enterprises and large NGOs with international access to funds, to NGOs that were local with limited access to finance. We observed that despite the need to control and make effective the joint effort of all the PFAs, the PMU did not have the authority to take penal action against any non-compliant or inefficient agency. It could at most mark a particular organisation on its blacklist for its shortcomings. The governance structure did not have any provision for representation by direct beneficiaries or local institutions, although a stated objective was one of participatory management. Hence, the project took an essentially top-down approach to development.

An objective of the PMU was to serve as a platform for mutual learning from experiences on the field. If, for instance, a PFA faced a particular problem, the PMU could be used as a forum for brainstorming. Experience sharing was encouraged in the meeting we witnessed. Rarely do so many varied NGOs get an opportunity to share experiences and learn from one another. However, much would depend on the degree of cooperation and mutual respect. If the PFAs viewed themselves as competitors whose relative performance in this project would determine their overall strength in getting future funds and new projects, then of course the effectiveness of mutual learning and experience sharing would be limited, if not totally absent.

We also came to know that there were a number of pre-existing property-related issues which were adding to the problems of claims and rights in the proposed use of land in the watershed activity. People were trying to establish their usufruct rights according to the provisions of the Indian Forest Rights Act of 2006. This led to many legal issues about land ownership, and the PFAs would have to work within this ambiguity of ownership and legal wrangles.

As convener of the PMU, the NABARD official had the onerous task of coordinating a large number of heterogeneous organisations at the operational level. He had to make their actions and performance comparable and comprehensible. The PFAs were sceptical about complementary government interventions like the Mahatma Gandhi National Rural Employment Guarantee Act (MGNREGA). During MGNREGA projects, the availability of labour for the construction of the watershed was a problem as the wage rate was higher and, presumably, in certain cases the opportunity to shirk work was higher too. The PFAs were also quite doubtful about the ability of the community to acquire the requisite skills to explore and experiment with new sources of livelihood. There were complaints about the ineffectiveness and inadequacy of capacity building efforts. The NABARD official was wary of the PFAs as to whether they were reporting accurately or complying with all the norms and procedures.

The Poor of Piparna

The Piparna watershed area had its expanse spread in Chitrawas and Rawach panchayats of Gogunda tehsil in Udaipur district, adjacent to the Kumbhalgarh wildlife sanctuary in the north. Around 98 per cent of its population belonged to the Gameti and Garasiya tribes. The average landholding of the households was less than a hectare and around 85 per cent of the land was cultivated only once in a year with a rain-fed crop, primarily maize. The remaining 15 per cent of the land was used to cultivate maize and chickpea in the kharif season, and wheat and chickpea in the rabi season (with irrigation through traditional diverted stream channels and shallow wells). Most of the private uncultivated land was used as private pastures, usually with a moderate cover of grass and some trees. This land primarily augmented the fodder stock and on certain occasions provided a source of minor timber. There were also some commons, mostly *charagah* (grazing) and revenue wastelands, which could be used for open grazing. However, they were encroached upon and used as either cultivable lands or private pastures. The average annual rainfall of this area was 615 mm. The yearly variation in rainfall and its intensity was high and unpredictable. The minimum and maximum temperature varied from 4°C to 47°C. The watershed comprised five habitations covering three revenue villages — Chitrawas and Piparna of Chitrawas panchayat and Rawach of Rawach panchayat. Piparna village, the largest among these, had a population of around 1,300 and was located at a distance of 38 km from Gogunda town and around 73 km from Udaipur city, and was accessible through metalled roads. The nearest bank was the rural branch of State Bank of Bikaner and Jaipur, located in Saira which was 24 km from the area. There was a primary school in Piparna with a single teacher. There was a secondary school at Chitrawas, a higher secondary school at Saira and colleges at Udaipur city. Educational attainments were poor with 77 per cent of the population illiterate. Of the 289 literates in the village, over 60 per cent had only attended primary school. There were just four to five people in the village who had studied up to class 12, and the only college-going person was a woman.

Animal husbandry and sale of non-timber forest products (primarily fruits such as *sitafal and ratanjyot*) were the other major livelihood sources for the community. Since cows do not yield adequate milk, earning opportunities from them was limited to selling calves and dung cakes as fuel. Buffaloes were primarily reared to produce milk, which was mostly consumed by the household and sold occasionally. The nearest assured dairy collection centres were in Samal and Padrara, which were around 10–18 km away from the habitations. Goats and poultry were reared primarily for meat, and it provided scope for small but frequent incomes round the year from the sale of the animals. Tribal customs dictated frequent household consumption of goat and poultry meat for social occasions. In this village access to basic amenities was far below that of most of the other parts of Udaipur district and opportunities for a secure livelihood throughout the year were limited. People's dependence on wage-earning activities was high and if the ends were not met with the opportunities available within the village, they tended to migrate to the neighbouring urban centres for employment.

FES, the NGO facilitating the NABARD watershed scheme in Piparna, had been working in this area since 2002 and had intervened on issues of conservation, governance and livelihoods. They were also involved in organising village institutions for the protection and development of commons, particularly around forestlands and charagah lands. We visited Piparna village in early February with representatives from FES (see Plate 5.1). There was a small gathering of menfolk from the village with a few women wearing their *ghunghat*s (headscarves) very low. There was a curious lack of enthusiasm in the group as they sat with expressionless faces (see Box 5.1). The FES representative explained how the seeds of the watershed project were sown in Piparna after observing the watershed in nearby Rawach. They explained how mobilising enough people for the initial shramdaan itself had been a challenge as many of the households in this village were prone to distress migration. We asked the villagers why they agreed to the shramdaan given their abject poverty. They responded that through this their cultivable lands would be bound better as bunds

Plate 5.1: Meeting the Beneficiaries at Piparna

Box 5.1: A Long Wait

Ramchander, a small farmer with a big moustache, appeared to be in his mid-50s and had a frail look about him. He was a member of the VWC of Piparna. He described how even five years ago there were no roads in the village, and was happy to see some progress, although the village was still not electrified. The villagers had to go as far as Saira to recharge their mobiles (about half the households had mobile phones). Chitrawas, nearer than Saira, was electrified, but few residents could afford electric connections. Only selected houses of Chitrawas (including that of the local member of the legislative assembly or MLA) had electricity. Ramchander narrated, in matter of fact voice, that the local MLA, who hailed from the same village, was in the process of converting some of the common pasturelands into a stadium. This land, according to him, was considered one of the best protected fodder lands. When asked why the local politician was hurting the interests of the villagers, Ramchander's reply was revealing. He claimed that sports activities were needed too and that a minister was given the power to do what he wanted. Electricity would come one day, just as the roads had come. Waiting patiently was the only strategy. The watershed had also been conceived and initiated by outsiders. He accompanied us after the meeting to the highest point of the watershed where the bunds were being done and the soil treated. When we got there he was out of his depth to answer our questions. The PFA representative was ready with all the technical answers. A young person, possibly in his early 20s was following our small group. He was introduced to us as a night guard to protect the construction work going on. In contrast to Ramchander, he was knowledgeable and shared many technical details about the watershed with us.

would be created on the land boundaries to retain water and prevent loss of topsoil. Moreover, they would earn some minimal *mazdoori* (wages).

They went on to recite (almost by rote) all the benefits of a watershed, and explained the process of working from ridge to valley for watershed development. Further, they emphasised how this intervention of FES was superior to the government intervention in 1986 to develop the watershed, as this was more inclusive and there did not appear to be a budget constraint for high quality work. Mahabir, the *sachiv* (secretary) of the VWC, discussed its role, which included convening meetings, developing master plans and getting everyone to sign on them, and supervising watershed-related construction work. If the committee was not satisfied with a piece of work, they were empowered to put payments on hold, and insist the work was properly redone.

While pleased with the idea of the watershed, the men expressed their desire for more wells for irrigation, and more goats and household poultry, for supplementing their livelihood. According to this group, more animal manure would also improve their agricultural yields, as organic manure was better than urea, which ruined the topsoil. Moreover, women at home could take care of such ruminants, and household demand for milk would be met. The discussion then moved towards the goats that FES had provided at subsidised rates to many of the households, and whether it was worthwhile to breed Sirohi goats, which were not indigenous (see Plate 5.2). Some concern was expressed that the quality of goats (in terms of expected weight attainment) had gone down of late, which meant they would

Plate 5.2: Stall-feeding of Sirohi Goats at Piparna

fetch lower prices, although their usefulness as a source of organic fertiliser did not diminish. Goat dung was a much sought-after fertiliser in Udaipur city and nearby towns. Although sheep did less damage to vegetation as compared to goats while grazing, goats were preferred by the villagers due to a higher market price for goat meat. There was concern raised that fatalities for goats and poultry were on the rise as veterinary care was non-existent in the village. FES had been unable to train a villager as a para-veterinarian because nobody in the village met the prerequisite of having passed the higher secondary examinations in the science stream.

The villagers had formed pasture societies to protect their commons, where they employed four watchmen on rotation at Rs 1,600 per annum each to guard against unauthorised ingress. Fines were levied for trespassing. While the engineering for the watershed had been completed at higher levels, the process was ongoing in some of the pasturelands we visited. FES appeared to have put a lot of thought into meticulously planning the bunds and trenching operations. They were even considering solar energy possibilities as a means to electrify the village using the common grazing lands to put the solar panels in. They also asserted that at the micro level they had observed a rising water table, although this was not reflected in satellite images yet. According to the FES the villagers were aware that financial inclusion had now provided a means to take loans to improve economic well-being. Housing loans were not on their radar as they believed that one needed a permanent government job to make a house. The FES claimed that the villagers had expressed a need to set up a dairy close to the village as they were fond of *khaati chaas* (buttermilk), which they currently obtained from neighbouring villages in exchange for firewood. However, FES was of the opinion that the villagers would have to put higher priority focus on developing their pasturelands in order to ensure that their ruminants had enough fodder (1 hectare could yield up to 6 metric tonnes of grass) so as to provide sufficient milk for making khaati chaas in the village itself. Then they would no longer find it necessary to cut trees to trade firewood for khaati chaas.

When speaking separately to the village women, it was initially difficult to get them to open up to start a conversation. When they did speak, all of them articulated the urgent need for drinking water. They did not share the menfolk's decision to rear goats, claiming that it would mean more work for them as they were responsible for the upkeep of domestic animals. It was also pointed out by the women that taking the goats to graze was usually the responsibility of the oldest girl child of the family, who would then be forced to compromise on her education as a result. Girls were not being married off before 18 any longer, as till then the girl was eligible to earn through MGNREGA and contribute to her family's income. The women's real dream was to have a good hospital in the village, as the nearest one was in Saira. With respect to schooling, the women admitted that only two out of every five children went to school, while others tended to farm animals, although this trend was changing rapidly as people realised the necessity of education for jobs. They unanimously felt that *kheti* (farming) was the only option if you failed to survive in school. However, there was an air of despondency when talking of possibilities of a job after a good education — statements like *Bhagwan jaaney padhega to kya hoga, sheher mein naukri nahin milega to kheti hai* ('Only God knows what jobs will be obtained in the towns after an education, farming is always there as a last resort') abounded.

We asked the women whether they were part of the VWC or involved in any way with the village governance, to which one of the men (who had been hovering around us) responded that Piparna's panchayat had only male representatives. Malteebai, who belonged to Rawach village (also part of the watershed), was present in the gathering and she spoke up to say that she was a member of the Chitrawas village panchayat and also a member of the VWC. Her contribution to the watershed had been primarily to pass on information about meetings and decisions taken at the meetings to the women in the village. According to her understanding, benefits from the watershed project included stopping water from running off by digging trenches, conserving the soil and giving roots of trees more support and ensuring that fertiliser does not get washed away. She was among the more affluent villagers with 5 bighas (1.25 hectares) of land and was the proud possessor of the only biogas plant in this neighbourhood, which had been in operation since 2003.

We enquired about the SHGs in the village. While there were none at Piparna, there were only two SHGs in Velukhet and another two in Merkakhet, hamlets of Chitrawas village. On an average, monthly contribution for SHG members was pegged at Rs 25, and loans were provided at an interest rate of Rs 2 per Rs 100 borrowed per month. While the SHGs had a bank account, visits to the bank were infrequent and the money circulated among the members as consumption loans. Festival expenses were high in the village, for example, a total of Rs 20,000–Rs 30,000 was spent on Holi celebrations, or to celebrate the birth of a male child. All such cultural expenses were financed through loans.

Padla: From a Lost Opportunity to a New Beginning?

Padla, about 50 km from the city of Udaipur was one of three villages covered under the Devpura-II Watershed under the IGWDP. The watershed covered an area of 934 hectares and the total population of the three villages was 2,110 in 350 households of which 346 households were tribal families. Males comprised 52 per cent of the population. Illiteracy was high with the literacy rate just about 41 per cent. Female literacy rates were only around 20 per cent. Of the 934 hectares, 495 hectares was government land, of which 149 hectares was under the care of the forest department and 346 hectares was revenue and panchayat land. The remaining was private land, of which a little less than 50 per cent was rain-fed and irrigated area only 10 per cent, the rest being wasteland. The area was extremely dry with an average annual rainfall of 55 mm. The major crops were wheat, maize and pulses. When we visited, the watershed project had entered the interim phase and the civil works construction at Padla was complete. Pastures had been developed, women had received one round of training for alternative skills and five farming families had been given Sirohi goats — 25 goats and two bucks (see Box 5.2). Only two SHGs had been formed with 22 members, with a savings of a little over Rs 28,000. The facilitating agency was the Rajasthan Rural Institute of Development Management, an associate of BAIF, a big NGO associated with many projects across India.

The hilly terrain of the area was extremely dry and rocky where even the sight of grass was rare. Trees were few and far between. Even in early February the sun felt more like summer. Compared to Piparna, Padla was economically better off with electricity and most people had mobile phones. The houses were scattered and population less dense. The BAIF personnel looking after the project were excited to share with us details of the civil construction works on the

Box 5.2: Of Goats and Gains

Shikhar was one of the few people who had obtained Sirohi goats from the project in Padla. This farmer had pooled his land along with six others to form a 5 hectares pasture on which they had been helped by BAIF to sow fast-growing grass that would yield about 1,000–1,500 bales of fodder. The grass would be ready for grazing 45 days after sowing. During this period any person allowing his animals to graze in the pasture would be penalised. A penalty system was prevalent for common pastures, where a very nominal monetary fine was charged by the government. As a result, people considered it legitimate to allow their goats to graze in the commons as long as they paid that nominal penalty. Shikhar and his group of farmers would have to ensure that this did not happen.

In the interim, while the grass was being grown, he showed us that the goats had been tied to a feeding stall where an innovative way of feeding was being experimented with. Green fodder (leaves and twigs), hanging from a horizontal pole, was offered to the goats, and they could stand, raise their heads and feed. He had acquired the goats at Rs 1,000 per head of goat, which was only 25 per cent of the market price. The subsidy came in the form of a grant from the project because his family was below the poverty line. A goat kid would sell at Rs 1,500–Rs 2,300 depending on its weight. The weight would, in turn, depend on how much the kid was fed. The farmer was worried. The usual norm for feeding was (apart from green fodder) about 200 gm of maize or wheat grains per feed. They could, at that moment, afford only about 50–100 gm. When asked whether he was confident about there being enough of a market for all goat breeders to sell at a profit, the man was not sure. According to him, since the buyers were coming to the village to buy goats, this was a seller's market.

very rocky and fairly steep hills of the neighbourhood. They were engineers and it appeared that they found the challenge of creating the bunds and treating the soil much more attractive than dealing with people (see Plate 5.3). In fact, we had to politely insist on setting up meetings with beneficiaries.

Looking at the stark landscape it was difficult to even imagine that the project was supposed to turn the land into green pastures, growing fodder plants that would transform the lives of the local people for whom water was a luxury of life. From a nearby hilltop, the view was

Plate 5.3: Meticulously Constructed Watershed Structures in the Rocky Terrain of Padla

breathtaking. Stark and barren rolling hills for miles on end where the watersheds were being created greeted us. And in the middle of this sweeping panorama of undulating terrain stood a very high chimney tower of the Zawar Mines, only about 15 km away. This was originally owned by Hindustan Zinc, a public sector company. The mine had since been privatised and the new owner was Vedanta.

The men who came for the meeting were all landed, though their holdings were small, between 2 to 5 acres. We had expected the people to be excited about the prospects of getting more water. When asked about the watershed and how that would affect their lives and incomes, they gave very general answers such as the water level would go up, there would be more greenery and the forests would be protected and people would not cut trees. One of their main concerns was the availability of drinking water though. They were not sure how the watershed might help resolve their drinking water problem. They wanted an overhead water tower but also realised that this would be expensive to distribute to each household as the houses were scattered and inter-house distances were significant.

The proposal to build a watershed had come from the BAIF people who went door to door to seek support for their cause. It took two months before a gram sabha could be convened to discuss the issue and agree to offer shramdaan. We observed that the men were cross-checking amongst themselves about facts of the origins of the work on the project as if these were a recollection of things that happened a very long time ago. Yes, the watershed might bring benefits in terms of incomes and livelihoods, but people would have to work hard for it. However, the people had become very lazy compared to the past. Life had changed in the opinion of an old gentleman: 'People did not have to work as hard as I had to in my youth'! Nobody objected to this statement though there were quite a few young people present.

We asked about the low literacy rates despite the village having a secondary school, to which the menfolk had no firm answers, although all of them seemed to be aware of the instrumental value of higher education in obtaining jobs. In this context, one person (a retired security guard of Zawar Mines) pointed out that Hindustan Zinc had started a higher secondary school near the mine which was about a dozen kilometres only from the village.

The story of the impact of the Zawar Mines was interesting. When the mine began operations around half a century ago, they were looking for employees who would have to go down 300 m daily for work. The local villagers were afraid of doing this work. Hence, the mine brought in migrant workers from faraway places like Tamil Nadu and even Nepal. The local people were interested in desk jobs but were not qualified for them. The one person who did get a job as a security guard (and had since retired) was sitting in the group. When the villagers realised that the miner's job was not as risky as they had originally perceived, it was too late. One or two people were hired, but by then the migrant workers had their cartel, and refused to train the locals for mining work. They did acknowledge that it was due to Hindustan Zinc's efforts that electricity arrived in the village, a higher secondary school was set up, and health-care facilities improved with the setting up of a hospital near the mines that could be accessed by the local villagers too.

They were unaware of any pollution-related problems emanating from the mines which produced mainly zinc but also some amounts of silver and lead. They noticed that after a few years of mining the groundwater level had dropped significantly. In fact, people who lived on higher terrain had to come down because of the lack of water. They explained to us how about six months earlier (sometime in the middle of 2010) 3,000 miners had been laid off but were not sure why. (We later learnt that this occurred soon after the privatisation and found press reports [*Udaipur Times* 2011] that mentioned that these miners were organising themselves, looking for compensation and alternative employment.) The villagers were concerned because it brought down local wages. For this they blamed the mines. They also thought that since the action of the mines had brought about an adverse economic impact, the company should have had the social responsibility (in fact the retired security guard used the term CSR) to create a compensating positive impact on incomes in the village. However, the villagers had not done anything to induce such a reaction from the company. Zawar Mines existed like a big giant who they did not like, but they could not make it disappear from their lives altogether.

Our conversation with the women from the village, a group that included one lady who was in the VWC, also touched upon the role that Zawar Mines played in their lives. However, the women spoke a lot more positively about the company. According to them the company had brought to the neighbourhood greater access to education and improved health facilities. They arranged a number of skill training programmes for the village women. The training had not, however, translated into supplementary income for the women. There were only two SHGs. One of the groups had around Rs 7,000 in hand and around Rs 18,000 in the bank. All the women SHG members were illiterate and had no clear idea about the state of their SHG account. They had to depend on other people to fill up forms and maintain records. The group was contributing Rs 50 per head per month. They were internally allowing members to borrow at the rate of 1 per cent per month. They were clear about the reason for the formation of the group though — to gain access to credit. The other SHG had Rs 1,500 in cash and the members present (again all were illiterate) were unable to tell us the balance in their bank account or what the purpose of their savings was. Possibilities of attending adult education courses were there but the women complained of the burden of housework. One or two complained about having to take the animals out for grazing, a tedious job which left them with no time to get an education. Cow milk seemed to be the only regular source of additional income, selling for around Rs 30 per litre. Here again, it was pointed out that the Zawar Mines had set up a collection centre near the village for the villagers to supply their milk. The forest was the source of their fuelwood and they did not seem to be aware of the need to reduce felling of trees in an unplanned manner.

When they were asked about the importance of educational opportunities for their children and what kind of future they wished for their next generation, all of them said that they would like their sons to become doctors, collectors (civil servants) or teachers. They hardly spoke about their daughters and appeared to have no special aspirations for them. However, we learnt that all their daughters (the young ones not yet married) were going to some school or the other. It appeared that educational attainment improved marriage prospects. One lady wanted her son to get a job in Zawar Mines. When the others were asked about Zawar Mines, most of them said they had no objection if their sons got jobs in the mines. Unlike in neighbouring Piparna village, everybody had access to television and villagers did watch serials. Mobile phones were owned by every household. Liquor was a social problem, along with domestic violence. The women pointed out that *peena* and *peetna* (drinking and beating) were the only two activities of the men.

The watershed was going to be of help when completed. The women had not contributed shramdaan for the watershed. They farmed it out to people who were willing to work for low wages (Rs 80–Rs 90) while they earned Rs 135 that was available as the daily rate for MGNREGA. The women seemed to recite the benefits without being sure of how they would be achieved and what they would signify in terms of livelihoods and the quality of life. The benefits of the watershed, according to the women, included higher rainfall, more water and improved soil which would help agricultural production and hence incomes. The benefits, however, were yet to be realised. The women pointed out that migration for casual work was prevalent. Most people went to Udaipur city (relatively close by) to work in construction projects, possibly explaining their relative affluence. They commuted on a daily basis.

Overall, Padla was more prosperous than Piparna, but awareness and energy of the residents seemed to be lacking here as well. The NGO came with their engineers and social workers and the villagers were aware of that. However, the project clearly belonged to BAIF and the villagers were completely helpless without them. The benefits would come if someone gave it to them. And they waited for change to happen.

Stillness and Change

When we talked to the beneficiaries in Piparna and Padla villages, their involvement was markedly low and lukewarm to say the least. It was evident that someone was taking the trouble to build a watershed and they had to do their bit; they would simply follow what they were told to do. The region itself was heterogeneous in terms of educational attainment and access to infrastructure. In Piparna there was no electricity, and a handful of mobile phones. The women were mostly illiterate and inhibited about talking to us about the project, their perceived needs and their assessment of the changes taking place. In contrast, about four-fifths of Padla village had electricity. Most people had mobile phones and there were quite a few television sets in the village. The degree of involvement was still low. For both villages the real good life and better prospects lay outside the village in a distant future.

This relative lack of people's involvement could have been due to the scale and design of the project that entailed a complex control mechanism. The technical aspects of the project, like the civil works involved, the financial flows and attaining the physical targets, were more amenable to control than human beings and their interrelationships. We noted that the energy of the NGOs was much more focused on these quantifiable issues. A consequence of this was their lack of engagement with the locals. The temporary organisation was for all purposes delinked from the identified set of beneficiaries as far as decision-making was concerned.

Another implication of the scale of the project was the impact of this on the business model proposed as a supplementary livelihood source through goat rearing. No one was sure what kind of market would finally emerge if the entire area of the five districts adopted goat husbandry. Would there be enough demand for the large-scale supply of goat meat? Would prices remain high enough to cover costs?

There were a large number of peripheral issues that were weighing on the PFAs and NABARD alike. First, as mentioned earlier, there were a number of property disputes that needed to be settled before work could progress. Second, the large number of facilitating agencies meant that internal problems of some of them could have an impact on the delivery of project outcomes. Small issues like an internal transfer of a field worker from the Rajasthan project to another state was having a delaying effect since the new person was taking time to 'warm up' to the project in progress. These all-India transfers held true for the big PFAs with operations in multiple states. Third, we found that some of the smaller PFAs had trouble retaining good people as they were poached upon by the bigger PFAs operating in the neighbourhood.

The IGWDP at Udaipur was the only large foreign-donor-funded project that we visited. It was a top-down expert-opinion-driven project aimed at diversifying the livelihood portfolio of people by creating watersheds and introducing goat husbandry. A lot of changes were discernible in the physical landscape of the region — the green shoots in the new hilly terrains, the stone bunds, the Sirohi goats, and the wells for storing water, yet there were hardly any signs of ownership noticeable amongst the beneficiaries. They waited in silence and in hope. Would the changing landscape ultimately stir life into the stillness of the locals? We left Udaipur with a feeling that adequate finances, competent management and availability of water might not be enough for creating enduring change.

Part II

Empowerment and Entrepreneurship

Participatory processes are considered to be an important feature of development interventions. Participation comes from individuals as well as the community of beneficiaries. The degree of participation of people and its effectiveness is influenced by the sense of empowerment that individuals qua individuals, and individuals in the collective community, display. Empowerment is reflected in the ability of people to make conscious choices, take decisions, be able to engage with other people as equals and generate new ideas. Empowerment, in these senses, leads to desirable, enduring and acceptable outcomes. This is the instrumental value of empowerment in the context of development. However, empowerment has intrinsic value too, whether at the individual or the collective level of the community. It is about self-realisation, the ability to communicate and relate to others, a sense of confidence and understanding, and participation in networks of trust and tolerance.

The degree of empowerment is determined by many factors such as education, wealth, social status, gender, and facilitative institutional mechanisms. Inadequacies in some of these determinants can act as constraints for individuals as well as groups to exert effective control over their living conditions and their future (Alsop, Bertelsen and Holland 2006). For instance, an uneducated woman in a remote village would be less empowered than an educated man in the city of Mumbai, only because of the different opportunities that their circumstances throw up.

A simple manifestation of empowerment is the ability to articulate one's needs. A higher level of empowerment would go beyond mere articulation of a need to taking initiatives to fulfil the need. For instance, being able to voice the need for water is one kind of empowerment, while getting hold of a shovel to dig a well is another. One can observe different levels of empowerment when people participate in community meetings. Some come up with novel ideas, while others ask for more information or critique other people's ideas. Instances of empowerment are also evident in people working together with a common objective, convincing other people to participate and demonstrating ownership towards an initiative. Expressing dissent or criticising the existing power structures is another form of empowerment. The highest level of empowerment may be observed when a community is capable of transcending the limitations of the immediately available opportunities. One manifestation of an individual's empowerment is his choice of becoming an entrepreneur and taking advantage of the opportunities that development interventions throw up. This empowers the individual by meeting one's material needs and also acts as a means of expression for self-realisation and creativity.

The acknowledgement of entrepreneurship as an indication of empowerment has been the reason behind promoting credit linkages and disseminating information about microenterprises as a means of livelihood. This has been a common method of augmenting immediately available opportunities of beneficiaries. Entrepreneurs who emerge through this process would be considered to be relatively more empowered than others. These entrepreneurs could be individuals or a set of individuals with a shared objective. The specific process through which they emerge, their impact and the constraints they face may widely differ. The chapters that follow are narratives on how development interventions have affected the lives of some people through empowerment and entrepreneurship in dissimilar contexts.

In all the interventions we observed and studied, women's empowerment was an integral element of the projects. The ubiquitous self-help groups (SHGs) of women were supposed to provide the basic platform for empowerment in terms of control over financial resources, over community decisions and, ultimately, their own self-realisation. In Chapter 6, we recount the story of two women entrepreneurs from two different parts of the country; women who were able to use the platform of the SHG and move beyond the basic saving activity and bank linkage. They did so in different ways and with unique outcomes. In the process, however, they were able to realise their own ambitions in a fulfilling manner. As their ventures progressed, they were also able to touch the lives and families of many other women.

Chapter 7 is an account of a group's empowerment that helped them to not only enhance their income from the traditional livelihood of fishing, but also to free themselves from the bondage of usurious credit. The men were consciously chosen by an individual who empowered the group members through his leadership. The group achieved a good deal of mutual trust and understanding. Though willing, they were unable to transcend the constraints of their circumstance because of the limited opportunity-set they had access to. As entrepreneurs, they required more expensive physical assets but their own wealth set a limit to their ability to access the formal credit market.

The story of an attempt to empower entire communities is narrated in Chapter 8 where the village itself is considered as the entrepreneur, and a business model is woven around it. The endowment of natural beauty and a traditional lifestyle were the capital assets the villagers collectively owned. Leveraging these assets in a fruitful manner, however, could lead to potential conflicts. The private ownership of assets, such as an easily accessible, relatively modern house and a spare room, could conflict with the distribution of common gains (net revenue).

The narratives in this section tell us about three alternative routes to entrepreneurship. The cases of two women from the hills are stories of people born with entrepreneurial talent, who, given an opportunity, seized it and flourished. The fishermen from the shores of the Arabian Sea achieved entrepreneurship as a response to their livelihood needs and economic environment. Our stories of ecotourism are examples of instances where entrepreneurship was thrust upon an entire village.

6

Control and Creation
The Worlds of Two Women

The empowerment of women along with other gender-related issues are now at the forefront of discussions on development. Being a woman poses a distinct set of challenges that have to be overcome to achieve some freedom in exercising control over one's life. Gender itself is a challenge in a male-dominated world. The other challenge, arising out of crushing poverty, is related to her dual role as a caregiver in the home and a bread-earner outside it. To overcome some of these challenges, the concept of the self-help group (SHG) for women based on mutual support has been widely promoted. An SHG is supposed to inculcate the discipline of regular saving as a habit, even if the quantum is small. Even minor activities like coming to meetings, keeping minutes and records of financial transactions, lending to one another, handling money responsibly, and responding to group members' needs and concerns all contribute to building self-confidence. The SHGs are also the basis for accessing markets — starting from credit in banks to selling products in local markets, to even running a microenterprise like a small *kirana* shop in a village. The activities of the SHGs are explicitly supported by the Panchayati Raj Institutions (PRIs) thus granting them social legitimacy.

Women take great pride in participating even if their participation is nominal. We had seen women take more than a full minute to pen down their signatures on the attendance register for SHG meetings, but the pride and self-confidence with which they did was memorable. The SHG provides a sense of solidarity with other women and members enjoy a sense of security knowing that there is one source of financial assistance where the decisions about the quantities or the interest rate and repayment period is determined jointly by all of them. It is in this sense that the participation (albeit in a very limited way) is important to the functioning of the individual woman. There are different levels of empowerment that this can achieve — from a control over resources, to a voice in decisions to a freedom to realise their potential as an entrepreneur or be able to give shape to their creative abilities beyond the routine drudgery of household management. However, not many rural women can leverage their empowerment to go beyond the confines of the village.

We narrate two such cases, where the woman was able to make the most of the given circumstances to have her impact felt far beyond the territorial confines of the place from where she began her journey. One woman in Himachal Pradesh used SHGs to scale up a dairy enterprise with aspirations for getting into big business and big politics. The other used the SHG route to build a textile enterprise with her family's help. Her creative interest in textile designs found expression through her enterprise. They are two distinct faces of empowerment demonstrating two very different capabilities.

Marketing Ambrosia in God's Abode

Nestled in the Himalayas, picturesque Himachal Pradesh, often referred to as *Dev bhumi* or God's abode, has been ahead of most other states of India in terms of human development indices like education and health. The indicators of gender balance are better than those of many other states. Quite expectedly, it has been at the forefront with respect to women's empowerment programmes, with many active women's SHGs functioning from as early as 2000. We travelled to Solan to study the social change brought about by the SHG movement. Solan is a congested market town in the Solan district of Himachal Pradesh, handling a lot of business as well as tourist traffic (see Map 6.1). Among the many women whose lives had been transformed through involvement in the SHGs, one woman stood out as having completely taken charge of both her life and the lives of many others across the state. What follows is the story of Jyoti Dhiman, a leader emerging from the SHG movement.

We first saw Jyoti at the coffee shop of our hotel, where we had scheduled a meeting with the representative of the National Bank for Agriculture and Rural Development (NABARD) to plan our itinerary for the next few days. From a distance we could see an animated

Map 6.1: Solan District in Himachal Pradesh

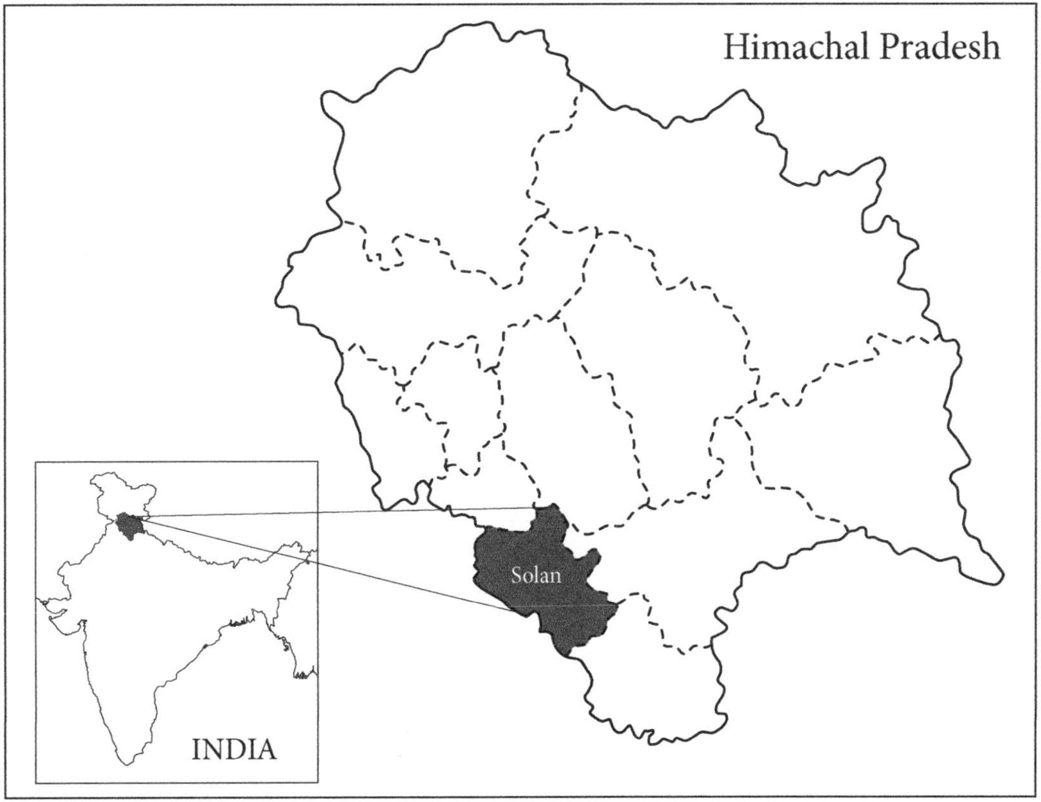

Himachal Pradesh

Solan

INDIA

discussion taking place; later, we came to know this was about setting up a stall for Jyoti's SHG at a handicraft mela in Solan town. Jyoti had come to know that the NABARD representative would be at our hotel, and without any delay had seized the opportunity to meet her to discuss the stall. What struck us most was her confidence, zest and energy. She excitedly shared with us her achievements, playing an active role in influencing us to look at SHGs in her village and others associated with her activities. We were curious to know more about her and visited her home the next day.

Jyoti was a middle-aged woman from Paplota village of Solan. She had been married off by her parents at the early age of 16. However, she kept returning to her parents' home, and then started living there permanently with her children. Her husband worked for Bharat Sanchar Nigam Limited (BSNL) and was posted in another town of Himachal. She had studied till the second year of college, but could not obtain a degree given the pressures at home. Initially, she was involved in some tailoring activities in her home, and then worked as an *anganwadi* worker for the Integrated Child Development Services (ICDS). She soon joined the SHG movement with the belief that she, along with other women, could do something productive in search of self-realisation. By the time she had formed her own SHG she was already a mother of three. Recognising that it was her education that had helped her stand on her own, she had ensured that her children went to school and her eldest daughter was now completing her graduation.

Jyoti's involvement with SHGs started around 2000 when, along with 10 other women from Paplota, they started an SHG called Jagriti. Jyoti took it upon herself to ensure that Jagriti (and other SHGs in the neighbourhood) functioned effectively as credit-facilitating bodies. To ensure that members of SHGs were truly engaged, they set up rules such as returning the deposits (sans interest) of women who displayed disinterest in the SHG by not coming to weekly meetings. In genuine cases of withdrawal, however, individual savings with interest were returned to the concerned person. Transparency was critical: Jyoti recognised early on that money could be a huge source of mistrust, and ascribed this as a key reason why women would not come forward to take up administrative positions in their SHGs. Her initiative was given due recognition when NABARD appointed her as pradhan of a Mahila Mandal formed by it. She was just 25 years old at that time. Within the next four to five months, Jyoti had facilitated the formation of over 20 SHGs. NABARD had to act as guarantor as she linked each of these SHGs to the banking system. It was around 2006, when NABARD suggested that she form a Kisan Club, which could act as an a Self Help Promoting Institute (SHPI), which would not only facilitate SHG formation but also act as their guarantors. Thus, Jyoti graduated from being president of Jagriti SHG (a post she still holds) to being Mahila Mandal pradhan and president of the Jagriti Mahila Kisan Club. As an SHPI, Jyoti's Kisan Club had facilitated the formation of at least 65 SHGs registered with NABARD and 120 other SHGs, registered with ICDS and other non-governmental organisations (NGOs).

Jyoti and her band of women were involved in numerous activities. Routine savings with the SHG and access to credit meant that the women could try alternative livelihood opportunities. Some tried their hands at making soft toys, dolls, candles or bags, while others took advantage of government schemes to grow exotic vegetables in polyhouses, or mushrooms (Solan is also known as the mushroom capital of India). Yet others took up milk production, which involved improving milk yields of domestic cattle as well as finding markets to sell the milk. Jyoti took it upon herself to coordinate all SHG activities, from taking up cudgels with uncooperative bank officials (*lakeer ka fakeer*, literally 'slave to the written rule') to approaching relevant NGOs for assistance. Having set up all these SHGs, Jyoti was now looking for a means to scale up her activities, leveraging her circle of influence. She recognised the window of opportunity in setting up an organic dairy, and approached NABARD for finances under their Rural Innovation Fund. She set up a pasteurising and milk packaging unit, which cost her around Rs 2 million (see Plate 6.1). She obtained a grant of Rs 975,000 from NABARD, and another loan of Rs 900,000 from the district central cooperative bank, with the rest of the money coming from the funds of her Kisan Club. Around this time, she realised that to reduce her tax burden she would be better off setting up a company under Section 25. Thus, the Jagriti Mahila Kisan Samiti (JMKS) was formed. Since its formation in 2008, her cash flows were steady and she was consistently repaying her loan, while continuing

Plate 6.1: Milk-packaging Machine at Jyoti's Gau Amrit Processing Unit: The Promise of Overtaking Amul

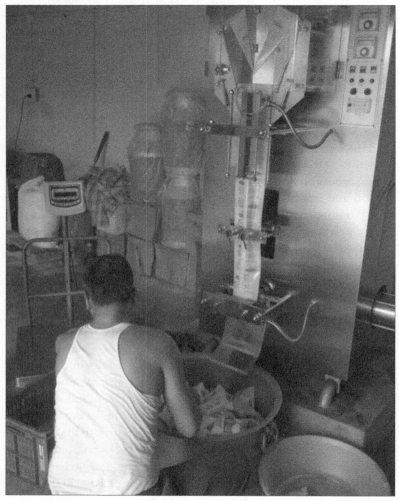

to invest more in her dairy unit. However, the unit was not profitable yet. Jyoti realised the need to scale up and to increase the offering of value-added dairy products. Meanwhile, she had branded her dairy products as Gau Amrit (Ambrosia from the Cow), and sold packaged milk across her state.

We had an interesting discussion on this idea of Jyoti's. We asked her why she had set up the dairy unit and what her future plans were. She replied that she wanted to create an 'Amul', like the one in Bihar, and then 'Bill Clinton' would visit to congratulate her on her good work (the Amul Milk Cooperative is in Gujarat and it was Bill Gates who had visited). Thus, while not completely informed of similar business models, she had a fairly clear idea of where she wanted to go, and clearly realised that recognition by eminent personalities would help her leverage her initiatives even further. Jyoti had won several awards, from 2008 onwards, at the district, state and national levels for her innovation, social service and achievements.

Around a year after Jyoti's venturing into a dairy unit, in 2009, the Doodh Ganga initiative was launched by the government of Himachal Pradesh with funding from NABARD. Under this project, SHGs were being provided loans for setting up dairy units of up to 10 animals with a total cost of Rs 300,000. While the entrepreneur (member of an SHG) was required to spend 10 per cent margin money, half the loan for the project was made interest free. Further, if the entrepreneur ensured regular repayment, 50 per cent subsidy would be provided on the total interest payable on the net loan component. NABARD also would extend support for the collection, preservation and processing of milk. The state animal husbandry department would ensure that quality veterinary services were available to all entrepreneurs who purchased cows under this scheme. The Doodh Ganga initiative was an instant success, and resulted in a substantial increase in milk production and empowered many poor women to become self-reliant through dairy farming.

Jyoti and her group decided to avail of this Doodh Ganga Project for scaling up their operations. She began to initiate the formation of a loose (informal) federation of women's groups across the entire district. The purpose was to pool their collective resources and energies to expand the dairy activity and look for other income-supplementing opportunities. This would ensure a steady supply of milk for Jyoti's Gau Amrit dairy. She began to organise SHGs across the district, travelling tirelessly and convincing women about the gains from working together. While there clearly was a private gain to Jyoti's enterprise in federating the SHGs, this was also a means to ensure that all the SHGs that Jyoti had helped put together could sustain themselves by taking advantage of the Doodh Ganga scheme.

Jyoti had called about 30 other women who had been working together in the federation to her home to interact with us. She was collecting milk from around 150 groups of women. Her business model was simple but robust. She would collect milk from her 'federation' of SHGs. It would be brought to her pasteurising unit in cans. The milk would be tested and the price fixed according to the quality and the fat content. She would pay immediately and not keep credit. The milk would then be pasteurised and packed. Later in the day, mini trucks would move to markets in the neighbouring towns for delivery. She processed about 500 litres of milk per day.

In the meeting, Jyoti proudly informed us that her Gau Amrit processing unit now employed 10 people of whom three were women. She was facing a skill constraint and was on the lookout for trustworthy people with managerial skills. In the interim, she had asked her brother to give up his little business to help her in marketing Gau Amrit. She paid between Rs 15 to Rs 18 per litre of milk she collected, depending on the quality. The wholesale price for processed milk was around Rs 22 per litre and the retail price fetched around Rs 28 per litre. A quick estimate of the daily gross revenue would be around Rs 10,000 to 12,000. In comparison, her competitor, the Milkfed, the dairy run by the state government, paid the dairy farmer only Rs 10–12 per litre of milk. Other competitors were Reliance Pure, Vita, Amul, and Verka. Jyoti realised that as a new and small entrant into the milk market her margins would have to be lower, and she would have to keep her overheads lower than the state-run Milkfed. To compete with Milkfed, Gau Amrit was trying to reach as many relatively inaccessible areas for collection, leveraging the network of federated SHGs. The networked supply could provide up to 15 quintals of milk every day. As a result, Jyoti claimed that she now had to cope with excess supply of milk that she could not pasteurise and market, since her processing capability was limited. The local market also was narrow and competitive. So, her next phase of planned expansion would be to produce ghee and paneer with the excess milk that she could not market locally.

She talked about the pasteurising and packaging unit of Gau Amrit that we saw, and pointed out that she had also bought four mini trucks for collection of milk and transportation. However, during the hot summer months that year, she had sustained a loss as the milk spoiled during transportation and she was contemplating buying refrigerated trucks, although they were more expensive and had half the capacity of ordinary trucks. She intended to invest around Rs 3.2 million in Gau Amrit for setting up a paneer processing unit, and ghee, butter and curd processing unit, and increasing the cold storage capacity. Since she had been commercially successful (though still in debt), she saw a clear case for expansion. She also knew that to realise her ambition she had to work hard, and, perhaps, face tougher challenges in the process than if she had been a man.

She related, in a satisfied tone, a story of how she had persuaded the wholesaler in Solan to distribute her product. It took time, patience and a lot of persuasion to gain entry into the closed circle of the dealers and their suppliers. She was cheated at times. Once a dealer made a spot payment for five crates of milk but gave her a wad of counterfeit notes. This was when local markets bailed her out, where her reputation and quality assurance were enough for people to buy Gau Amrit. In trying to penetrate the existing milk markets, she quickly realised that political friends came in handy and worked with local politicians. She was able to persuade the chief minister (CM) to inaugurate her unit. As a result, Gau Amrit was better known as *CM Sahab ka Doodh* among the locals. Other marketing strategies involved screening a movie on local television channels on how Gau Amrit processed milk. She was able to use the government's television channel, Doordarshan, through NABARD's good offices. She also used the rural marts sponsored by NABARD across the state as advertising kiosks. They also faced trouble from local police with respect to transporting processed milk. Jyoti's was not shy of using her influence among local politicians and administrators. Once the senior police officers and the CM were made aware of the harassment Gau Amrit's trucks faced at check posts, the roadblocks surprisingly disappeared. Dealing with politicians and bureaucrats was not new for Jyoti. In the past, when she was active in SHG formation, she had the temerity to orchestrate the transfer of an uncooperative sub-divisional magistrate and extract an apology from him through a local Member of the Legislative Assembly (MLA). She claimed that she could walk into any bureaucrat's room in Shimla, the state capital, if the need arose, and proudly asserted that she was always given priority when she went to meet a politician or local administrator, as they considered her efforts to be synonymous with the success of Doodh Ganga, an initiative close to the heart of the current CM.

With Gau Amrit gaining in strength and visibility, she was approached more than once by Reliance Fresh, a big retail chain, to buy out her business. There were pressures on her to yield but she stood firm and refused. From her discussions, it was not clear whether her political friends came in handy in this instance. She said that she wanted to keep growing till she became like Amul. Then she might consider selling it and think of new ventures. We finally asked whether she would take up politics as a career; she smiled enigmatically and replied 'not immediately', as she still needed to devote time to strengthening Gau Amrit as well as support her SHGs. That the state CM's household used Gau Amrit was evidence of her strong political links. According to her associates, she had close ties with the district Bharatiya Janata Party (BJP) and was once offered a ticket to run for the state assembly. She confidently brushed them off, mentioning that many political parties were insisting she at least compete for the panchayat elections, but her refrain was that she would support all political parties provided they supported her SHG movement in return.

While on the topic of SHGs and their focus on women, Jyoti quickly mentioned that Gau Amrit also needed men to succeed, and, in that context, the Doodh Ganga Yojana provided credit to men either as individuals or as part of a Joint Liability Group (JLG). This was especially relevant as many banks did not lend to non–SHG members, and men could now avail of loans to start dairy farming from NABARD through the Doodh Ganga Yojana. With her assistance, six out of 40 JLGs were linked with the bank. Thus, her Kisan Club continued to act as a guarantor for new SHGs (and JLGs), which constituted an additional risk for her (see Figure 6.1). To ensure a steady supply of good quality milk, Jyoti also diversified into selling feed material and additives such as calcium for the cows at the doorstep of the dairy farmer at wholesale rates. This was very successful. Moreover, she counselled anyone who bought a cow to also buy insurance to protect themselves from financial adversity should the cow die. She was also exploring the sale of cow dung as biomass feed to several of the SHGs that had installed biogas units.

Figure 6.1: The Activity Net of Jyoti's SHGs

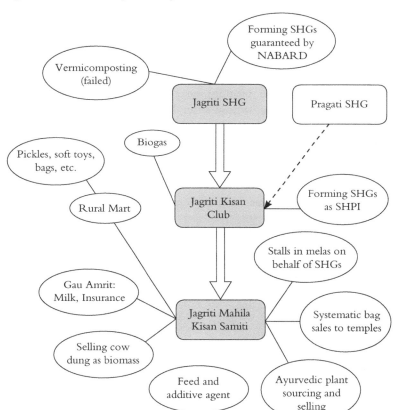

When talking with Jyoti and her close associates we realised that Jyoti was doing all the talking with the women around her nodding in agreement, but remarkably quiet otherwise (see Plate 6.2). We changed tack and addressed our questions to the group of women sitting with Jyoti. We still found Jyoti responding. So, we explicitly requested her to let other people answer and she finally took the cue to remain silent. Still, any comment or response to a question was either prompted by her, or the respondent made eye contact with Jyoti seeking approval before responding. It was apparent that Jyoti's personality towered over most of the women. The women, most of whom owned a few cows, told us how they had tided over financial exigencies in their families through their own income, and were not dependent on their husband's income alone. Another lady talked about how the attitude of bank officials towards her improved as a result of her operating their SHG bank account. Yet another gave credit to Jyoti for the formation of their SHG. They had acquired new skills and enhanced their incomes. Jyoti's mother proudly narrated Jyoti's success story. Jyoti introduced us to Nitya, whose sister lived in Shimla. Nitya's sister was a vital link in the Gau Amrit marketing chain as her network was being used to slowly expand the consumption of Gau Amrit in Shimla through a door-to-door supply. Currently around 120 milk packets were sold daily through Nitya's sister's network.

Plate 6.2: Jyoti with Representatives from her Federation of SHGs

After the meeting, where the NABARD district development manager (DDM) was present observing our conversation, she remarked that not all was as well as it appeared. There were a lot of women who disliked Jyoti's overbearing nature and thought that they could have got a better deal if they had had more power vis-à-vis Jyoti. Nevertheless, the DDM hoped that Jyoti's business venture Gau Amrit would thrive and grow because of NABARD's interest in it, but was quite aware that one day Jyoti's style of operation could lead to a fracture in her network. She also conjectured that Jyoti was aware of some dissidents in her merry band of 500 dairy farmers and 5,000 to

6,000 SHG members. Among them, there were at least 15 equally competent women who could challenge her leadership. But given her social standing and support networks of SHGs involved in all kinds of activities, the probability of such a challenge seemed low.

Jyoti's sense of responsibility towards the SHGs she helped federate was evident from her interest in the stall that JMKS was setting up in the local trade fair at Solan. The JMKS stall had little to do with Gau Amrit; instead it showcased the different activities that the SHGs were involved in through selling dolls, bags, handicrafts, and organic beauty products. Jyoti had developed a systematic supply chain through which handmade bags from the SHGs were sold at the local temples. Despite her busy schedule, she had succeeded in using her influence in bringing Baba Ramdev, a popular yoga guru, to conduct a *yog shivir* at Paplota village more than once. She used the opportunity to explore potential profitable options for the SHGs in Paplota from supplying the ayurvedic herbs that grew in and around the village to Baba Ramdev's ashram. Her self-confidence was apparent as was her remarkable ability to network. She had a keen eye for spotting potential business opportunities.

Weaving Dreams into Colour

Arunachal Pradesh, at the easternmost tip of India, is literally the 'land of the rising sun'. We drove towards Ziro, through the lush green rolling hills, crystal clear streams, and pristine environment. Around 43 km from Lilabari airport in Assam, Ziro is the headquarter of Lower Subansiri district and is one of the oldest towns in Arunachal Pradesh (see Map 6.2). Famous for its gentle hills covered with pine trees and green rice fields all around, it is home to the Apatani tribe, who are dependant on permanent wetland cultivation and forest produce for their livelihoods. Traditionally, the womenfolk were responsible for weaving clothes for their respective families, which led to this becoming a cottage industry for the tribals (IGNCA 1999). The women of this area are good weavers, who use both traditional patterns and original artistic designs. As we came into Ziro, a shop displaying several bright *galeys* (skirts) and shiny knives drew our attention. This was a retail outlet of the Arun Kutir Udyog Cooperative Society (AKUCS), whose president we were to meet the next day.

Map 6.2: Lower Subansiri District in Arunachal Pradesh

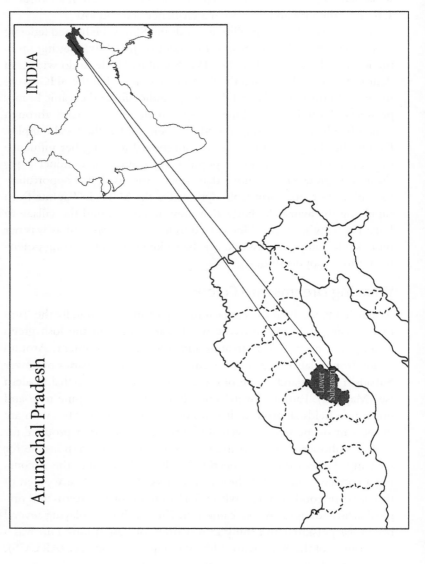

Arunachal Pradesh

INDIA

Lower
Subansiri

The next morning, we were at Anshu Yansenpa's residence, from where all the activities of the AKUCS were conducted. She had already called us and expressed her inability to be there to welcome us; she had to attend a meeting in a town around 4 km away, where she was part of a development advisory committee. She had asked us to look around the cooperative and promised she would join us by noon. Some training classes on knitting were on in one of the rooms, with the master trainer moving from one machine to another, supervising the ladies in training. In another room, an elderly lady in traditional Apatani garb was weaving a colourful *galey* on her loom (see Plate 6.3). Later we learnt that the lady was Yansenpa's mother. We spoke to

Plate 6.3: Weaving of *Galey*s at Yansenpa's Residence

Dani Nancy, one of the 'master trainers' employed by AKUCS, who had been with them for over five years, and was also a member of the managing board of the cooperative. A distant relative of Anshu Yansenpa, hailing from East Siang district, she had been staying with the Anshu's since 2006, assisting them in all their activities and focusing on the weaving side of the business. She enjoyed her engagement. Not only could she work freely without disturbance, she also got the opportunity to go out of her home state and meet people. She had trained over 300 people and was pleased that most of her students were able to weave as much as 10 a day. An average weaver could weave 5 m daily after takitng care of household chores, which meant she could earn as much as Rs 600 in a day at the prevailing rate of Rs 120 per metre for a traditional *galey*.

There was a flurry of activity as Yansenpa arrived and the household quickly made arrangements so we could interview her. Yansenpa was serene; the rushed return from the meeting had no effect on her composure. She settled down and started telling us about the genesis of AKUCS. She was the president of AKUCS, a network of weavers and handloom merchants. Her husband, Anshu Jamsempa, was a deputy director of the textiles department in the government of Arunachal Pradesh. They met when Yansenpa was a trainee in the department of textiles in one of their regular training schemes on knitting. She was very happy to be there and learn new skills. As a child she loved nothing better than to sit in front of a loom and weave her own innovative patterns and work on handicrafts. This was an opportunity to learn how the knitters from Ludhiana worked with wool, learn more about ergonomic looms and know where to source the best yarn from. Yansenpa enjoyed every moment of this.

Very soon, with the support of Jamsempa, AKUCS was set up with her as president in 1992. Funds worth Rs 50,000 were obtained from the Rural Industry Service Centre scheme of the Khadi and Village Industries Commission (KVIC) to set up the cooperative. She bought two looms for Rs 4,500 each, while continuing to attend training in the textiles department, and employed two weavers in her home to give shape to the numerous patterns in her mind. The fabrics produced were an instant hit, with customers willing to pay good money for the innovative weaves. Many loyal customers soon started placing bulk orders for custom-made weaves, which meant that Yansenpa had to meet a constant string of orders. Meanwhile, Jamsempa and Yansenpa married in 1994, and started living in the same premises (Jamsempa's house) from where the cooperative functioned. In 1996, Yansenpa got a break when there was a 'contingency' (temporary) position open in the textile department, and she started working there. By 2003, with a salary of Rs 1,500 per month, she was on track for a permanent position in the department of textiles, notwithstanding her limited educational qualifications; she had studied only till class eight. As a training instructor in knitting and weaving, she trained several batches of young women from far-flung villages in Arunachal, with growing confidence, deriving a deep satisfaction from their progress. Yet, by this time, the activities of AKUCS started demanding more and more of Yansenpa's time, as did her seven children (five girls, two boys). Yansenpa confessed that raising her children was never a problem, as she had all the assistance at home with several of her sisters and sisters-in law taking full responsibility of the children. However, Yansenpa had to make a choice between her regular government job, which provided satisfaction and security, and engaging full time in AKUCS, which gave her the freedom to innovate and take risks. Supported by her husband, she chose to plunge headlong into developing AKUCS into a thriving entrepreneurial venture.

The initial idea to set up a business venture with textiles and other indigenous arts of the Arunachal region came from Jamsempa. Yansenpa told us how she was happiest when she was designing new weaves. The success of the small experiment in her home encouraged her to go ahead with setting up a small shop in Ziro. The rent for the shop was around Rs 1,000 per month, which she could afford, and she had enough place in her residential premises to set up the handloom infrastructure. The Anshu family had plenty of agricultural land which made them rather well off. Moreover, with Jamsempa holding a fairly responsible position in the bureaucracy, the family was well connected to influential people such as the manager of the local State Bank, the district collector (DC) and other top bureaucrats. To start with, AKUCS was given a grant of Rs 450,000 to procure looms and conduct training sessions on weaving and knitting by the KVIC, a competence that Yansenpa had gained in her government job. Successful completion meant more such schemes, and AKUCS's credibility going up. This in turn meant that more banks would offer loans;

they even got a one-time grant of Rs 8.3 million from KVIC to set up adequate training facilities. Yansenpa proudly shared with us that at that time (2011), AKUCS had around 20 regular employees, 10 of whom were salaried (others were part of the Anshu household), and was networked with 250 women weavers through 30 SHGs. These weavers worked from their homes and visited AKUCS if the need arose. At present, she had restricted the number of weavers associated with AKUCS by insisting that the weavers reside within a 7 km radius from the AKUCS premises. This was important given the inhospitable terrain of Arunachal, to ensure that the weavers were regular in delivering their consignments, and for AKUCS to take care of the weavers' well-being.

Yansenpa also helped the SHGs involved with her cooperative to apply and get loans from banks, as a guarantor, with her husband assisting with the paperwork. So far she had acted as guarantor in more than 25 instances. She also assisted individual SHG members in taking loans from banks. AKUCS had undertaken the responsibility of providing government-issued weaver cards and facilitating insurance schemes for the weavers associated with it. The cooperative ensured processing of insurance claims on behalf of the weavers. In addition, the cooperative facilitated the provision of almost 800 artisan cards, which would enable the weavers to access bank loans and avail travel discounts when travelling to exhibitions or workshops across the country. Depending on the economic conditions of the weavers associated with her, she provided some with yarn if they could not afford it. There was a market for her products — in addition to the small shop in Ziro, she had now invested in a large store at Itanagar, which was under construction. For her store she stocked a variety of other local handicrafts ranging from knives to baskets, in addition to what AKUCS produced.

We could not meet Jamsempa when we visited Yansenpa; he was away on work. However, it was evident that although she was managing this cooperative, he was in charge of all the paperwork. At the time of our visit, key ongoing projects with AKUCS were the Scheme of Fund for Regeneration of Traditional Industries (SFURTI) of the KVIC for supporting regional traditional industry, and the Cluster Development Education Scheme to impart training. However, she was unable to show us any report or financial document, as Jamsempa, who took care of these, was not available. She was not even aware of where to locate them in her office, and offered to call her husband to find out where they were. Her approach was open — she did find a register with minutes of meeting of the cooperative that she promptly showed us. She had little idea about the revenue flow of AKUCS — from her discussions we inferred that the revenue was quite irregular, although, on an average, it made a monthly surplus of over Rs 50,000. Her concern was more about the irregularity of the flow rather than its inadequacy.

AKUCS was run by a board of 10 members, including Anshu Yansenpa as president, Anshu Jamsempa as secretary, and five other women who were all related to her. It also included the current DC, executive and joint directors of the textile department and the local bank manager. We met many of the board members as they were in her premises supervising the ongoing work. Two of them were master trainers in knitting, based on training they had obtained at Ludhiana. Others supervised day-to-day activities at the cooperative as Yansenpa often had to attend project review meetings, follow up on schemes and other meetings as she was on the board for many development initiatives owing to her position as president of AKUCS. Moreover, she had to travel at least once a month to display AKUCS's products at exhibitions held across the country. So far, they had not started exporting their wares as there was a huge domestic demand to be met, and through their exhibitions they reached many foreign buyers anyway.

What were her ideas about the future? Would her seven children expand the scale of AKUCS's operations? Yansenpa proudly smiled and told us that was not how she had planned things. While she might leave behind a thriving business for her children to run — she expected that this would be no more than a fall back career option. She, however, preferred her children getting government jobs. Three of her daughters were professionally trained (or undergoing training), as a dentist, law officer (in a government position), and doctor. Another was pursuing graduate studies and the youngest daughter was in secondary school along with the two sons. The younger siblings would like careers like their older siblings; none knew how to weave, nor had displayed any interest in AKUCS. Yansenpa did not seem worried about the future — she talked excitedly about how she needed to buy some power looms to scale up. She was on the lookout for appropriate government schemes so she could apply for a grant. She had already applied to NABARD for a grant to buy automatic knitting machines. She dreamt of having a permanent outlet in Delhi for AKUCS, but realised that she had to diversify as well as increase her scale of production for that to be a viable proposition. Would she take a loan to fulfil her dreams? She said no — she was not comfortable with loans; besides, if you were patient, you would get government assistance in the form of grants — you just needed to know where to look.

Different Faces of Empowerment

A process is empowering if it helps a person to develop skills so that she can solve her problems independently and take her own decisions. In this context, both Jyoti's and Yansenpas's stories are about empowerment, yet the context and conditions of empowerment are quite different. Jyoti's struggle conforms to the conventional understanding of empowerment of a woman in a world dominated by men. This world was neither of her choosing nor making, but she used all available opportunities to gain control over her life. The outcome of her struggle is the power she can now exert over administrative, political and economic decisions. Yet empowerment is not just about the ability to exert power *over* others, it is also about the power *to* act in a way that allows a person to realise their aspirations. This is the kind of empowerment that we saw in Yansenpa who developed a business model around handicrafts and weaving, essentially to fashion an outlet to express herself.

The process through which Yansenpa evolved as an entrepreneur is different from the way Jyoti evolved, yet in both cases the final outcome was that the women emerged as influential people with respect to development in their states. Jyoti has been winning numerous awards in recognition of her inspiring abilities, and now realises she has the potential to nurture political ambitions. Yansenpa is on numerous boards and committees that seek her advice and tap into her experience on how to engage people to work towards a common development goal. Both women are leaders, yet their styles are dissimilar; Jyoti appears to be autocratic in her functioning while Yansenpa appears to be more accommodative and approachable. Yet each style is appropriate for its respective line of business. While Yansenpa needs to foster creativity and empowers agents through her leadership abilities for her handicrafts business, Jyoti's style fosters efficiency and clear communication, which is critical for a confederation of suppliers of a perishable product. The women associated with these leaders are empowered as they learn to execute decisions quickly, and through their economic independence.

Over time the women's traditional relations with their peers and people around them have changed, and they have been able to garner mutual support. Of course, there are always a few dissidents. Among the various women in the SHG federation, not all would be beholden to Jyoti, nor appreciate her propensity to control. Yet, they were never openly confrontational in their attitude. It has been socially and economically beneficial for these women to be associated with Jyoti and seeing her meteoric rise may inspire one of them to also try something similar. Yansenpa has had the unstinting support of her husband, yet the challenge and daily grind of running a cooperative for handicrafts is one which she had had the courage and gumption to take up, which is creditable. Through carving out an avenue for herself (ably supported by her husband) to express her creative talent, she has demonstrated to women of the northeast, where most people are exposed to handicrafts in their homes throughout their growing years, that following your creative urge could be a means to achieve self-reliance. Both women have provided the people in their circle of influence a sense of self-worth and dignity through providing them opportunities to earn a livelihood by doing things they like best.

Despite different emphases and perspectives, discussions on empowerment have for the most part remained rooted in the local, in the needs of the poorest of the poor, constraining the transformative ability of the empowerment approach (Parpart 2011). Jyoti and Yansenpa, our protagonists from Himachal Pradesh and Arunachal Pradesh, do not conform to the poorest of the poor image. While Jyoti came from a landed household and her husband had a permanent government job with full support from her family, Yansenpa's husband was a key bureaucrat in the state's textile department, and she also had an enabling infrastructure on the home front. Yet, triggered and enabled by some development intervention, both these women took charge, albeit in different ways, not only to change the course of their own lives, but also to improve the lot of several other men and women, some of them being the poorest of the poor.

7

Between the Moneylender and the Deep Blue Sea

Stories from Fishing Communities in Kerala

Kerala, with its long coastline and famous backwaters, provides opportunities for both offshore as well as inshore fishing as livelihoods. This chapter examines how fishermen engaged in both kinds of fishing earn a livelihood from renewable natural resources. The fieldwork was done in the region, around the town of Alappuzha (see Map 7.1). The region shares typical features of coastal areas that provide ample aquatic resources that could generate important livelihood opportunities for the people. However, uncontrolled economic development and a high dependence of the poor on natural resources for their livelihood have resulted in the degradation of resources and loss of biodiversity. As a result, the capacity of these ecosystems to provide sustainable livelihood opportunities has been diminishing.

There are many different forms of dependency between resource users and aquatic resources. Some people rely almost entirely on marine resources for income, employment and food, while some use them as part of a diversified portfolio of livelihood options. Others depend seasonally on marine resources or use them as an intermittent safety net when access to other livelihood opportunities is absent.

Rural households typically engage in livelihood diversification. Wealthier households own assets related to fishing, such as boats, nets, traps, and they may have control over access to the best fishing areas. They own more land and livestock than other groups and may also own non-farm businesses such as shops and even accommodation for rent in tourist spots. On the other hand, poor households have access to fishing opportunities only as hired crew on boats owned

Map 7.1: Alappuzha District in Kerala

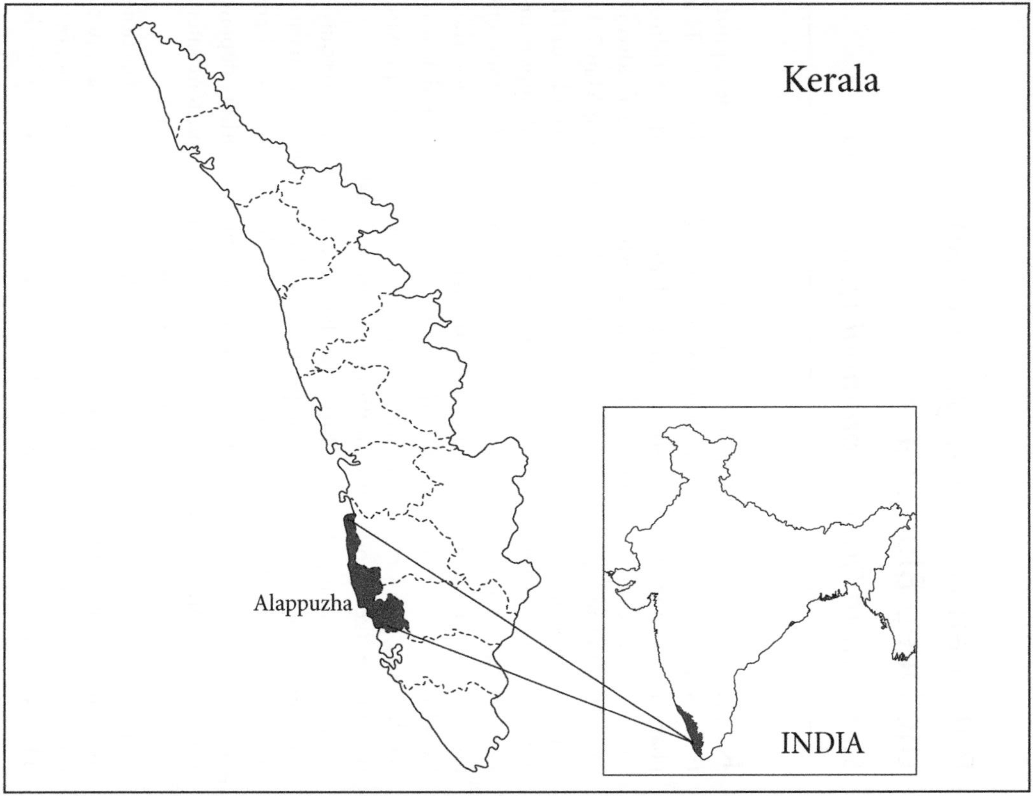

Kerala

INDIA

Alappuzha

by others. They independently engage in inshore fishing since it can be carried out without boats. Even if boats are used, they are very small and much more affordable than offshore fishing vessels. As the poor do not have much capital to invest in fishing activities, any gear (nets, boats) owned by them is generally constructed by them or by the members of their household. Some of them have access to tiny plots of land, mainly used for subsistence cropping. Fishing is typically done for food and as a means of generating surplus cash for consumption requirements.

Like in small peasant farming, the social organisation of small-scale fishing often uses sharecropping contracts. Owners (who are also the local moneylenders) use small amounts of capital to lease their gear in exchange for a share of the fishing products. The technology for capturing and distributing fish is artisanal in the traditional use of technology and equipment. Share contract fishing is seasonal and is generally combined with other fishing activities on a smaller and more independent basis, and also with agriculture and handicrafts. All of these are secondary activities, while fishing under sharecropping is the primary activity. Fishing under sharecropping contracts produces fish for both cash and food. These fishermen have little cash available to invest in fishing or any other activity. A lack of access to credit is an obstacle to growth. For poor communities this means that economic opportunities are likely to be quite restricted.

Alappuzha and its Surroundings

Alappuzha (erstwhile Alleppy) was, once upon a time, the biggest sea port in Kerala handling large exports of spices. The small city had a large grid of artificially dug canals and waterways through which much of the hinterland connectivity was established. A few kilometres from the coast is the huge Vembanad Lake and the large rice bowl called the Kuttanad area. It was once called the Venice of the East because of its vibrant network of canals and waterways. Apart from the large economic activity that surrounded the port, fishing was a major source of livelihood. On the coast was the vast opportunity of accessing the Arabian Sea, and a bit inland, the Vembanad Lake offered a large commons where sweet water fish could be obtained. Around the region, famous for its backwaters, tourists flock to live in the houseboats and float through the area. The local market for fish is available throughout the year since the people of Kerala love to eat fish.

Now the port is dead. A rusted quay jutting into the ocean is a reminder of a once active landing point. The lighthouse still warns ocean-going vessels of the coastline of the district, all 82 km of it. The local people blame the labour unions who they say became too active; some say there were vested interests that took away the activity from Alappuzha port to Kochi, about 70 km to the north. All this was after India's independence, when, according to an old fisherman, 'local politicians started meddling into economic life with their own agenda of greed and power'.

With the decline of the port, fishing became more significant in terms of livelihoods for a greater number of people (see Plate 7.1). Fishing is still important and the scale can vary from a single fisherman on a raft to outboard engines on canoes, to more heavy duty vessels with inboard engines, and, finally, the modern trawlers that can do deep-sea fishing with sonar equipment in international waters. Every few kilometres on the ocean front are auction centres where the fresh catch is auctioned off on a daily basis. In the locality though, like the port, the really big auction centre is at Kochi. There is freedom to

Plate 7.1: Fishing Boats: How Far Will They Have to Go for the Next Catch?

choose one's selling point, and the ubiquitous mobile phone is a versatile instrument of arbitrage. The smaller vessels can find it costly though to go much further from the point of origin, and can de facto be tied to a smaller geographical space.

Fishing is controlled by vendors and moneylenders and this mafia-like nexus is difficult to break even when banks and non-governmental organisations (NGOs) work together. The fishermen are mainly Christians and the district is politically very polarised. According to the secretary, Gandhi Smaraka Grama Seva Kendram (GSGSK), a well organised NGO that works in the region, there is a powerful nexus between politicians and religious leaders in the region and developmental projects that emanate from the state capital of Thiruvananthapuram are what he calls 'Big System Projects' that are largely insensitive to local needs and local problems. He thinks that such projects are essentially 'anti-human'. The only viable alternative, according to him, is the Gandhian concept of a village republic. However, the stories we teased out of the villagers nearby were not exactly reflective of an idyllic egalitarian republic.

A retired professor with a PhD in agronomy, another member of the think tank of GSGSK believes that the biggest threat to fishing comes from the growth of the tourism industry. Hoteliers and developers offer large amounts to fishermen to relocate and the 'fishlands' are being eroded and gradually destroyed. A large one-time payment is of no sustainable use. Most of the fishermen are already in debt, and after they repay the debt any residual amount is blown up in having a good time. When we talked later to the fishermen though, their perceived threat was entirely different. Tourism at least offered a handsome compensation. The real threat was the trend of a steadily declining size of the catch, especially after the tsunami. Fishing is the most important income-generating activity of fishermen in the coastal area of the district. The GSGSK was actively engaging with the local fishermen in trying to build their capacity to avail of credit and expand their productive activities. Self-help groups (SHGs, only women) were rare among the fishing folk, but the Yojana Sasray Samitis (YSS) for men only were numerous and quite active. Though female educational attainments are supposed to be high in the state of Kerala, women in fishing villages of this district rarely went out of their homes to work.

The Story of South Cherthala Panchayat

In South Cherthala Panchayat, in the village of Arthunke, GSGSK had given a small loan to a Joint Liability Group (JLG) of fishermen to partially finance an outboard engine. We met the members of the JLG and talked to them to understand the consequences of being able to afford an outboard engine. Andrew (referred to as Andy), a local fisherman, had formed a federation of 22 fishing YSSs, and when we met him he was the president of the federation. From the members of the 22 YSSs, three JLGs had been formed called Misshiha, Purappad and Immanuel. Each JLG had obtained Rs 100,000 from GSGSK as microfinance. The loan had been taken for a two-year period. Andy their leader planned to form 10 more JLGs from the 22 groups in the near future. He had hand-picked members from the 22 groups to form the three JLGS with an eye on their savings behaviour and reliability. They initially saved enough to start buying some equipment and then used the loans to repay the moneylender, locally known as the *therakan*, who charged 10 per cent per day on loans. It was claimed that the therakan's presence and the practice of usury were widespread amongst fishing communities in the entire state (see Box 7.1).

Andy appeared to have great leadership skills in mobilising and organising groups in his village. According to Andy, 'What hurt me the most was when after a long night's effort I brought in my catch from the sea which was nobody's private property, the therakan would have complete rights over it because we had used his equipment'. Andy was helped to a considerable extent by Maggie who worked for GSGSK. She had grown up in the neighbourhood and came from a fishing family. Maggie was in charge of the sub-centre of GSGSK in South Cherthala. It was Maggie who had first broached the idea of a microfinance loan for Andy and his men. When Andy and his friends had begun to repay the therakan, four moneylenders from the neighbourhood along with some local toughs went to Maggie's house one night and threatened her with dire consequences if she did not stop organising the fishermen. Maggie was courageous enough not to be cowed down. According to her, the therakan's bosses were spread out across the country, from Chennai, Bengaluru and Mumbai to even as far away as New Delhi. When we asked her how she tackled them, her reply was revealing. She had told the moneylenders that

Box 7.1: A Therakan's Prey

We met Stanley when we were talking to Andy and his band of fishermen in Arthunke. Stanley was old and frail. His weather-beaten face bore a helpless expression as he followed us around, completely unaffected by our indifference towards him. Andy introduced us to Stanley saying he was not a member of any YSS but now wanted to join desperately. Andy had still not allowed Stanley to become a member of any YSS because of his habit of not saving.

Many years ago, Stanley, after passing his class 10 exams, had obtained a state government job as a bus conductor. He had not accepted it because he felt it was better to be free and take up the traditional family livelihood of fishing. He now deeply regrets that decision. He has four children. His son has passed class 12 and is working as an electrician in Thiruvananthapuram. Of his three girls, two are unmarried. One is a nun and the other teaches in a teachers' training school. Stanley spoke to us in a sad and weary voice. He claimed he belonged to the therakan; his boat, his net, his fish, the clothes he wore, and everything that was there in his house. He was completely bonded. He had taken an initial loan of Rs 10,000 which had now accumulated to over Rs 250,000 worth of dues. He had been in the clutches of the same moneylender for over 20 years.

When we asked why he had not joined a group earlier, he gave a number of reasons. He claimed that at that time he did not fully understand what groups were supposed to do, and had no time to find out either. He also said that when he did find out about the groups he thought he would not be able to save as he had sizeable financial commitments. Having observed the success of Andy and the fishermen in freeing themselves from the clutches of the therakan, he knew there was a way out. We were not so sure; it was probably too late for him.

the NGO was not a threat but a competitor. She challenged them to lend at 4 per cent per annum rather than at 10 per cent a day. It was a challenge to compete in business!

How were the JLGs doing? The GSGSK had helped this federation (with Andy as president) obtain the auctioning rights for one year in the Arthenkul landing area. Each village had a fish landing centre where whoever brought the catch could auction it off to buyers. The group that managed the auction centre for one year received a 1 per cent commission on total daily sales. This was an added income opportunity for Andy's group. The proceeds from the auction commission were benefitting a total of 145 families, many of whom who had gradually come out of the clutches of the therakan. Their average income had gone up only marginally. However, they felt much more secure because the catch was now theirs and the boat, engine and nets were again their private property.

Did they see any threat to their security? Yes, according to the JLGs. Their catch was steadily declining. According to Clarence, who has been going out to sea for 45 years (one could almost see the sea salt on his thick eyebrows and white hair), there has been a 30 per cent decline in catch during his fishing career. The only thing that was saving them was the rise in fish prices due to a growing and buoyant demand.

Why was the catch declining? Apart from the tsunami effect, which they claimed they did not fully understand and yet they had seen a clear decline after the tsunami, there was another reason too. The more trawlers and boats with inboard engines that went out to sea meant that there would be less catch left in shallow waters. There was a ban on deep-sea fishing during June, July and August so as not to disturb the reproductive cycle of the fish, but this was only valid for trawlers and not for boats with inboard engines. Another fisherman, James, observed that ideally all fishing should be stopped during the three months, but alas the banks and moneylenders never paused for three months. So the government had allowed both outboard and inboard engines to be used for fishing during June to August. Trawling, however, was forbidden during those months.

As fish becomes scarce in shallow waters, outboard engines costing around Rs 150,000 each would have to be replaced by inboard engines that cost around Rs 4–5 million each. Clarence was certain that the banks would not give them that kind of loan, so they may have to go to back to the therakans once again. Andy had been very strict with his group about maintaining and honing their savings habit. If they could not get an inboard engine in the near future would they have any real options left? Andy stared at the sea, but his friends said that if they needed to supplement their incomes Andy could become a therakan and use their resources to lend money to other poorer fishermen and earn high interest rates. Andy controlled all the repayments to the NGOs and enforced a 3 per cent savings of their daily income.

Andy kept this in the bank and used it to give interest-free loans in case of unanticipated needs of members. When Andy was organising the group, most other members did not want to take yet another loan from the NGO, but had started looking for jobs not related to fishing. Andy promised to take all the risk himself in terms of repayment commitments. Andy was 55 years old, a seventh class dropout, and had stopped going out to sea for the last four years. His wife was a home-maker. Andy's son was a hardware engineer and worked for a large company in Ernakulam. His daughter had a master's degree in English with a BEd and worked as a schoolteacher in another town. While Andy does not regret his fishing career, he was extremely happy and relieved that his children had gone off from the village.

We had one last question for Andy. Why does the government not help the poor fishermen? There is a government federation (Matsyafed) that could promote new schemes. Andy was of the opinion that help was inadequate and sporadic, and it always came attached to some political obligation. He said there was not much to choose between the therakan and the government's help!

North Cherthala Panchayat

Not far from where Andy and his friends lived, GSGSK had helped another group of fishermen (one YSS) obtain a loan of Rs 2.5 million from Federal Bank in North Cherthala Panchayat.

The Thyckal Mekhala Sasraya Samithi (MSS) is a federation of 23 YSS in North Cherthala Panchayat. One of these YSS called New Star, under the leadership of a young fisherman in his mid–30s, called Charlie, took a loan for an inboard engine. The YSS had started 10 years ago, around the year 2000, with 19 people, which were now reduced to 12. The YSS initially had two boats with outboard engines (engine capacity of about 10 h.p. per boat). The engines had been financed through a loan of Rs 1.2 million from GSGSK in 2006. They could go up to 12 km on these boats. The revenue earned per trip would depend upon the size of the catch and the price received in the auction. According to Charlie and his men, on a good day the revenue could be as high as Rs 45,000 and on a bad day there would be no catch at all. The cost per boat per trip would be around Rs 7,000. Each boat with an outboard engine could carry 30 people. Since the group had 12 members they could carry 48 extra people. These extra people were employed by the group, and the contract was on a sharing basis. The sharing rule was that 40 per cent of the net revenue would be taken by the 12 boat owners (to be shared equally amongst themselves). The remaining would be distributed among the other 48. If the net revenue was negative, the group would still have to pay a minimum of Rs 50 per day per person to the other 48 people. Average net revenue was estimated to be between Rs 10,000 and Rs 15,000 per day.

The group began to save and repay. After repaying Rs 400,000 (with Rs 800,000 still outstanding from the initial loan) the group decided to expand their scale of operations by acquiring a more powerful inboard engine. They approached GSGSK. GSGSK asked them to repay the Rs 800,000 outstanding first, then save some more money (to be used as margin money for a future loan). They did so in four years time and looked around for a good deal on an inboard engine boat. Around September 2010, they obtained a loan of Rs 2.5 million from Federal Bank, arranged for and guaranteed by GSGSK. The total outlay was Rs 4.2 million, which included a second-hand boat with an inboard engine, and new nets for deep-sea fishing. This was considered a very good buy given market prices and the condition of the second-hand engine. The residual amount of Rs 1.7 million was raised from their own sources. Given the economics of the outboard engines they previously had, it would not have been possible to save Rs 1.7 million in the short span of four years. Some of them did supplementary non-fishing jobs to augment their income, while others possibly took personal loans from the moneylender. They were not very explicit about the source of the additional funds. They insisted that the money was from their own sources. The inboard engine boat also had three carrier boats which the group purchased from their own resources. The bigger boat had a capacity of 409 h.p., and could go up to 60 km into the sea and carry up to 60 people. The pattern of business was the same as before. The group now took 40 people on the boat with the inboard engine. They were employing 28 (40 minus 12) people on a sharing basis. The New Star YSS led by Charlie was a much younger group than that of Andy's. Their initial endowment of assets and incomes were obviously larger than the JLGs led by Andy in the South Cherthala Panchayat.

The Federal Bank loan of Rs 2.5 million carried equated monthly instalments (EMI) of Rs 65,000. When we met the group, the first four EMIs had been paid on time. During the previous four months they had used the boat for 100 days and their total gross revenue had been Rs 2.8 million. Their maximum revenue on a day has been Rs 200,000 so far. September to December was considered off season for fishing. They estimated that during the season a good day's catch can go up to even Rs 3 million. They usually took their catch to the Kochi auction where they got better prices. They avoided the Alappuzha district landing points. They used the mobile phone to find out the going price at each centre and were now considering using the carrier boats to sell at more than one landing point to maximise their revenues. Auctions costs were 1 per cent commission charge for the auctioneer. The cost of running a trip on the more powerful engine was around Rs 10,000. The estimated net revenue in the first 100 days of use was Rs 1.8 million, implying daily average net revenue of Rs 18,000 to be shared by boat owners and workers. They hoped to improve upon the earnings as they got more used to the new boat and its operations.

When asked about the best season for deep-sea fishing they said it was June, July and August. The reason cited was the regulatory ban on trawlers during that period of time. The trawlers were banned during those months to allow fish to spawn. The inboard engine boats, though not as large as trawlers, are quite large compared to the outboard engine boats. When asked whether the inboard engines also disturb the reproductive cycle of fish, the fishermen smiled wryly. They explained that the ban was not applicable for them since the boats they used were traditional boats that were exempt by the regulator. They clearly knew that their best opportunity to catch fish was at a time when the bigger boats were absent. It did not matter whether the fish should be allowed to spawn or not! Their economic improvement was already perceptible, even in the off season, by moving to a bigger capacity boat. They were extremely optimistic about their future prospects.

What was the political ambience in their village? They had not experienced any political meddling. Local politicians were very easily accessible and responded to their demands. There were a number of fishermen's unions with different political affiliations. But there was no compulsion to join them. Members of the New Star group had decided against joining any union. The group members were all high school dropouts and all had individual bank accounts, and medical and life insurance policies. Their wives were all homemakers and a few of them sometimes did coir work to supplement their incomes. Their children went to an English medium school in the neighbourhood. One group member's son was going to a marine engineering college and had trained in Visakhapatnam and Mumbai ports. None wanted their children to become fishermen, and they would be very happy to see their children get jobs anywhere else in India. To them economic development was all about rising incomes and secure jobs, the best options being in government or in the public sector.

Charlie explained that the initial success of New Star's inboard engine was being viewed as a success story in the neighbourhood. Quite a few fishermen's YSS had approached Charlie for advice on how to raise finances for an inboard engine. Some people had also wanted to join New Star YSS but he was not in favour of it. When Charlie was asked if he was afraid of competition from big trawlers and other inboard engines coming into existence, he appeared quite confident. He replied, 'I don't know much about the future, but in my lifetime there will be enough fish in the sea for all to live on'.

Our field trip was just after Christmas and each fishing household had received a Rs 250,000 grant for improving and renovating their houses. This was part of a tsunami rehabilitation package from the Japanese government, as part of their overseas development assistance. The Thyckal village was full of freshly painted houses in bright cream, yellow and purple, Christmas decorations were still shining new and everybody seemed to be sharing the optimism evident in Charlie's quiet confident smile.

The stories of Andy and Charlie are tales of entrepreneurs who empowered themselves and their teams to change the conditions of their livelihood. They took risks, organised people, networked for greater access to finance, and as a result increased their incomes. For Andy and his mates, the empowerment they achieved by freeing themselves from the grip of the moneylender was probably not enough to allow them to sustain this improvement due to the dwindling fish stock. Their access to only limited amounts of finance was inadequate to fish in deeper seas. Charlie's story, on the other hand, was one of empowerment that allowed him and his mates to achieve higher incomes. They did not perceive any immediate constraints on their abilities to earn.

Possibility of Integrating Value-added Operations

In Alappuzha town, a fish-processing centre called Matsya Bandhu (literally, friend of the fish) had been started with a grant from the Japan Fund for Poverty Reduction as part of the tsunami rehabilitation package (see Plate 7.2). The implementing agency chosen for starting operations was GSGSK and the centre still did not have its independent legal entity. It was slated to become an autonomous registered society once they got more SHGs involved. Currently, there were 10 SHGs (102 people plus their families) as shareholders with 4,001 shares per individual. The GSGSK had formed 10 JLGs from the 102 families. The SHGs had been selected from four local

Plate 7.2: Matsya Samrudhi: A Government Initiative to Add Value to Fishing Produce

panchayats that were affected by the tsunami. The four panchayats actually got together on a consultative basis on how to choose the beneficiaries. Local participation ensured that the choice was acceptable and deemed to be fair. The grant component of the financial outlay was Rs 4.9 million and another Rs 2.9 million as loan had been obtained from Corporation Bank with GSGSK as guarantor. Of the 102 people (and their families) who were beneficiaries, about 80 per cent came from fishing families, but the women we interviewed were all from non-fishing backgrounds — their husbands were doing non-agriculture work as weavers, drivers or masons.

The centre had started commercial production since June 2010. The centre bought fish from auctions in nearby fish-landing sites. The fish was then trucked to the centre where it was cleaned, sorted, frozen, and packed. Then the fish was sold to buyers (exporters) in terms of an annual contracted price of Rs 85 to Rs 90 per kg. The remaining fish would be sold in a cleaned and ready-to-cook form in the local retail market at an average price of Rs 100 per kg. The ratio of contract selling to retail was about 80:20. A small portion of the fish was also being sold locally as ready-to-fry cutlets and ready-to-eat bottled pickles. We were told that the Rs 100 plus price per kg included a 20 per cent premium over the local retail price and people were ready to pay that because the middle-class market wanted ready-to-cook, time-saving solutions. The average daily purchase of various fish (three or four varieties constituted about 90 per cent of the weight) was 2,000 kg at an average price of Rs 40 to Rs 50 per kg.

All work at the centre was done by the shareholders (the 102 women), who have all been trained in the daily operations. Each day a maximum of 45 people could work in the centre and their daily wage was Rs 150. All 102 persons got employment on a rotational basis according to a well-maintained duty roster. Net profits were to be distributed equally amongst the shareholders, over and above the wages earned. The centre claimed that they had worked 150 days in the last six months though they had not actually purchased fish on all the days. In the initial stages, the contract buyers were being identified and agreements drawn up. In the first six months their gross revenue had been Rs 2.6 million and they had been able to meet all their costs as well as loan repayment obligations. For the forthcoming year (2011) they were expecting a gross revenue of over Rs 10 million. They also expected to become a separate legal entity, distinct from GSGSK. They were applying for a direct export license as well as planning to open 10 retail outlets in Ernakulam town, about 70 km away. Clearly the GSGSK was ensuring that some fresh investments would be made out of the net profits, and not all of it would be distributed back as dividends.

We interviewed the president of the centre, Ms Malini, and the treasurer, Ms Jaya. Both seemed very optimistic and proud of their endeavours. They emphasised that the 102 women cut across caste, religion and political affiliation. There were only three male employees (all from GSGSK) who drove the truck and went to the auction to buy the fish. One lady in the focus group (obviously a Muslim from her headdress) said quite proudly that in Kerala such groups were made from a sense of fairness and need and not on the basis of politics or religion. There seemed to be an urgency to learn much more about the business such as keeping accounts, branding and brand promotion, pricing strategy, the product mix, and the search for distant markets. They were also beginning to learn spoken English. For them neither the size of the market, nor the size of the catch from the sea appeared to be a concern. We asked them about the possibility of also sourcing sweet water fish and brackish water fish. They said they were not seriously considering that because the market for marine fish was more organised and easier to access.

Inshore Fishing and Cage Cultivation

One increasingly popular way of creating a more organised market for sweet water fish was the novel method of cage cultivation. A few kilometres drive from the coastline took us to the huge Vembanad Lake. The lake is obviously a common property resource. The lake's (at least in the western part that we visited) shoreline is cragged and little creeks flow into the land. Though essentially still a part of the lake it is claimed as personal territory by the owners of the adjoining land. These inlets are usually choked with hyacinths. The method of cage cultivation was interesting and quite novel (see Plate 7.3). A cage made of nylon net with a plastic frame of dimensions 1 m by 1 m and a height of 3 m was inserted into the hyacinth-filled water. A bamboo trellis prevented the cage from moving around in the water

Plate 7.3: Cage Fishing as a Supplement to Livelihood Activities

and the bamboos were tied to some trees or posts on the land. This cage allowed sweet water to flow through it and was supposed to be full of nutrients for the fish. We visited one JLG with 10 members who had taken a loan of Rs 150,000 from GSGSK returnable in eight months. The cost of each cage was Rs 6,000 but could be used for eight years. There was another initial cost of Rs 20,000 for the bamboo framework, plastic pipes and seed eggs. The feed for the fish had to be bought and the expense was estimated at Rs 1,000 a month. The production cycle was also eight months (same as the loan period). This JLG was growing the famous *karimeem* fish of Kerala known as the pearl spot. This outlay would give them an expected output of 900 kg to 1,000 kg per cage and the expected price would be Rs 250 to Rs 300 per kg. This JLG was banking on the houseboats on the lake buying their produce. The JLG members did not want to go in for elaborate marketing exercises. They were confident that the tourist traffic and the houseboats would ensure revenues. The numbers implied that in the first cycle of eight months, the JLG

(10 members, all of whom were marginal farmers) would make a net loss of Rs 4,000 per head, and would have to repay the loan. This would require deep pockets. However, from the second year, with no additional fixed costs required, the net profits would be around Rs 22,000 per head for an eight-month cycle.

This was an interesting case of fishing emerging as a livelihood diversification strategy and where private landowners adjacent to a common property resource were encroaching and treating parts of the lake as personal property. Cage cultivation seems to be experiencing a rising trend. The only apprehension the JLG members had revolved around the possibility of houseboat owners or resort owners getting into the act of cage cultivation and stopping their reliance on small fishermen supplying the much sought after karimeen of Kerala for the tourist trade.

The Bigger Picture of Fishing in Alappuzha

We learnt about the many other problems that plague the fishing industry in the district. First of all, there is a clear lack of urgency in ensuring that marine resources are tapped in a sustainable and renewable fashion. There is an inadequacy of infrastructure and poor governance and enforcement of policies. Growing urbanisation and tourist population growth had increased pollution (especially the non-biodegradable type in the form of plastics) which was taking an irreversible toll on some fish species and their reproductive behaviour. Fishermen had an ambivalent attitude to the tourist industry. The attraction of short-term demand and incomes often blurred, though not entirely erased, the long-term possibility of spoiling the common resources that held the key to their livelihoods.

The government's deep-sea fishing policy also left much to be desired both in terms of clarity as well as in monitoring its effectiveness. The Government of India accorded permission to liberally import used vessels of running condition for fishing in the Indian seas. This decision was tactfully utilised by many Indian and foreign businesses involved in the industry. The result was that many a foreign ship extensively exploited valuable fishery resources to the extent of reaching a depletion of the harvestable stock of some species. There had been a growth of unauthorised new fishing vessels. The existing marine fishing fleet of Kerala was, according to many of the fishermen, far above the desired level. A large number of mechanised and motorised fishing vessels were being constructed without permission from the authorities. There had also been, as claimed by the smaller fishermen, an increase in the use of banned fishing practices and banned gear such as bottom trawling and night trawling (Harikumar and Rajendran 2007).

The backwaters of Kerala face excessive and unauthorised fishing pressure too, along with illegal and detrimental fishing practices. Fishing by using explosives and poisons was widespread in the backwaters. The number of stationary gears has reached many times the authorised number. Many had less than 5 mm size meshes. The species that made up the bulk of the commercial catches during recent years now showed signs of depletion or were even under the threat of extinction due to the effects of various anthropogenic activities.

Rising aquatic pollution remains a problem. Backwaters, rivers and even the seas are the ultimate reservoirs of the waste generated by modern civilisation. Lack of facilities for monitoring the marine and estuarine pollution was becoming a severe threat, which posed a serious hazard to aquatic living resources. The non-biodegradable pollutants would alter the aquatic ecosystem to a considerable extent.

Fishing and Sustainability in Alappuzha

Against the backdrop of unplanned exploitation of a renewable resource, described earlier, and the ubiquitous moneylender, the stories from the real people involved were not too heartening either. Andy's story is particularly telling as he and his band of small fishermen with inadequate resources were perhaps turning full circle from freeing themselves from the clutches of the moneylenders to becoming moneylenders themselves so as to augment their incomes against the ever increasing threat of competition from the big boats and trawlers leading to dwindling fish stock. The richer fishermen led by Charlie were more comfortable precisely because they had more access to resources, and they could not much care about the marine stock of the future — their idea of sustainability was severely limited, perhaps because they were confident that their children would not be in the same profession. As far as inshore fishing as a supplementary livelihood was concerned we found that the method of fishing created 'property rights' on a common resource like the Vembanad Lake. Unlimited cage cultivation could well imply over-harvesting of the sweet water nutrients and that it could cross the carrying capacity of the lake. No one seemed to be concerned with the long-term effects. The edge was clearly with the people who had resources, particularly land and access to finance. In the Kuttanad area, too, we saw how collective action failure to exploit a livelihood diversification strategy could lead to greater inequalities in income and wealth (see Box 7.2).

Box 7.2: Mixing Paddy and Prawns

> Kuttanad, a sprawling 33,000 acres, is famous as the rice bowl of Kerala. Amidst the innumerable intersecting canals of the backwaters, paddy is actually grown on land that is below the sea level. There are well-defined property rights but small holdings and fragmentation prevents potential innovation in diversification and supplementary livelihoods from benefitting a larger number of paddy growers. Small holders grow one crop of paddy in the winter. During the rainy seasons there is flooding of the lands and the brackish water has to be constantly pumped out. The cost of the pumping process and the maintenance of the bunds prevent any possibility of a second crop unless a sizeable number of small holders collectively agreed to share the costs. This was difficult to achieve as Dev (a well to do landlord with 10 acres of land) claimed. He showed us that adjacent to his single contiguous plot of 10 acres was a large area of 100 acres owned by about 300 people. The sheer numbers would make it extremely difficult to get a consensus on an agreed upon collective action.
>
> Dev's innovation, as an individual farmer, was that in the monsoons he used his 10 acres of land with flooded brackish water to raise a crop of scampi. The production cycle of scampi was eight months. In fact, while he was producing his winter crop of paddy, he used about 1 acre of his land as a nursery to keep the scampi (prawns) eggs and babies, to be transferred into the total 10 acres after the paddy had been harvested. This innovation had given him a rich source of additional income and wide national acclaim. He was doing this for eight years when we visited him at the end of 2010. He had got a German firm to certify his process as internationally acceptable, and had tied up with two large firms in Hyderabad and Chennai to buy his scampi harvest.
>
> This was a good example of a sustainable innovation with multiple cropping of paddy and scampi. The small holders could not benefit from

Box 7.2: (*Continued*)

Box 7.2: (*Continued*)

multiple cropping of paddy or from a mix of paddy and scampi. Reaching an understanding of whose land was to be devoted to a fish nursery or to the distribution of scampi harvest was an indomitable task. Collective action failure by the small holders had led to a claim that the brackish water used by Dev was actually reducing the productivity of the small holders' paddy cultivation. On the other hand, some larger farmers were beginning to show interest in emulating Dev's model in their relatively larger single plot holdings.

8

Packaging Heritage to Unpack Ambitions
Himalayan Homestays

The state of Sikkim, tucked in the eastern Himalayas, is well known for its natural beauty and biodiversity. It encompasses Khangchendzonga which is the third highest mountain peak in the world. Elevation of this region ranges from 300 m to 8,500 m above sea level. The vegetation varies from tropical to alpine, and Sikkim is known as a treasure house of flowering plants, particularly the varieties of rhododendrons (36 species) and orchids (600–1,000 of the world's 5,000 species). Among the 10 most critical biodiversity hotspots in the world, Sikkim has about 600 butterfly species, 1,200 moths, 144 mammals, 39 varieties of reptiles, 550 species of birds, nine amphibians, and 16 kinds of fish (WWF 2014). Less than half a million people live in a little over 7,000 sq km of the state.

Obviously, Sikkim has been a preferred destination for domestic and international tourists. The hub of all activities lies in Gangtok, the state capital, where tourists first arrive. Visits to other places — short stays, trekking, camping and day trips to places of interest — are usually organised from here. Tourism is a major industry and the growth of visitor arrivals in the past decade has grown by over 150 per cent (ECOSS 2007).

The government of Sikkim realised that the benefits of growth of traditional tourism, while contributing to state domestic product and employment, were not percolating to the poor in terms of opportunities and incomes. Unemployment rates in Sikkim were the highest in the country in 2013 according to the *Annual Employment & Unemployment Survey Report 2012–13* released by the Labour Bureau of the Government of India (*The Times of India* 2013). Moreover, there was an urban-rural gap in tourism where the gains were accruing more in urban areas to hoteliers and transport operators. The Government of

Sikkim, by the 10th Five Year Plan of the Government of India, had begun to shift its emphasis from traditional tourism to more sustainable activities in the form of ecotourism. Ecotourism, it was felt, would provide more livelihood opportunities for the rural poor, conserve natural wealth, and also reduce the pressure of rural-to-urban migration of jobseekers. The promotion of ecotourism would also open up more tourist centres and allow for more diverse activities. In 2002, the Ecotourism and Conservation Society of Sikkim (ECOSS) hosted the South Asia Regional Conference on Ecotourism in Gangtok. Since then, Sikkim has become an important centre for ecotourism, with the state government, a number of non-governmental organisations (NGOs) and even the United Nations Educational, Scientific and Cultural Organization (UNESCO) contributing to the gradual shift from traditional tourism (which is still very large) to a more sustainable approach involving the appreciation of natural beauty and traditional culture.

Ecotourism

The primary economic advantage of ecotourism lies in the diversification of livelihood that helps increase rural income by conserving natural capital. The success of the diversification strategy depends on the 'buy-in' of the local people to the idea of promoting ecotourism as a supplementary activity. Ecotourism can be of various kinds. It is often described as a multifaceted activity which includes farm-based tourism, health tourism, ethnic tourism, and nature tourism. The demand for ecotourism services would depend upon the aesthetic value of the natural assets of a region, its cultural uniqueness and historical heritage. Support from government and other social organisations is important to provide, and coordinate, the initial resources required such as some capital assets, education and training, and experiential learning through visits to other ecotourism sites. Finally, it is of utmost significance that the youth get engaged with this activity if it is to be sustained over a reasonable period of time.

The ENVIS Centre, Sikkim, website, sponsored by the Ministry of Environment and Forests, Government of India defines ecotourism as:

> [A] purposeful travel to natural areas to understand the cultural and natural history of [the] environment, taking care not to alter the integrity of the ecosystem, while producing economic opportunities that make conservation

of natural resources beneficial to local people. In short, ecotourism can be conceptualized as any tourism programme that is: (*a*) nature based, (*b*) ecologically sustainable, (*c*) where education and interpretation is a major component and (*d*) where local people are benefited (ENVIS Sikkim Centre 2013).

The ecotourism projects we studied were essentially homestays in East and South Sikkim districts (see Map 8.1). This is a decentralised approach where tourists stay with local families in their homes, appreciating diversity in their culture and traditions. The village community pools in resources to offer small-scale services to harness some direct benefits to the village. For instance, visits to local heritage buildings or nature treks or camping expeditions are organised. A clear code of conduct is given to each tourist at the time of registration and displayed prominently in the community centres and guest rooms (see Plate 8.1).

Pastanga

The drive from Gangtok to Pastanga in East Sikkim took us almost two hours through beautiful scenery and bumpy roads. The breathtaking view of the Teesta River was interrupted by the sight of heavy earth-moving equipment and a horde of hard-hat construction workers who were involved in building the latest phase of the Teesta Barrage Project. There were mud slides on stretches of the road, and the hillside looked denuded. The construction of the barrage was widening the gorges, and hillsides had been blasted to attain the required engineering specifications. It was as if a giant claw from above had uprooted part of the lovely natural beauty — and the claw was not Nature's making but very much an integral part of the design of the process of human development. This intervention — the breaking up of mountains and altering courses of rivers — was as much about economic development as the idyllic image of ecotourism protecting nature and serving human society.

Pastanga was one of the pioneers of the ecotourism experiment in Sikkim and, at the time of our visit, had acquired quite a bit of experience. Khedi Eco-tourism and Eco-development Promotion Society (KEEP) was involved in ecotourism in Pastanga from 2002 and had been awarded the Best Village Home Stay Award by the Department of Tourism of Sikkim. Pastanga's entry point on the motorable road

Map 8.1: East and South Sikkim Districts

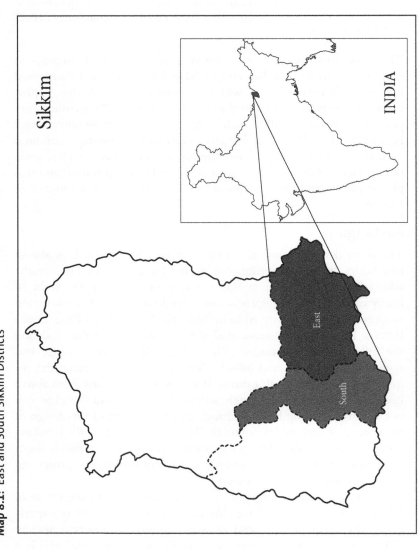

Plate 8.1: Code of Conduct for Ecotourists

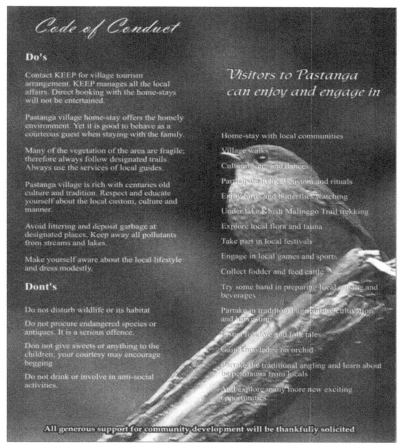

Source: Khedi Eco-tourism and Eco-development Promotion Society (KEEP),
    Pastanga.

was the community centre built by KEEP, a local non-governmental
organisation (NGO) that partnered with ECOSS for ecotourism.
This building also housed a telecommunication centre funded by the
National Bank for Agriculture and Rural Development (NABARD)
which had a desktop computer attached to a large satellite dish antenna
allowing Internet connectivity. The purpose, we were told, would be
to facilitate connectivity across a set of other villages that also organised

homestays. It would allow booking by potential tourists from all over the world, and the villages could cooperate to ensure that the visitors were not turned away as long as there was accommodation available in other sites. A spin-off from having a computer would empower the local youth to become computer literate and keep records of visitor arrivals, financial transactions and other business documents.

At the community centre, we were greeted by two teenagers, Sujata and Manoj, both studying in high school. Our designated contact, the secretary of KEEP, was away on a family medical emergency. They were keen that we go with them on a short trek but warned us of leeches and soft footholds because of the heavy rains. As we chatted, Manoj shyly shared with us that he wanted to study economics and become an officer in the Reserve Bank of India (RBI). Sujata wanted to leave the village by marrying someone in Gangtok.

The community centre was used as a common area for meetings and cultural programmes, and also served as a dining area if required. There were a few posters depicting the natural beauty of Pastanga and its neighbourhood. Apart from the computer, there was some camping and trekking gear strewn carelessly. The hall looked shabby and forlorn. There were a few handicrafts on display, almost all made from bamboo. The area had a large variety of bamboo trees and the name Pastanga was connected to this feature.

In contrast to Manoj and Sujata, there was a curious lack of energy amongst the villagers who met us to talk about their ecotourism experience. The general discussion veered away time and again from the prospects of ecotourism to a discussion on what outside agencies like the government of Sikkim, NABARD and ECOSS could do more in terms of providing grants for the project. There was resistance to taking loans for ecotourism, whether for community activities or for improving basic facilities in individual homes. This might have been an indication of the poor prospects perceived by the villagers, or a reflection of a more deep-seated aversion to loans. When we talked to the NABARD official who had been involved in the project, the assessment was that the latter reason was more accurate, as Sikkim is a DONER state with a plethora of grant-based projects.

C. T. Rai, a well-to-do member of the Rai community, who worked in the health department of the government of Sikkim, had first mooted the idea of village tourism to the villagers. KEEP was formed with a capacity of hosting 40 guests at one time in Pastanga. Initially, the business model was that 40 rooms across the KEEP members' households would be made available for stay and any guest would be charged Rs 500 per night. The Rs 20,000 thus earned would be shared equally among members. To start with, a fund of Rs 20,000 was created to develop the facilities for the homestay. At present, an annual contribution of Rs 100 per member (comes to around Rs 5,000 annually) was collected towards a fund for the upkeep of the homestay facilities. Using these funds, a community hall was constructed across the road on donated land.

ECOSS was introduced to KEEP by C. T. Rai, as the organisation was perceived to be a good source to contact tourists and train villagers in various tourism-related skills. They sent several tourists to Pastanga and organised their exchange between four such villages. They did not charge any commission for their intermediation. They provided training to the participant households and shared valuable feedback from the tourists.

However, economic development has strange ways of creating collateral damage. New roads to facilitate tourist movement were built by the government. To make space for the road, demolition of the community hall was necessary. KEEP was not compensated for this loss. The compensation was given to the original land owner. That was a huge setback. The hall, where we were received, had been subsequently constructed using voluntary labour and donations from KEEP members. It was made on land that was purchased by KEEP some years back to construct modern residential quarters for village tourism. The dire need for a community hall led to the construction of a simple but sturdy building in its place.

The Rai community dominated this village and most had traditional homes for hosting guests. There was provision for hot water in buckets and hot water bottles for the bed at night. According to tradition, toilets were detached from the main living quarters, and access to the traditional (original) Rai kitchen with wood stove was restricted. An open kitchen with gas stove and dining facilities was available for guests.

The family of the village pradhan, who was our host, opined that the number of guests, averaging six a month, visiting Pastanga was optimal — they would find it difficult to handle more guests. Also, fewer guests meant it was easier to deliver satisfactory hospitality levels. When we visited, the pradhan was preoccupied as his cow was unwell. His wife was a very competent hostess and took good care of us. The rooms allocated to us were clean and comfortable, with fresh bed linen with the KEEP logo on them (see Plate 8.2). The natural beauty outside and the warm hospitality more than made up for the lack of amenities, like a television or hot water kettle, in our rooms. The fresh flowers in a vase on a small worn-out table had a human touch that was usually absent in the impersonal ornate decoration of an average hotel room. The recently constructed detached toilet was clean and airy with a refreshing scent of pine.

Plate 8.2: A Well-prepared Bed and Clean Monogrammed Linen for Ecotourists

It was unfortunate that our hostess took ill the next morning as she had stayed awake all night with the pradhan and the ailing cow. We were surprised to know that she suffered from the typically urban diseases of diabetes and hypertension. Sujata (who was our guide and who did not belong to the pradhan's family) helped out with all the necessary household chores next morning.

She mentioned that often guests asked for added services — so it was important to reiterate in the marketing brochures that the village-stay provides no more than basic amenities. Sometimes the inability to communicate with guests became a problem and the hosts wished they were more educated. Variety in cuisine was also an issue — there was a perceived need for training to make continental food.

At the present level of costs, KEEP would break even if they hosted four guests in at least two homes (that is, a total of eight guests) every month. However, they were willing to extend all services even if they had just one guest till the time that their business was established. For example, requests from more demanding guest for non-alcoholic beverages and packaged snacks were entertained even though it was tedious for the hosts, who had to take a long hike to the nearest store to provide them.

In general, the experience of the hostess was *ramro laagchho* (enjoying the experience), as she got glimpses into the lives of different kinds of foreigners (see Box 8.1). Although language was an issue, the

Box 8.1: Window to the World

Sarita Rai, a middle-aged lady from Pastanga village had come to be a part of the cultural evening that KEEP had hosted for us. She was a mother of two daughters; both were going to college at Gangtok. She herself was a primary school dropout. Traditionally dressed and at ease with her surroundings, she shared with us in broken Hindi how she saw the ecotourism experience. Her house had been used for homestays several times and she had the privilege of hosting some foreign guests. According to Sarita, the inability to speak English was not a constraint. 'Language can be an obstacle when it comes to taking care of guests but only notionally so. I can see the expression on my guests' faces and know whether they are comfortable or not. I have enough sensitivity to know what to do to keep my guests happy.' She was amazed to see that even English could be spoken in different ways (the village had visitors from Italy, Switzerland, Germany, and Guatemala).

She was very happy with the exposure that the villagers were getting as a result of the ecotourism project. In a voice mixed with pride and just a tinge of despair, she told us: 'I wish I was born a few years later, so that I could get all the opportunities to learn and grow that my children are getting. I wish I could be educated, go out and see the world, be independent of the village and be able to live like "them" (the foreigners).'

guides were well conversant with English and hung around to translate if needed. Our hostess — she understood a little English by now (although she has no formal education) — understood Hindi well and could speak broken Hindi. She hesitated to speak in English with the guests for fear of making errors while conversing. However, she managed to say yes or no with ease, implying that she understood English reasonably well. The impact of having house guests had been that she had learnt to speak with outsiders, which was contrarian to her introvert nature — even the extent to which she interacted with her peers had gone up. Moreover, she found that the exposure her children were getting was an extraordinary learning opportunity. Language was not a barrier for her children and now they had an opportunity to choose ecotourism as a possible livelihood. They also got a chance to practice English conversation which would be useful no matter what they did in the future. Would she like to have more guests than the current flow? She felt that would be difficult because of the additional burden from cooking and household chores.

We looked at the feedback from previous guests. Some of it included difficulties with bed length (they had standardised beds of 6.5 ft length, but once had a 7 ft tall German guest), complaints about hard pillows and low ceilings, and suggestions on how to manage garbage. A Guatemalan guest stayed for over 45 days with them and spent time teaching environmental responsibility in schools. They had implemented compost pits for their biodegradable wastes, a suggestion from another tourist. Some other guests helped create the KEEP logo so as to give the venture a professional look. The logos had to be machine-stitched onto the linen. Since this capability was unavailable locally, it had to be sourced from Siliguri (over 100 km away).

KEEP ensured that all participant houses got to host the guests in turn. Members without adequate housing to host guests worked as guides and porters. Others contributed to organising cultural programmes for guests. For large groups who would like to eat together, the provision of meals was contracted out to a group of KEEP members and served in the community hall. There were only two to four families in the village who knew how to make handicraft items. The displays in the community hall were products made by these families, and guests could purchase them if they wished.

Lingee–Payong

Lingee and Payong are two adjacent villages in the South Sikkim district, at a distance of around 60 km from Gangtok. Payong is at a higher altitude than Lingee, and it takes about 3 km to 4 km of driving by road to get from one to the other. Lingee (derived from the verb 'to call') is dominated by the Lepcha (tribal) community and Payong (derived from bamboo) by the Chhetri (Brahmin) community. Surrounded by rivers and waterfalls, the villages are located near a beautiful ridge of the Mainam Wildlife Sanctuary. The initial proposal for developing Lingee–Payong as an ecotourism site came from the people of Payong.

Lingee–Payong boasts of a population of around 5,000 and has eight to nine schools in its vicinity. Livelihoods come from agriculture, teaching, government service, and government contracts. Most teachers are on transferrable jobs and not native to the villages. Prior to 2000, people in this area were cardamom farmers, and cardamom being a high-value-cash-crop, they were relatively wealthy. However, some viral disease struck resulting in a decline in productivity, which was as high as 95 per cent. As a consequence, people started selling timber from their rich forest resources as an alternative source of income. The villagers claimed they became the largest supplier of timber in the entire South Sikkim district.

During those difficult days, two youngsters from Payong attended a skill development workshop in Gangtok, organised by the government, on trekking. Both were graduates from the nearby North Bengal University. This was where they got the idea of starting an ecotourism venture (see Box 8.2). On hearing about ECOSS, they seized the opportunity and the Comprehensive Village Tourism Centre came into being.

Around the same time, assisted by ECOSS, villagers of Lingee formed a farmers' club with the objective of improving cardamom yields. At that point, ECOSS mentioned the ecotourism idea. The Lingee Tourism Development Cell (LTDC) was formed with 26 members, each of whom were assigned separate responsibilities. A membership fee of Rs 100 was charged to all members. The first priority of this group was to provide livelihoods and minimise school dropouts. They felt that both these objectives could be attained by leveraging nature as a source of income and as a mechanism of

Box 8.2: Equal Opportunity for All?

It was a clear summer evening in Payong, and the residents of the village had put together a cultural programme as part of the ecotourism experience for us. Everyone was involved in the event; while the children danced and sang, the adults chatted with each other and with us, explaining the cultural contexts of the performances. We observed two young men, Raju and Kanchan, sitting slightly away from the crowd, observing the proceedings of the programme in silence. After the children had left, they were still sitting in their corner, in deep conversation with each other. We were curious whether they were locals or ecotourists like us. It turned out that Raju was indeed from the village and was studying law at North Bengal University about 100 km away, and his friend, Kanchan, was from a neighbouring village. They had met at the university, where Kanchan was studying political science. Initially, Raju had taken a lot of initiative to bring ecotourism to his village. He had heard about the possibilities of ecotourism at his university and had taken the trouble of undergoing training as a tour guide for trekking at one of the state government training programmes. Now he felt left out and slighted because despite having played a key role in mooting the idea of ecotourism, and campaigning for support, he had no part in organisational or operational matters. The pradhan and the village panchayat had, in his view, taken full control. He was now trying, with his friend Kanchan, to convince ECOSS to take ecotourism to the latter's village.

Raju spoke about some of his ideas to sustain the ecotourism initiative in his village. For instance, a more finely graded menu of services with specific prices could be made available to potential tourists. This, he thought, would help visitors make better choices. He also indicated that it was essential that each participant in this project stands to gain financially for every tourist arrival. Even with a single guest, some part of the revenue, however small, ought to be distributed equally. The remaining could be shared according to effort and costs of services rendered, especially services that involved importing of materials from outside the village such as processed food and sodas.

When asked why he felt he was excluded from decision-making, he quietly commented: 'The differentiations of caste, community and class continue to act as a drag on greater inclusion and greater momentum in scaling up the activity; the poorer a household in the village, the lower its capability to be included in ecotourism activities.'

providing exposure to the children on what the outside world was like. This would influence them to stay in school to learn good English or get an education that would enable them to get a job in faraway cities like the tourists who visited them. The Lingee resident who headed the LTDC was of the following opinion:

> Just by itself, tourism is a loss — nature is spoiled and only few people profit, but village tourism is one way that we can conserve nature by preventing logging, provide alternate livelihoods and educate our children. So we win in every way. In addition if the village gets publicity we may access more funds. Our culture is showcased and preserved and there is exposure in both ways.[1]

Implementing the idea of ecotourism was being thought about simultaneously in both the villages. It was ECOSS that noted the problem of scale and suggested that the two villages come together for the project.

A hurdle faced by the project was the insecurity of the Lepchas who would rather have had a separate ecotourism project for Lingee. We noted that all the data presented in the reports on ecotourism prepared by ECOSS related to socio-economic data from Payong alone, which had better human development parameters. However, the report claimed that it represented both Lingee and Payong. This undercurrent of separation was evident even when we met a group of volunteers from both villages who had come together to attend a course in spoken English.

ECOSS strongly felt that the biggest challenge in Lingee-Payong was just keeping the communities together. Many interested families backed out from the project when they found an alternative livelihood opportunity. Getting the communities to develop a sense of ownership towards the project was difficult, according to both ECOSS and NABARD officials. Most of the villagers were not that poor that they felt compelled to collaborate so as to get better access to finance. Here again, as in Pastanga, the aversion to access loans and take business risks was evident. Other challenges were finding and acquiring land for a common space for interaction. Coordinating trainings and ensuring participation in the face of continuous migration from the villages to the city was an added concern.

Now that the ecotourism project was taking off, we observed that everyone (participants as well as non-participants) wanted to host tourists in their homes to make money. ECOSS was willing to facilitate

---

[1] Personal communication with the authors.

loans to individual households for improving their facilities such as better rooms or access to the Internet. However this had few takers.

We stayed in the house of the pradhan of Payong village, an intelligent, witty and hospitable personality. The cuisine was local and cooked at home. The meal comprised different preparations of all parts of the pumpkin plant, including its seeds. The utensils, crockery and cutlery were clean and relatively new without being ostentatious or ornate.

The pradhan claimed that one of the benefits of the project was a reduction in the number of people who made a sport out of injuring small game and birds with a catapult. However, it was still not clear what monetary benefits ecotourism brought, or could bring in the future. The best case scenario, as calculated by him, was eight homes housing two guests per month for an average of four days, that is, 64 person–days a month. At present, the rates they charged were lower than those charged at other homestays because the quality of amenities provided by them was not up to the mark. They were still charging on a somewhat ad hoc basis (evident from our bills as well) and were yet to work out the economics of it all. At the time of our visit, they had identified 16 homes in the two villages for hosting guests. The criteria for selection included quality and size of house, proximity to the metalled road, education level of the host, availability of refrigerator and training received by the host. Expenditure to make the houses guest-worthy was between Rs 60,000 to Rs 70,000 per house on an average, inclusive of furniture. Attached toilets were part of future plans to improve the homestay experience.

The Village as an Entrepreneur

The project of ecotourism in Sikkim was designed such that an entire village or a significant proportion of its population would act as an entrepreneurial organisation. This would entail a change in the way in which a primarily agrarian community functioned. The activities were new, as were the roles and responsibilities. It would also call for a clear understanding of the business model underlying the activities and the division of roles and responsibilities. Therefore, such a venture would require a well documented and established governance structure. To be really dynamic, the organisation would need local leadership who would be able to adapt the basic business model to the context and peculiarities of the community.

The economics of the project was much more complex than what appeared on the surface. The basic model was based on a two-part pricing strategy. There would be a daily flat charge for food and accommodation. This would include a room to stay, with clean linen and towels, and access to a hygienic toilet and hot water if needed. The food comprised local cuisine and mineral water would be available. Over and above this base price, there would be optional add-ons like a cultural evening where local talent would present traditional art, music, song, and dance. There would also be possibilities of going on treks, visits to local sites of cultural interest like temples, traditional houses or caves, and local camping trips. The degree of difficulty and the duration of these activities could be customised to meet the needs and interests of tourists. A guide would be assigned for each trip, and porters would also be made available.

We observed some potential problems. First, ecotourism involved pricing of household services, for which there were no clear benchmarks or prevailing market rates. What would be a reasonable cost-plus-pricing strategy to adopt? Too high a premium might deter business, while too low a price may signal entry for low-end tourists, which could run counter to the whole objective of promoting ecotourism.

All participants would require training in a variety of skills. These included cooking and serving, room preparation, knowledge about the local environment, and communication skills. Over and above this, the households who volunteered to keep guests in their homes for the night would require capital investment in creating the necessary facilities. These expenses would be borne individually. The overall services and facilities provided by each home might not be identical. The experience was not supposed to be like a regular hotel where rooms with similar tariffs were similar in size, shape and comfort. If this was indeed the case, should the homes have charged the same price or should there have been price differentials since the 'services' on offer might not be exactly the same.

The pricing of optional services was even trickier. First, it had to be kept in mind that such services would typically be customised to the need, physical ability and interests of the guests. Hence there could be a range of services requiring a wide spectrum of prices. This in itself could be difficult to benchmark and then calibrate. The added problem here was that direct costs, such as depreciation of any equipment (for instance, camping gear) and the opportunity cost of time of the guide or the porter, were likely to be very low. However, the guests who opted for these services would have been willing to pay for what their intrinsic valuation of a natural asset was. On the other hand, for the people facilitating the service, nature was only of instrumental value to earn a livelihood. Where should the price have been pegged?

The capacity of the service provision would be limited by the number of people who volunteered to participate. Consider a village of 100 households where 20 households volunteered to be part of the ecotourism project. Not all the 20 households might have had the assets (household space) to accommodate guests. If 12 households had the capacity to handle two guests each, then the village would have a maximum capacity of hosting 24 guests at a time. The remaining eight households, presumably with fewer assets, could volunteer to cook or clean up after the guests departed, or act as guides, or become porters. Somebody would have to mind the office — receive arriving guests, register them, maintain records and finances, and organise logistics like transportation and journey bookings. It would be necessary for each volunteer to acquire an assortment of skills as they would be handling multiple tasks.

The scale of activity and the ability to sustain a flow of visitors without having some common-built property that could be shared by the homestay providers was another concern. Since the capacity of the village was fixed, and inflexible in the short run, the village's ability to host large groups was limited. We were told of how they had to reluctantly turn down a college students' group because of capacity constraints. Yet this had come in a season that was slow and unrewarding. The resources of households that volunteered for ecotourism could be inadequate to finance the construction of a common hall. Pooled resources of the entire village could however suffice. In such a situation, the common space would be community-owned and multipurpose in nature. Then there was always the issue of a conflict of interest. For example, consider a situation where a large group of guests was visiting and at the same time the non-participating households of the village wanted to use the hall for a social occasion. How would the priority of usage be determined?

Another problem arose from the topography of the region. In these sparsely populated villages, the houses were not exactly adjacent to one another. They were some distance apart and moving from one to the other involved a steep climb or a long walk. Even for groups that could be accommodated within the village, guests could demand to be as together as possible. Such large groups might not prefer staying in houses that were 300m–400m apart and where each kitchen could provide meals for only two or three people.

Since all receipts accrued at a central point, revenue sharing was a concern. The revenue sharing model had to be decided ahead of business, and it had to be transparent and equitable. When some revenue was actually earned, how was it going to be distributed? How much would the porter get per day of activity? How much was cooking time worth? How much should the general office have received, and how much should have been set aside for common area maintenance?

Other essential infrastructure, like the power supply, road connectivity to the village (from the nearest highway) and the local availability of the basic necessities, that the tourists would require would be key determinants in positioning the site as a preferred ecotourism destination. The villages we visited were good in terms of such infrastructure, but the adequacy of these or their maintenance was beyond the control of the villagers. Similarly, the Internet would be a good way of reaching out with regard to sales and marketing. However, the setting up of such communication facilities could be expensive and beyond their means.

The revenue sharing models at both Pastanga and Lingee-Payong were ad hoc, and no proper justification was given when we asked about the logic of distribution. The only equity factor that came out of the discussions was that for services that required only labour and local knowledge — like a guide or a porter — priority would be granted to landless members of the village, or at least ones who were relatively poor in the locality. However, our guide (chosen by our host) in Lingee-Payong was a schoolteacher who spent considerable time giving private tuitions and owned a house. In Pastanga, the guides provided were the two teenagers, who, it later turned out, were not regulars but temping in for the secretary of KEEP.

As mentioned earlier, the pricing was arbitrary. In Lingee–Payong, after much deliberation, the villagers came up with an amount. They were extremely tentative about it, although we had made it patently clear that we would pay whatever they charged for their services. There was some confusion about whether there was to be a consolidated bill, or separate bills for the separate services provided. A hint of an argument was discernable about the valuation of each service.

Clearly, leadership was lacking in the entrepreneurial ventures of Pastanga and Lingee–Payong. It appeared as if the scheme was thrust upon them by an external agency and they were struggling with it. If the project did not take off and scale up to its full potential, the interests of the villagers would not only decline, it could lead to frustration and pessimism among them. The villagers were extremely risk averse anyway. Their unwillingness to take loans and their unusual dependence on grants prevented an enterprise, in the true sense of the term, from emerging in the villages.

The success of the ecotourism initiative could lead to an empowerment of the villagers in a variety of ways. One form of empowerment would be in terms of rising incomes through one's own effort and enterprise. Ecotourism activities would also require the acquisition of new skills by each participating member. The running of the venture would encourage independent decision-making at many levels. Perhaps the most significant empowerment would come from exposure to tourists, from far and near, of different cultures and with diverse worldviews.

Showcasing Culture

An integral part of the ecotourism package was the showcasing of culture. This living experience was aimed to be different from learning about culture through books and films. From our observations we noticed that there was a variation in the ability of the villagers to showcase their heritage.

In Pastanga, the cultural get-together was inclusive in the sense that they were constantly trying to involve the guests — asking us, as guests, to sing along or even dance with them. The event was held in the community hall which was warm (it was a particularly damp and cold evening) and people from all age groups got into the act. After a while we were offered the local alcoholic beverage. It was not clear whether we would be charged for it, or if it was part of the ice-breaking ritual, since we declined the offer. The decline was influenced by the list of dos and don'ts given to us at the time of arrival. Interestingly, one member turned up quite inebriated, and was heavily critical of the whole effort of the ecotourism project. We learnt that he was an influential member of the community. The show, however, went on, with the local organisers generally tolerating him. There were wry smiles when they commented that he did this often!

What was interesting in Pastanga was that the older folks, especially the women, found the experience of hosting ecotourists culturally empowering and educationally enlightening. They thought that there were many things that could be learnt from the visitors, particularly the foreigners. We expected that the gaze of the visitor would be on the cultural 'other', but realised that the gaze was in both directions. The cultural 'other' observed the observer with equal curiosity. Glimpses of modernity, as seen through the guests, were reflected upon by the women. The encounters of heritage-living with modernity would have a long-term effect on the local culture. Ecotourism showcased culture as an asset that did not change.

The cultural programme at Lingee–Payong was more formal with the performers using a separate paved courtyard as the stage. The overwhelming majority of the performers were students in high school. All the traditional dances and songs were performed with grace and confidence. The commentary was competent in explaining the context to us. On completion of the programme, when we congratulated the performers on such a fine effort, their response to the applause was not very animated. One young man, studying in class 12 approached us somewhat shyly and announced that this performance was nothing compared to the skills he was capable of demonstrating in doing contemporary Bollywood dances. The others joined in and the discussion veered towards Hindi films.

All the young men and women who had performed told us that they wanted to leave the village as soon as their schooling was over. Some wanted to go to college outside Sikkim. They were willing to go anywhere in India to study, the worst case being going to North Bengal University in Siliguri. One young man said his ambition was to appear on the popular TV show 'Dance India Dance'. They were clearly doing the traditional dance and song routine at the behest of the elders. Upon enquiring whether the practice of the traditional arts was common in the village — the answer was surprising — the arts were being encouraged only after ecotourism began. However, the performers were reluctant young people who expressed no desire to continue with this tradition.

A part of the cultural exposure on offer was a visit to a traditional Lepcha house, claimed to be over a hundred years old (see Plate 8.3). The traditional house was very different from the typical modern cottage or bungalow one might see in the hills. It was a *pucca* house but with some unique features of preserving the heat inside and making the most use of the heat available from the burning of fuel for cooking. While we were being shown around, we came to know that the tourism department of the Government of Sikkim was giving soft loans to build traditional houses for expanding the capacity of the homestays. The government stipulation for the loan was that the toilet had to be made attached to the guest room, while leaving other features of tradition unaltered. This was clearly unacceptable to the locals.

Plate 8.3: Traditional Lepcha House, Lingee–Payong: One of the Tourist Attractions

We saw a construction where the toilet was adjacent to the guest-room, but its door was from the outside! An innovative compromise had been found to circumvent the diktat of the government. Most locals, when granted a soft loan to build a new house or extend their existing houses, wanted to build a structure that resembled the fancy ones that they had seen in Gangtok, which were Western and not traditional. If the rich in the cities could be allowed to live in modern houses, why were they being dissuaded from adopting the same styles? This question seemed to bother many a local resident.

The packaging of culture as an integral part of ecotourism struck us as unsustainable. This commodification of culture reflected an urban bias. Good living was more than staying in a Lepcha house for the locals. Mobile phones and the ubiquitous dish antenna for cable television had perhaps engendered that attitude. Moreover, the locals did not have a single uniform way of living. Their own lifestyles were obviously different from one another — determined by a complex set of issues such as economic status, degree of exposure to urban lifestyles, and the level of educational attainment. Thinking of the Lepcha or the Rai communities as culturally homogeneous could be misleading and erroneous.

The Future

Though the business model of ecotourism allowed for a part of the revenue to be kept aside for defensive investment in natural assets like preserving trees and preventing habitat loss, we did not see evidence of this. A herbal garden of medicinal plants had been made only as an exhibit for tourists. KEEP had neither considered commercial purposes nor conservation of traditional knowledge when making this garden. Deforestation was a major concern in the Lingee-Payong area, as forestry had become a source of livelihood prior to the eco-tourism drive. At present, we were told that the trees around us were 16–18 years old, planted under the state government's forest mission. We were also told that we would not be able to see older trees in this region any longer, as they had all been cut down in the recent past. The rampant cutting of trees had been arrested through awareness drives and provision of alternative livelihood opportunities.

The real preferred job was, however, in government. Opportunities to secure a government job were limited, so the ecotourism project was a good way to secure a livelihood option for the next generation. The children did not share the same opinion though. For them, as we learnt from our series of discussions with the local youth, going to the city for a different life and better incomes was the shared aspiration. Nature was good and perhaps it was wise not to disturb it. But the good life was certainly not in the rolling green hills with an arabesque of rhododendrons and orchids. City lights were too enticing to ignore.

Part III

People and Participation

The participation of people in development projects is rather obvious. There will always be some people who benefit from the project, others who design the project, and still others who implement the project. In the past, a top-down approach was followed where 'development' was something that was provided (Streeten and Lipton 1968). Participation in project design and implementation was usually kept distinct from participation as a beneficiary (Angeles 2011; Dreze and Sen 2002). A more recent approach, sometimes referred to as bottom-up, involves beneficiaries in more basic ways. It empowers them to voice their needs and aspirations. Facilitated by development agencies, the beneficiaries contribute to designing, implementing and even evaluating the project. Hence the nature of participation is hands-on and involved. Extending this concept, participation is much more than a mere instrument for attaining a set of measurable outcomes. Ideally, this should enable people to organise themselves and engage in a broader set of issues that affect their lives and environment.

The consequence of participation results in individual benefits as well as social improvements. The latter may come from the creation of community-owned natural assets. There is a close relationship between the creation and sustainability of such assets on the one hand, and a sense of human ownership and care on the other. This relationship is based on collective participation and requires the concerned people to be empowered to have control over the utilisation, management and conservation of these resources.

The actual extent of participation depends on context. People's participation could be nominal, or it could be of a more substantial nature. Participation could evolve in a dynamic way, from conception to implementation of a project. While elements of participation, such as attendance in a meeting, can be systematically recorded, the quality of participation cannot be formally measured. In all the interventions we studied, creating village-level committees and attendance in the gram sabha meeting were insisted upon for decision-making. In addition, some form of active participation, such as voluntary labour to create a commonly-owned natural asset, was built into the project design.

What follows are four narratives which look at different forms of people's participation in varying contexts. The first story, situated in a village in Chittoor district of Andhra Pradesh, is about people's participation as agents who are offered benefits that are derived from creating individual natural assets and providing access to markets. Managing individually owned natural assets in this fashion does not always lead to a better environmental outcome for the community or the region as a whole. Common property is neglected and economies of scale from pooling resources are not reaped. Instead, some common resources like groundwater are over-exploited as a result of too much individuation. The consequence is the emergence of a fractured and fragmented community although individual well-being, measured in terms of income, improves. While the village is, in its own way, trying to create more natural assets, there is rampant granite quarrying around it. The villagers realise this contradiction but their participation is not organised enough to raise a voice against it.

Our second account is about some villages in the backward tribal areas of Valsad district of Gujarat where, like in our earlier narrative, people participated as individual agents. In this case the development agency realises the importance of integrating individual efforts into creating a larger cooperative organisation that is capable of reaping the benefits of scale. The organisational design is well thought out and procedures clearly documented. The design, however, entails a maze of activities and decisions at different levels and locations. This maze is quite complex, certainly beyond the grasp of most of the local participants. Hence the development agency cannot afford to let go of control at any level. It is like a puppet show where people participate, but only at the tug of a string.

Nestled in the dense forests of Raigarh and Jashpur districts of Chhattisgarh, two villages are participating in a Village Development Programme (VDP). This programme is designed to promote convergence of the set of existing development interventions of the state and central governments. Prioritising and choosing among the schemes and working collectively towards their implementation needs a shared vision. Here the nature of participation has to be more substantive than in the earlier two cases. People have to agree upon a common future image of the village. This requires a climate of trust and a concern for all. The relative power of the stakeholders is of great significance in constructing this image. It is determined by educational attainment, prior experiences of both the villagers and the external stakeholders. There could be a tendency for accentuating social and economic inequality. Addressing these is a challenge for all the stakeholders including the government and development agencies.

The verdant hills of the East Godavari district of Andhra Pradesh provide a perfect setting for a different form of participation, which is collective in nature. A micro-hydel power station is being constructed here by government agencies along the Yelleru River flowing past the village. All power generated will be sold to the grid. The underlying business model allocates a part of the net revenue to the village for creating public assets. A set of local women will be trained to run the power station after operations have stabilised, and the government agencies leave. Here, participation is for a public cause with no individual material incentives. The level of participation depends on the shared urgency to create a desired set of public assets, and since there is an absence of material incentive, the driving force has to be recognition by the community. This kind of participation requires individual sacrifice for the greater good. If it is successful, it has the potential of being truly transformational.

The four narratives are instances of different levels of participation with dissimilar outcomes for individuals and the community.

9

Natural Resource Management
The Limits to Conservation

Chittoor district, a part of the Rayalaseema region, lies at the southern tip of Andhra Pradesh between Chennai and Bengaluru (see Map 9.1). The area has mountainous plateaus with rocky and hilly regions, forming part of the Eastern Ghats and the Seshachalam Hills. The elevation of the district is up to 2500 ft. Ranking 18 out of 23 districts of Andhra Pradesh in 2007–8, it is considered a backward region. The people in this district are mainly from four different tribes. The Yanadis, originally a nomadic tribe, are the poorest and constitute the majority. The others are the Erugula, the Sugali and the Chenchu tribes.

The district is prone to drought and water is a scarce resource, with the groundwater table declining by almost a metre annually during long periods of low rainfall. Mango production is a key activity, although groundnut, sugarcane, banana, tomato, and paddy are also grown. Animal husbandry is another economic activity in addition to agriculture and horticulture, with the district being the leading producer of cow's milk in the state. This area has very good road and transportation networks. This makes it easy for milk from Chittoor to be marketed in Chennai, Bengaluru, and Hyderabad, and even as far away as New Delhi. The region has been experiencing a steadily rising demand for milk. The District Rural Development Authority (DRDA) has established 51 bulk coolers in the district that help procure about 150,000 litres of milk per day. The rearing of Nellore sheep is also encouraged as they can survive on scanty vegetation and graze in a less damaging manner. Inadequate grazing land, poor quality feed, unavailability of a good breed, prevalence of disease and unorganised marketing channels are impediments to sheep farming. The veterinary

Map 9.1: Chittoor District in Andhra Pradesh

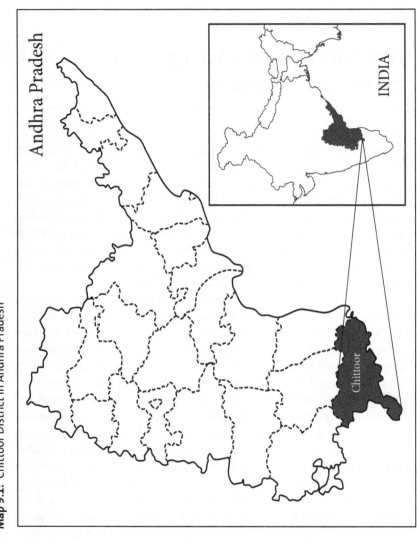

infrastructure of the district is overstretched, with a scarcity of qualified veterinary graduates. With reduced paddy cultivation and use of combine harvesters, the quantum of paddy straw has declined leading to a perennial shortage of crop residue as fodder. Of late, fodder cultivation is being encouraged through *subabul* plantations on fallow land or on denuded rough terrain, and cultivating *azolla* in tanks as a fodder supplement. Although a lot has been done to improve financial inclusion in the district — for example, the introduction of microcredit plans, financial linkage through self-help groups (SHGs), and identification of new avenues for credit dispensation — there still remains room for improvement.

It was against this backdrop that National Bank for Agriculture and Rural Development (NABARD) considered improving Chittoor's animal husbandry sector as well as integrating some activities that taken together could complement agriculture through its Umbrella Project for Natural Resource Management (UPNRM) scheme. This was supplemented by its efforts to facilitate bank linkages for the poor, marginal and landless farmers through the promotion of SHGs and Joint Liability Groups (JLGs).

NABARD defined the goal of UPNRM as one that aimed to enhance the livelihoods of the rural community for equitable and sustained increase in their quality of life through improved natural resources and increased private investments. To achieve this, the policy framework would have to identify financial instruments to support this activity. Also, 'NABARD considers it of utmost importance for the beneficiaries to be actively involved in a project throughout its life from its inception through planning to implementation and post-project management' (NABARD 2014a).

The principles that would guide the programme had been identified as the following. First, it had to be pro-poor by directly addressing socio-economic disparities and ensuring equitable access to natural resources. Second, it would have to be well-governed through people's participation in a transparent and responsible way. Finally, the approach to the programme would be need-based and integrated in the sense of ensuring convergence with existing public initiatives and ongoing government schemes.

MASS: A Locally Rooted Non-governmental Organisation (NGO)

NABARD identified a local NGO called Mitra Association for Social Service (MASS) for coordinating the programme. MASS was already involved in NABARD's Integrated Tribal Development Programme (TDP) covering over 1,000 tribal families of the Yanadi tribe in the Palamaner region of Chittoor. The TDP covered soil conservation, horticulture, education, and health in addition to credit provision and capacity building. The UPNRM in the Palamaner region could be dovetailed into the TDP, obtaining synergy through convergence. MASS had originally started as an organisation that fought for land rights for the poor and dispossessed. As they were successful in obtaining land rights for landless people, MASS got involved in granting and strengthening children's and women's rights through forming and facilitating women's SHGs. They realised, however, that ensuring a land *patta* (ownership document) did not really help the tribal unless he was told how to use the land for his livelihood. This led MASS to help in generating, strengthening and augmenting livelihoods of people.

The prime movers of MASS were Suchitra, the secretary, her husband Rajesh, who coordinated the projects, and Abraham. Abraham was a land-rights activist who had campaigned in almost every village in the region. Rajesh, an accountant by training, was shy and reticent, while Suchitra was articulate, energetic and very passionate about the activities of MASS. MASS had now grown to a size where they had 20 full-time employees, many of them tribals or from the backward classes, recruited from the villages where MASS carried out development interventions.

The UPNRM at Chittoor

Under the UPNRM, loans for cattle were given to only those individuals who committed a minimal plot of land (0.2 acres) for growing fodder, to ensure adequate supply. Farmers without land were provided loans for a local variety of sheep for rearing in the commons. There was reportedly a large demand for mutton that could be met with these sheep. MASS had also mandated that the animals be insured through a nationalised insurance company during the time of purchase. They installed fodder-cutting units in common places in the village, sold good quality dry feed, and made available a mobile veterinary unit for general animal health. It also promoted the breeding of hybrid cattle like Jersey and Holstein cows through artificial insemination (see Plate 9.1). Azolla is a variety of algae, rich in protein, that grows very rapidly. A small dose added to the feed of cows increases the protein intake of the animals and raises the quality of the milk they produce. MASS facilitated azolla production units for farmers and provided exposure, knowledge and training as and when necessary. The cold chain developing in the district was a distinct advantage. The credit line for buying animals of proper quality would be provided by MASS through the Grameen Bank and the liability of the individual taking the loan would be shared by a group (a JLG). The other advantage, over and above the income supplement, was the boost it would give to the cross-bred germplasm for better rearing of calves.

The intervention also included the possibility of building a 1 m³ biogas unit and vermicomposting facilities of 5 tonne annual capacity

Plate 9.1: Cattle Wealth, Insured to Smoothen Income Flows

for interested households. The mini biogas unit could provide quality cooking gas to a family of four or five. The construction would be subsidised by a scheme of the Non-conventional Energy Development Corporation of Andhra Pradesh Limited (NEDCAP) and the slurry obtained from it could be used for vermicomposting. It would save women from the laborious effort required to procure and use firewood. The vermicompost would save farmers the cost of inorganic fertilisers and could be used for enhancing horticultural productivity and spreading the use of organic farming.

The UPNRM was estimated to supplement the gross income of the direct beneficiaries by around Rs 72,000 per annum through dairy farming and horticulture. Regular returns from the sale of milk were expected to be around Rs 4,000 as income per month per family. The ongoing TDP where horticulture was being promoted would also augment incomes by around Rs 2,000 per month per family.

Families who had two milch cattle could expect to earn at least Rs 48,000 per annum. This was the net amount after taking into account insurance premium, veterinary care, fodder costs, and repayment of loans. It was calculated by assuming an average productivity of 9 litres per animal per day for around 280 days a year at the rate of Rs 12 per litre. This was a conservative estimate, from the figures given to us by MASS, and corroborated by the villagers. In case of an exigency, the liability towards repayment would be no more than 50 per cent of the net annual earnings. These families (if they were tribals) would also be practising horticulture on their land. Most people planted mango and *amla* on their plots, although a little persuasion was needed for amla plantation. The tribals were not too familiar with growing and harvesting amla, but it was promoted by MASS as it had a gestation period of just a year as compared to four years for mango. Annual revenues from mango and amla for cultivation in an acre of land were expected to be at least Rs 30,000 and Rs 25,000 respectively. For sheep rearing, the landless were given a loan of Rs 54,000, payable in six years at 15 per cent interest. Annual earnings from the sale of mutton and manure were expected to be over Rs 30,000, net of insurance premium, veterinary care, fodder costs, and repayment of loans. In case of an exigency, the liability towards repayment would be no more than 60 per cent of the net annual earnings. The villagers were not inhibited to access credit and their curiosity to know more about newer financial products and loans struck us as remarkable. Having successfully repaid the small loans disbursed by MASS, the farmers were keen to take more loans. The menfolk of the village were quite comfortable with the idea that the loans for animal rearing were granted to women only. They believed that women were better managers of finance. Women always kept sight of the liabilities associated with loan repayment and planned their expenditures accordingly. The concentration and focus with which the women were signing the attendance register after a meeting was evidence of their commitment and sense of responsibility (see Plate 9.2).

Plate 9.2: A Signature Move towards Empowerment

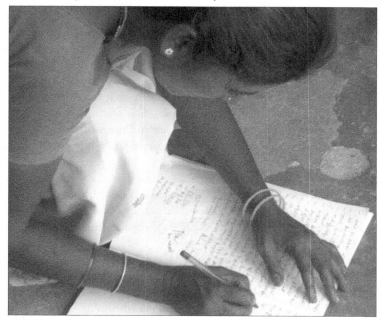

The area chosen for implementation was a contiguous region of tribal hamlets in Palamaner, Baireddypalli and Bangarupalyam Mandals. In the chosen area the majority of the population was from the Scheduled Castes (SCs), Scheduled Tribes (STs) or Other Backward Classes (OBCs), and was generally very poor. It was decided that the beneficiaries would be at least 50 per cent women and at least 50 per cent from the Yanadi tribe. The Yanadis in the Chittoor region were allegedly resettled from the erstwhile Madras Presidency (currently Tamil Nadu) in the 1960s and given individual plots of land. Many of these plots were unsuitable for cultivation, and many were on almost vertical slopes of a hilly terrain! MASS described the Yanadis as unenterprising, unintelligent but honest.

Experience at Bandladoddi

MASS was already involved in implementing a TDP at the Bandladoddi village of Bangarupalyam Mandal when they started implementing the UPNRM. It was a 'mixed village', with 147 families, of which 40 were Yanadis, 61 were SCs, 22 were OBCs, and 24 were from other castes. Most of the members of the older generation in the village were illiterate or just functionally literate. The TDP involved developing individual tribal lands for horticulture, especially mango, amla, *sapota*, and groundnut. There were large markets for these crops. Often, for mango, the processing units would send their own men and equipment for plucking and packing so as to ensure that the fruits were not damaged. However, the relative inexperience of the tribals at horticulture coupled with its long gestation period meant that there was a need for further intervention for ensuring regular cash flows for them. They were not used to systematic farming. They were more used to depending on the forests for their livelihood. As a result, many of them had to be taught basic activities such as how to hold a shovel or dig a pit. Moreover, the non-tribal residents of Bandladoddi who had not benefitted from the TDP wanted assistance from MASS under UPNRM.

The integrated dairy farming approach of UPNRM with its robust forward linkages ensured that the villagers' incomes were supplemented. The renewable energy projects contributed to improving the quality of life. Around 31 families, with landholdings of less than 5 acres, were direct beneficiaries from the project, of which around 25 families were given loans for milch cattle and six were assisted with loans for sheep rearing (see Box 9.1). Families were selected based on their interest in this initiative as well as their capacity to take care of their animals. Thus, the six families who were given the 'sheep package' (20 ewes and one ram) were landless tribals who did not have the capacity or wherewithal of taking care of milch cattle.

Box 9.1: Opportunities for the Rich and the Poor

Lataamma, who lived alone, was a frail old tribal with no previous experience of raising cows. Despite this, she was provided an animal loan without any security. Being landless, she used to work as a daily labourer, earning Rs 100 a day on days that she got employment. Taking the animal loan meant she had to lease around 0.15 acres of land for fodder cultivation (a prerequisite for getting the loan), which changed her fortunes. Her cow yielded 6 litres of milk on an average, which was sold for as high as Rs 16 per litre and she did not have to leave her home for employment any longer. When we spoke to her she said: 'At the fag end of my life, I am happy to own this *big* cow which helps me earn income and repay my loan'. Despite her recent disappointment when the calf delivered by her cow died, she was hopeful of qualifying for a second animal loan. She said there were several other individual success stories from her tribe, and introduced us to a younger lady named Jaya.

Jaya was a relatively well-off farmer with 2 acres of sugar cane farms. She had obtained two cows with the animal loans. She had a biogas unit as well as an azolla tank. She also planned to invest in a vermicompost pit later, in her farm, away from her home, as it would be cheaper in the long run to use the manure for her fields. To start with, she used to sell the milk from her cows to an agent at Rs 13 per litre, but later she became an agent herself and received Rs 16 per litre from her sales. Her aspiration was to somehow get the milk to Tirumala dairy as they paid Rs 20 per litre. Although she had a bank account, she did not like bank transactions as going to and from the bank resulted in a lot of additional expenses. This was despite her handling monetary transactions ranging from Rs 5,000 to Rs 50,000 in a week as a milk agent.

Since many of the tribals in this village had been given their pattas in fallow or steep plots, it was impossible to farm on those lands. MASS worked with the tribals in inspecting the land and clearing it to make it fit for horticulture, and assisted in planting mango, amla, sapota, curry and other saplings there. They also provided a set of three borewells along permanent aquifers for every 20 acres of land for irrigating the saplings. MASS suggested that the locals construct water tanks to store rainwater to use in months of drought, but farmers had a clear preference for borewells.

While MASS promoted veterinary assistance through the state animal husbandry department, Raghu, the local MASS veterinary volunteer, was called on first for all medical emergencies. It also introduced fodder slips through Sri Venkateswara Veterinary University and installed chaff cutters through the State Agriculture Department. Moreover, its demonstration units of azolla had got good responses, as had its sale of superior quality feed. MASS sold and delivered feed at Rs 550 per bag to the villagers, although market prices varied from Rs 500 to Rs 570 a bag. The vermicompost units, whose use could result in savings to the tune of Rs 1,500 per year due to lower use of fertiliser, had not picked up due to inadequate slurry generation from the biogas units which served as the feed for the vermicompost. Also, in terms of location, farmers preferred to have the vermicompost unit away from their homes, which made the transportation of slurry a challenge.

We met several people as we walked around observing the individual biogas units and horticulture plots. The beneficiaries were especially pleased about getting the animal package loans (also service for collection of repayment instalments) and all other services at their doorstep. This saved them the inconvenience and humiliation of visiting a bank where they would have to wait in long queues and were jostled from one counter to another because they were not very knowledgeable and their transaction amounts were small. Some of these villagers were traditionally cowherds and shepherds who had to sell their animals to meet sudden family exigencies or for meeting educational needs. On receiving the loans for animals, it was easier for these families to quickly adapt to taking care of the livestock as compared to the families who were traditionally farmers or who depended on the forest for livelihood.

The beneficiaries wished for more direct support from the UPNRM for replacing damaged saplings, ensuring water supply though borewells and setting up vermicompost pits. Water was particularly a problem because of declining groundwater levels. We learned that because of the state government's policy of providing free electric power to farmers for seven hours a day, villagers left their submersible pumps on all the time to draw water even if they did not need the whole amount since they did not know what time of day or night they would get the power. They were not too concerned about letting the water run-off the slopes and get wasted.

It was apparent from our discussions with the beneficiaries that the supplementary income earned from livestock catered primarily to the rising education needs of the next generation. Moreover, with the DRDA intervening in the education sector with better schools and hostels, and women in SHGs also laying emphasis on education, it had got a boost in the village. They claimed that this had led to young girls often choosing their own grooms, which in turn had resulted in more manageable dowries. The mood was upbeat, with the relatively larger farmers sharing with us their desire to send their children to engineering college (there were over 60 engineering colleges in Chittoor) so as to be able to live in comfort in towns and cities. Moreover, there was a state government scheme to subsidise educational expenses, and local politicians met other college-related expenses borne by the farmers. Although this meant that many people from the next generation would be moving out of the village, it was actually welcomed by the older folk. At the same time, they felt the need to improve amenities within the village so that their grandchildren could spend quality time with them.

Yet, a few of the landless families, who benefited from sheep rearing, were not as optimistic and did not see a different future for their children (see Plate 9.3). Although MASS helped landless peasants by

Plate 9.3: Do They See Another Future? The Eyes Say it All.

recommending them for loans to run *kirana* shops, or getting them involved in other schemes, this group had been feeling neglected. Also, there were some local villagers who were not beneficiaries, but were curious about our visit and what it meant for them. However, they were not encouraged to participate in our meeting and were asked to go about their work rather than loiter around.

We had noticed incessant quarrying of land in the surrounding areas outside the village. When asking about it, we realised that the villagers had accepted that the stray stone or boulder could hurt them and the denudation was resulting in lower fertility of their soil. Their response had been to dig a trench fortified with stone bunds around the village so that the flying boulders and dust could be trapped. Some of the tribals even worked as labourers in the quarries. The quarries were claimed to be owned by influential and powerful non-local politicians, who had business interests which went far beyond the confines of the state. There was no question of confronting them.

Experience at Kutalavanka

We moved on to Kutalavanka village of Baireddypalli Mandal, where Raja (one of the MASS employees) hailed from. Here, the TDP and UPNRM interventions were started simultaneously. This was a village inhabited only by Yanadis and had 33 families, with a total population of 178. In our first meeting with a group of beneficiaries, we were greeted by a traditional welcome song. A short introduction of the UPNRM intervention was followed by another activist's song about the need to preserve the environment, to demonstrate commitment to the UPNRM and the spirit of solidarity among the group. We noticed that a local tribal (who had sung the welcome song a few minutes before that with great enthusiasm) was asked to join in to sing the second song but he refused. When pressed to do so, he withdrew and left the meeting in a huff. We were stonewalled when we asked about this individual's behaviour. We had overheard the word Maoist being mumbled a number of times in the confusion of several parallel conversations in a hushed manner. When we explicitly asked if his politics was different or whether he had Maoist connections, we got no answer.

In this village, seven landless peasants (including Raja) were given loans for cattle. Pitting work was started to prepare plots for horticulture. People worked as a community on each others' plots, including the landless peasants who had been given animals. With these interventions, distress migration from the village in search of work had reduced. Children could stay at home and could continue their education undisturbed. Maya, an old lady owning less than an acre of land, emphasised that in addition to going to school, children must contribute in taking the animals out and working in the fields, especially over the weekend. She was a rare person we talked to who did not have any aspirations for her grandchildren. She believed it was best for them to get used to farming and animal husbandry as a lifestyle.

Since biogas units were yet to be set up in the village, the entire village used firewood from their forests for their household fuel use. The state government cooking gas scheme seemed to have bypassed this village. Raja's influence in this village was obvious as the villagers were more vociferous about their demands and how the government seemed to have forgotten them. We wondered whether it was indicative of a lower frequency of interaction that MASS had with these villagers. We observed that this was quite in contrast to our experience at Bandladoddi.

Here, too, farmers were clamouring for borewells, asserting that their handpumps were not good enough. Landless peasants wondered whether there was a mechanism through which they could be allotted land. A widow asked whether MASS could also assist her with accessing her husband's pension. Another request was for assistance from MASS to set up drip irrigation systems in the farms. The villagers had observed that a set of four farmers had obtained assistance from the District Water Management Authority (DWMA) through a NABARD Rural Infrastructure Development Fund (RIDF) scheme to set up drip irrigation. Many people wanted cattle loans. Since animal mortality was a big concern, cattle insurance was a great boon (see Box 9.2).

When we wanted to continue our discussions in the village through the evening, we were asked to return the next morning by MASS. We were informed that MASS officials never visited Yanadi settlements after sun down because of 'cultural differences'. Alcoholism was a major problem as was the rising incidence of AIDS. According to MASS, their drinking habits and sexually promiscuous practices did

Box 9.2: A Complex Case of Cows and Culture

Gouriamma was a landless widow, with two daughters in secondary school. Her weather-beaten face, which had aged prematurely, told tales of the extreme hardship she had endured to feed and clothe her family. This was the third time that Gouriamma was asking for a loan to buy a second cow. Of the two cows (worth Rs 25,000–Rs 26,000) she had originally purchased, Gouriamma lost one within 25 days because of a fever. With insurance payment, and additional money, she bought a third cow worth Rs 29,000 again, which lived for only 13 days. It would be harder to get reimbursement from insurance once again although she claimed this was a genuine misfortune. Yet she had consistently been repaying her loan instalments by working as a daily labourer.

She seemed to be a little isolated from the rest of the villagers and muttered repeatedly that an evil eye was upon her cattle. She pointed out to us that the cattle deaths had occurred quite suddenly, without the animals showing any sign of ill health. She had looked after the animals adequately, and the veterinary assistant had never had to make any emergency visits except to declare her cows dead.

Suchitra, the secretary of the NGO, MASS, was a little concerned about processing Gouriamma's loan request once again despite her disciplined repayments. She had heard that both the instances of cow mortality were due to poisoning and not from natural causes; the veterinary assistant had never pointed this out. According to the village grapevine, the needle of suspicion pointed towards Sadhamma, whose husband was allegedly in a relationship with Gouriamma. While Suchitra spoke of this in a disapproving tone we were not quite sure how much this mattered in the moral codes of the Yanadi tribe.

not allow them to integrate with the rest of the local communities. They were mostly trucked out into the cities for construction jobs.

Experience in Kanchanapalli

In Kanchanapalli hamlet, a 100 per cent backward caste (BC) settlement with 40 BC families, all farmers, had been given some loan or the other under the UPNRM. They already had vermicompost units because of some prior intervention, and the UPNRM had been operational for the previous nine months. The biogas units had resulted in a reduction of drudgery for the women. Although many of the villagers had received the free gas stove and LPG cylinder from a state government scheme, they had now switched to biogas as it saved on LPG, which was expensive. Moreover, it was a boon to get all assistance at the doorstep rather than having to run from pillar to post from one government department to another. The villagers at Kanchanapalli had taken to azolla production without any persuasion (in contrast to the tribal villagers elsewhere) and fed their cattle azolla as they saw a clear improvement in milk quality. They had innovated in vermicompost production, mixing in these pits some of the bio waste from their biogas units and were getting good results.

Besides having 1.5 acre commons where fodder grass was grown, each cattle owner also cultivated 20 cents (a unit of land area equal to 1/100 of an acre) of land with fodder. They grew (rain-fed) groundnut on the rest of their land. This village had not got any assistance with respect to horticulture as it was not a tribal village. However, they would have liked MASS to assist them with tree plantation as well. In a short span of nine months, most of the farmers who were given loans for sheep had almost recovered their costs through the sale of lamb, which made it easy to service their loans. Even people who took loans for cows had serviced their debt fast and had paid back almost 30 per cent of the principal. However, for physical assets like a shed for cows or sheep they preferred a grant to a loan as their debt burden went up and the shed provided no direct returns.

Despite the menfolk's satisfaction with the returns on animals that they bought using the UPNRM loans, the women in the village complained that this was an added burden for them as the onus of taking care of the animal, feeding it and taking it to the pasture fell on the women and children in the family. This meant an added chore to working in the field, cooking, washing, and cleaning, which left even less free time. This was more the case as there was a high school nearby and all village children (whether boys or girls) went to school regularly. Most parents wanted their children to try to get government jobs on completion of their education, or work in the city or towns. Their unavailability in the fields was not too much of a concern. Besides, these children, being busy with school, knew little about farming. However, an alternative opinion expressed was that the children would get involved in anything provided they saw that it produced returns. Thus, if this generation could prove to their children that rearing animals along with farming could lead to prosperous lives then the children would be happy to follow a similar lifestyle. The menfolk were glad that due to the UPNRM intervention, their distress migration in search of labour opportunities during the dry months had come down and they could pay more attention to their fields.

In comparison to the other villages we had visited, this relatively recent UPNRM intervention of MASS appeared to be more integrated and seemed to have attracted a higher level of participation. Thus, a beneficiary who had recently bought a cow with the UPNRM loan was now requesting assistance to set up an azolla tank to improve the cow feed. There was a watershed management plan on the anvil, based on a collective requirement-mapping exercise in which the entire village participated. The village folk seemed very comfortable talking to each other and more than one person said that with all the government schemes for women, a girl child is actually a blessing, as it meant a bicycle for the family (if the girl was in high school), and access to cheap funds and assistance. Also several panchayat level jobs were available for women in education, health care and social services. For example, Bharatiamma, who had taken a loan for the sheep package, was able to get a job as a cook for the midday meal scheme for schoolgoing children. This job had a salary of Rs 3,000 a month and she earned an additional Rs 1,000 a month as the local *Sanghamitra* (a community resource person appointed by the DRDA).

However, they also rued the inaccessibility of rural banks and the unfriendly attitude that the bankers displayed towards them. Water and its availability was a major concern in this village. We heard the story of a farmer with 4 acres of land who had spent Rs 50,000 on a borewell, but it was not deep enough and ran dry. Improved water management was indeed high on their agenda.

The Challenge to Bridge Private Incomes with Collective Prosperity

The UPNRM scheme in Chittoor was a systematic approach to the use of natural resources in a way that took cognisance of their inter-relationships and complementarities. It was very effective in quickly achieving its objectives of increasing supplementary incomes of the participants through the creation and marketing of products from individually owned natural assets such as milk from cattle or fruit from trees. NABARD's concept note on UPNRM also indicated the possibility of extending the scale of these micro-interventions to cover larger areas and a wider set of activities. If this were indeed to be so, natural resources would have to be defined as a much broader set of assets that included public goods and commons.

Every group we engaged with in the villages spoke repeatedly about the lack of water as the single most important constraint they faced in organising economic activities. Almost all believed that this would fail to ease in the near future. The villagers, along with the officials from MASS, were of the opinion that there was overdrawing of water because it was very cheap to do so as a consequence of the state government's policy. Further, loans were being made available to a group of farmers to install bore wells, where three wells for every 20 acres of land for areas under the TDP of NABARD and one bore-well for four to five contiguous plots under the UPNRM were being allowed. Except for a recent intervention at Kanchanapalli, where we found some evidence of a plan for water management evolving, a community-based long-term arrangement was clearly absent. Water from these private wells was being used for irrigating the fruit trees planted on the erstwhile village commons. It is interesting to note that the income from the fruits would belong to the owners of the trees, not all of whom were the owners of water. Hence the ownership of water could emerge as a critical determinant of the distribution of income from common resources. The management of the environment is necessarily a collective task since it cannot be divided into individual property, beyond a point, without giving up the character of commonly shared natural resources.

The advisability of use of biogas plants as individual assets (created through a subsidy of the Andhra Pradesh government) was questionable because most households did not have the critical quantum of biomass to start the anaerobic digester to produce usable gas. A better planned public asset could have been a superior alternative, but this was not pursued simply because the philosophy behind the execution of the project was primarily focussed on individual incentives.

Property rights for a common asset would be usufructuary rather than making it disposable in a market transaction. Creating supplementary livelihoods from common property resources was about creating individual income streams by accessing markets. The typical conflict here would be about valuation of common resources used in the generation of income. The income incentive makes the typical individual look at the problem from a 'lone ranger' perspective that would actually underestimate the value of the resource. On the other hand, to preserve the resource as capital for the community, the valuation has to be a collective one based on how everybody contributes to its creation and conservation (Sen 2003). Pure market-oriented incentives may not suffice since the use of the available natural capital stock is a social choice. Sen observes:

> A central feature of the social choice approach is to require that the individuals' valuational inputs into making social decisions be concerned specifically with the actual alternative states from which the social choice is to be made. This is where the market analogy is particularly deceptive, since the market does not provide specified social states to the individuals to choose from. Given the prices, I choose my basket, and you choose yours; neither of us has to look beyond our nose. (ibid.: 2003)

Individual incentives work on the basis of endowments of some critical resource, be it a skill, a capital asset or land, the return to which can be improved upon through an available opportunity. In the UPNRM scheme studied, those who got loans for the cattle had to have some access to land for producing fodder. Horticulture was being promoted on plots in the hilly terrain. It was as if a fully integrated natural capital utilisation scheme was being created for people with land. Other landless people were given the option of taking a loan to buy sheep and graze them on the village commons. They could be taken to forestlands too. A long run implication of the scheme would be that the commons in the villages would be used more extensively to grow more fruit trees. Areas available for sheep grazing would shrink, and sheep owners would have to depend more and more on their access to forestland for this purpose thus making them more vulnerable to conflicts with the forest officials. The individual's participation in this scheme was not consistent with the attainment of the goal of managing natural resources *for the entire community*.

The geographical region under UPNRM in Chittoor district was the home of the Yanadi tribe, though many of the villages had mixed population including SCs and other backward classes. We found that the outcomes of the project were distinctly better for hamlets without any tribal population, followed by hamlets with a mixed population. In the fully tribal villages, the outcomes were relatively poor. By keeping its economic livelihood activities distinct from other social interactions with the Yanadis, MASS was unknowingly stereotyping the Yanadi tribe, which limited an open approach to participation. Individuals, even within a tribe, would be heterogeneous with different capabilities and assets. Development is about adopting and adapting to a new set of practices (not feasible earlier), like new agricultural practices, new livelihood practices, different sanitation or hygiene practices, different nutritional or educational practices. Indeed, the availability of new alternatives implies the need for a re-evaluation of the status quo. Who initiates the re-evaluation? Was MASS correct in limiting their engagement with the Yanadi tribe?

10

Creating Big Organisations with Small Farmers

Situated in the undulating terrain of the Sahyadri Range of the Western Ghats is Valsad district in the south of Gujarat, which contains some of the most backward villages dominated by Kokna, Warli and the Kolcha tribes (see Map 10.1). A Tribal Development Programme (TDP) for sustainable rural livelihood, called wadi, was started in 1995–96 in this area. It was part of bilateral cooperation between the Federal Republic of Germany and the Government of India, which was implemented by Dharampur Utthan Vahini (DHRUVA), an associate society of BAIF Development Research Foundation, and National Bank for Agriculture and Rural Development (NABARD).

Wadi is a Gujarati word for 'small orchard' covering 1 or 2 acres. The wadi was conceived as an individual orchard of fruit trees, which could be mango, cashew, *amla*, *sapota* or any other citrus fruits appropriate for the area. Apart from the planted fruit trees, the wadi would have a peripheral ring of forest trees. Each wadi would have at least two kinds of trees to minimise biological and marketing risks. The fruit trees were expected to bear income only after four to five years. During this time some expenses would be incurred in planting and nurturing the trees. The forestry plants would not only provide a safety fence but also cover the family's needs for fuel, fodder and small timber. Typically, 1 acre of wadi would have around 60 fruit trees and 400 forest plants. This would be adequate, it was felt, to ensure stability and security of livelihood.

The primary objective of the programme was to improve the incomes earned by the tribes living in the region. Many earlier interventions had succeeded initially, but the beneficiaries slipped back into poverty and economic vulnerability on the completion of the project.

Map 10.1: Valsad District in Gujarat

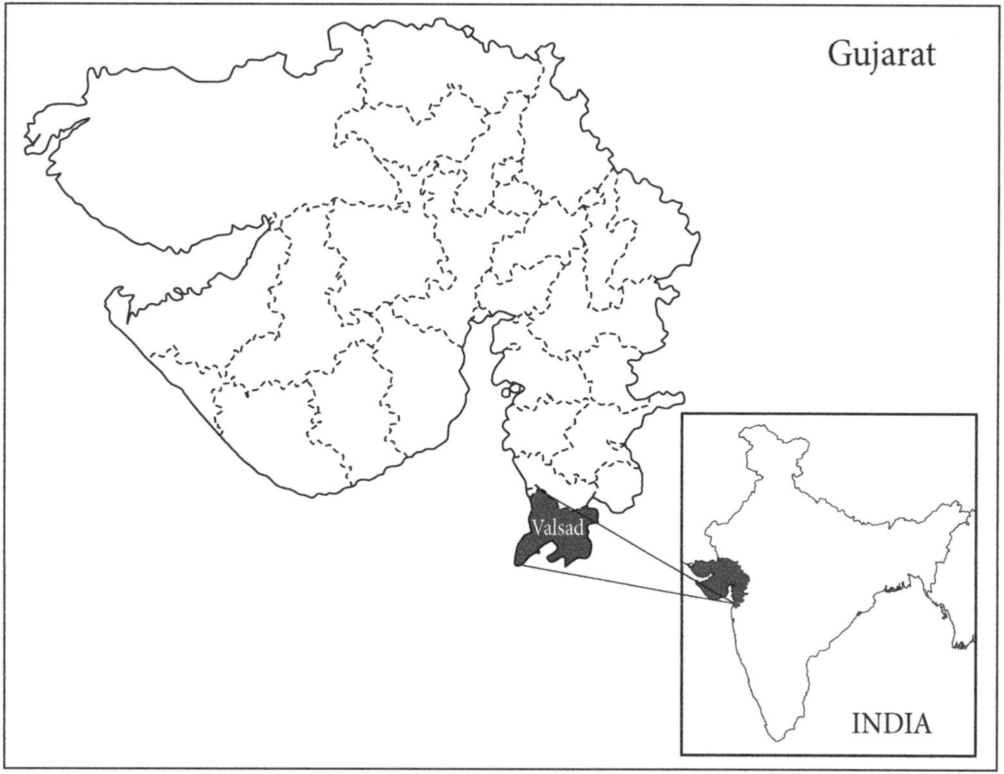

Gujarat

Valsad

INDIA

194 ✧ Another Development

To avoid such an eventuality, an organisational structure would be put in place that could pool together individual efforts so as to reap the benefits of large-scale production. This would enable the beneficiaries to attain larger reach in wider markets. Hence the wadi programme was designed to be sustainable beyond the lifetime of the initial intervention.

The real challenge would be to enhance income from natural resources, and yet reduce substantially the kind of uncertainties in income from weather, output and price fluctuations. Ideally, the intervention would have to be scalable and replicable in other parts of the region. Obviously, ensuring success would depend on the local people 'buying into the project', and taking active part in its implementation. Capacities would have to be built and capabilities augmented. Focusing narrowly on a particular aspect of income generation would not suffice; it would have to be supplemented by related activities.

The conditions of these tribal areas of Gujarat are harsh. According to the Gujarat WADI Comprehensive Tribal Development Programme brochure:

> The area is characterized by steep, undulating, inaccessible terrain, heavy rainfall with high run-offs. Remote and scattered habitations provide only harsh living conditions. Only one third of the area is cultivable with negligible area under irrigation. The harsh livelihood conditions lead to high morbidity. The vicious cycle of poverty-malnourishment — morbidity — low work capacity — increased poverty has made the tribals lose confidence in themselves.

Preconditions for the success of the wadi included improvements in water management and soil conservation in the region. These included construction of temporary check dams, the development of perennial springs and the use of pot drip irrigation as part of water management. Similarly, soil conservation measures like bunding and building of tree platforms would be important activities. Finally, the programme would require empowerment of people and the building of their capacities to implement the project. Hence, apart from training, focus would have to be on health, education, and women's development and building skills for micro entrepreneurial enterprises. The implementation would be done mainly through the people's organisations created for the purpose, the village Ayojana Samiti, made up of representatives elected from among the wadi participants for planning and executing the programme. Some specialists from within the participants would also have to be identified and trained such as the 'barefoot' accountant and a field guide with special knowledge of agronomy and horticulture.

The wadi programme also envisaged the need for credit by farmers, not only for activities related to the wadi, but also for other agricultural activities, non-farm microenterprises and even for unanticipated consumption requirements. The wadi programme in the Dharampur block covered around 140 odd villages and benefitted about 13,000 households.

Structure and Functioning of the Wadi Value Chain

The different stakeholders in this project included NABARD as the funding agency, DHRUVA, and the beneficiaries (farmers and the landless) represented through the Gram Vikas Mandals (GVMs), Ayojana Samitis and self-help groups (SHGs). In addition to actual wadi plantation and operation forward linkages were developed for marketing and processing by DHRUVA. Thus, DHRUVA set up two pyramidal structures, one for administration of the wadi project, which involved the flow of assistance from a nodal centre to individual participants. The other was to facilitate the flow of goods (mangoes and cashews) from the wadi owner to national markets through a network of cooperatives.

The administrative structure, in terms of flow of information and money (grants and loans) comprised of several hierarchies of community-based organisations (CBOs), starting from a flat base of wadi owners, producing mangoes and cashews. The wadi participants were all members of the GVM, who in turn elected members to the Ayojana Samitis. The intermediary in these interactions between the wadi owners and the CBOs were often the appropriate representative, such as the barefoot accountant, village field guide or the village health guide. The schemes implemented by the central office of DHRUVA at Lachhakadi were channelled through the relevant cluster office, to the Ayojana Samiti. The credit provided by NABARD to DHRUVA at 9 per cent was passed on to the Ayojana Samitis at a rate of 12.5 per cent (3.5 per cent service charges charged by the non-governmental organisation or NGO). The Ayojana Samitis, in turn, would provide loans to its members at the rate of 15 per cent. In addition, there was a Sahbhagi Vikas Yojana in place, which was based on using the savings of the wadi owners to provide credit to those members in need of loans, and to cater to working capital requirements of the cooperatives if required by the Ayojana Samiti. This scheme linked the credit flows with the flow of commerce from the wadi output.

The output of the primary producers was collected and processed through a network of cooperatives, which culminated in a cooperative-owned, BAIF-promoted multistate producer company called Valsad Agricultural Producers Company Limited (VAPCOL) for marketing branded finished products (see Table 10.1).

The 11 cooperatives, as depicted in Table 10.1, were formed such that they were at a distance of not more than around 10 km from the furthest wadi in their jurisdiction. Chosen representatives from the Ayojana Samitis, and a DHRUVA representative, made up the managing committee of the cooperative. These cooperatives, along with other BAIF-supported cooperatives in other states, were joint owners of the BAIF-promoted producer company, VAPCOL. Profits from VAPCOL therefore flowed back to the cooperatives, which could use it for financing working capital needs and providing credit to wadi owners on the recommendation of their respective Ayojana Samitis. They could also distribute dividends before the festivals of Holi and Diwali. Of these, Vasundhara, the oldest, owing to its location in the same Lachhakadi complex as the DHRUVA office, had assumed the role of the mother cooperative where a lot of the processing was being done for mangoes and pickles (Plate 10.1). Products from other cooperatives were sent to Vasundhara for branding before being distributed. The Mandwa cooperative also had several facilities to collect and process mangoes from other cooperatives because of its proximity to Dharampur town.

The flow of commerce was through a collection agent, usually a landless farmer, appointed by the cooperative, directly to the wadi owner, from whom the agent procured cashews or mangoes. The cooperatives gave the agent a commission based on the quantity procured (for example, at the rate of Rs 2 per kg of cashew procured in 2011), and they processed the wadi produce or sent it across to Vasundhara for further processing and branding under the name

Table 10.1: Schematic of the Structure of VAPCOL

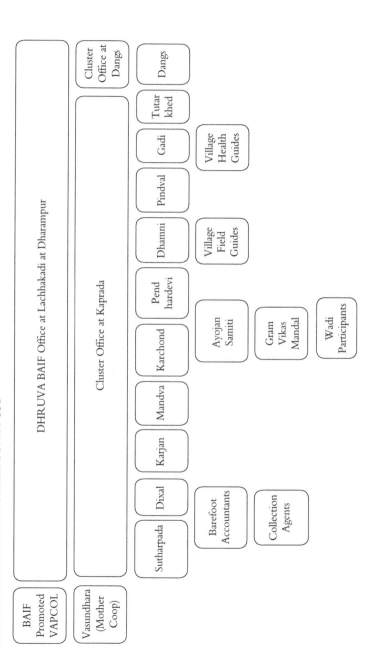

Plate 10.1: Vasundhara Processing and Packaging Unit

Vrindavan. For example, in 2011, the Tutarkhed cooperative chose four collection agents for procuring cashews. In general, women's SHGs were preferred as collection agents; otherwise people were chosen based on their local reputation and contacts. Vasundhara also received raw produce from the villages it represented. The product was then distributed and sold through VAPCOL, the producer company, at different outlets in different states. Around 30 per cent of the produce was sold through direct retail outlets of Vasundhara.

In addition to serving as a collection and processing centre for wadi produce, the cooperatives also provided discounts on bulk purchases on items such as roof tiles, oil extraction units for *mahua* seeds, pesticides, and fertilisers. They also acted as a source of credit for wadi owners, based on recommendations of the respective Ayojana Samitis. There was a plan to regularly hold annual general meetings of the cooperatives for greater interaction with wadi owners and improved transparency. The cooperatives provided employment opportunities to landless families to work in the cashew processing units, which were modern and well maintained. Each cashew processing centre could employ around 20 people. While cashew processing was a profit-oriented activity, other activities of the cooperative were not so profit-oriented.

Kishorebhai's Wadi at Tutarkhed

After a 90-minute drive from Dharampur (Valsad district) on a narrow, hilly, dirt track we arrived at Tutarkhed village. It is an arid region where some rain-fed crops like *ragi* and lentil are grown. Situated 50 km from Dharampur, it is one of five hamlets that make up a gram panchayat. There were 278 households in Tutarkhed, of which 145 households are involved in the wadi. Fifty-four households joined in the first phase of the wadi programme and then 91 joined in the second phase. There are 50 households that do not have orchards, but are connected with the wadi programme's peripheral activities. Of the 278 households (all tribal) 72 are landless. Tutarkhed has no banks, the nearest one is in Dharampur, and has only one primary health-care centre. The hamlet has only three television sets, but many of the residents have mobile phones. Many families possess two mobile phones, where one is always kept in the house, and the other is carried by whoever is going out a far distance or for a long time.

Three people from the hamlet were part of the gram panchayat. The GVM had five women members, but none from Tutarkhed. The Ayojana Samiti for this region had five representatives from Tutarkhed. We were surprised to find that there were no women's SHGs in the village. In the previous year (2010), the hamlet had earned total revenue of Rs 900,000 from cashews and mangoes. In 2011, the cashew produce was expected to be one-third of 2010's produce because of poor weather. The incomes of the wadi owners, it was pointed out, were not expected to fall that dramatically because the price of cashews would be higher. Since the primary producers in the wadis were all part of the larger cooperative structure of the wadi programme, it was only to be expected that the organisation would have some pricing power when the harvest was hit by an adverse supply condition. About 25 per cent of the landless got some support or the other from the wadi programme, especially as collectors of produce that had to be transported from the fields to the processing centres.

We stopped at Kishorebhai's wadi to know more about the wadi project from a group of direct beneficiaries. Kishore was frail and short and appeared to be in his late 40s. His house, attached to 1.5 acres of his wadi, was shady and cool, though not *pucca*. He was a beneficiary of the wadi programme, and this plot of land was where the cashew and mango trees were planted. Kishore had 20 mango trees in the lower part of his sloping garden, and 40 cashew plants in the higher parts. He had another 1.5 acres in two different locations (very steeply inclined) where he grew *ragi*, *urad*, *chana*, and *mugh*. One of five brothers, with an inheritance of 3 acres from the family property, Kishorebhai was illiterate with three daughters and a son. The daughters were married and lived in the village in their separate households. One of them was an *anganwadi* worker. His son, a fifth grade dropout, was married too. He worked on his father's fields, but stayed separately. He had three children all going to the local school, studying in classes four, six and seven. Kishore's son lived in a separate house, close to the other two plots that Kishore had and helped him with the wadi. Kishore had been able to purchase a motorcycle for his son, costing Rs 24,000. His savings of Rs 14,000 was not sufficient, so he had to borrow the rest of the money, Rs 10,000, from the GVM. The loan was to be repaid in one year's time. Kishore's son had purchased a mobile phone with money obtained from his wife. Hence Kishore felt compelled to purchase a mobile phone for himself too, which he did for Rs 1,500.

Kishorebhai agreed to get involved in the wadi project because of his conviction that this would bring him additional income that was a little more stable than his income from traditional agriculture. The person who convinced him and many others in the village was a field guide, Naraharibhai, appointed by DHRUVA (see Box 10.1). Kishorebhai started his wadi in 1998 on 1 acre of land, and subsequently added another 0.5 acre. In addition to land, Kishorebhai owned two bullocks, a cow and goats. He explained that his agricultural produce was for consumption by his family, which consisted of his wife and son, daughter-in-law and three grandchildren. They were actually net buyers of foodgrains. Fuelwood was obtained from the forest. Drinking water was accessed from a handpump installed in the village. Over the years he had experimented with two special nurseries in his land, one for herbal plants and the other for forest plants that could be used

Box 10.1: A Champion of Grass-roots Innovation

> Naraharibhai, who was educated and had a diploma in agriculture, hailed from Tutarkhed. He had seen wadi being supported by DHRUVA in other parts of the district. He was successful in convincing DHRUVA personnel to visit his village and start a wadi project there. When DHRUVA actually agreed to work in Tutarkhed, Naraharibhai became one of their field guides to assist farmers in starting the wadi. Naraharibhai was introduced to us as an innovator by the villagers. He was a marginal farmer, with too little land to have his own wadi. This did not deter him, and he turned to the relatively unprotected government forestland for all his experimentation. He was constantly trying out new techniques of farming, with an objective to increase the biodiversity of the species that grew there. Neither the forest officials nor the locals challenged him in any way, giving him space to try out new techniques of production and improving the productivity of existing botanical species in the forest.
>
> When we asked Naraharibhai what his gains were from participating in these activities, he replied, 'I get pleasure from seeing new plants grow. And if they can be a source of added income to the villagers, then it is even better. I did not get a job in the government agricultural service, but I must put my education to some use! Without any land of my own, this has given me great satisfaction. I like to teach people new ways of doing things.'

for the boundary for wadi plantations. He had also procured a diesel pump for drawing water from a nearby stream for his trees. The diesel pump cost Rs 18,000, of which half was a grant from the project and the other half was a loan that he was able to obtain as a member of an SHG which included his four brothers. They had been able to repay the loan in three years.

Kishorebhai's wadi yielded 1,700 kg of mango and 305 kg of cashews in the year 2010. The gross revenues earned were Rs 25,000 and Rs 13,800 respectively. Additional earnings every three or four years were around Rs 22,000 from selling some of the forest plants on the boundary. Kishorebhai's special nursery for herbal plant saplings fetched him Rs 7,000 annually. The special forest plants nursery had been fetching him around Rs 5,000 annually but he had decided to discontinue the sales after two years because of insufficient demand. Apart from the opportunity cost of his family's labour, his direct costs included diesel expenses incurred to run the pump. His diesel consumption for irrigation purposes was to the tune of 20 litres for wadi trees and 15 litres for his agricultural crops. Now, with the wadi being quite old, soil treatment would be needed for some tree platforms. The cost would be around Rs 300 to Rs 350 per platform. Other costs included costs of pesticides and fertilisers which were bought from the DHRUVA cooperative store at less than market prices.

After seven years of support for the wadi, DHRUVA decided to withdraw and allow the villagers like Kishorebhai to sustain the wadi on their own. However, according to DHRUVA, when they came to check on the status of the wadis after disengaging, they found that productivity had fallen in many of them, including the one belonging to Kishorebhai. DHRUVA then started a second phase of intervention called the Yield Improvement Programme (YIP) in 2008–9, which had a 50 per cent loan and a 50 per cent grant component. Kishorebhai decided to participate in this programme as his yield had slipped. However, he had no clear answer as to the reason why it had deteriorated. DHRUVA was of the opinion that the wadi owners were not very enthusiastic to maintain all the good practices. According to DHRUVA, there was a need to apply chemical fertilisers and pesticides in appropriate dosages at the right time, and they 'had to show the tribals that their organic processes are not enough. The plants need nutrition'.[1]

Prior to the wadi experiment, Kishorebhai would migrate to Vapi, Valsad and even up to Nashik in Maharashtra to work in grape farms. Collecting forest waste and earnings from selling labour in grape farms as a migrant worker would help him ease his cash constraints. A four and a half month trip to Nashik, for instance, would result in net savings of Rs 700 only. He claimed he was paid (in the late 1990s) a daily wage of Rs 15 only in the vineyards. He was better off now, not having to stay away from his family and with some assured supplementary livelihood from cashews and mangoes.

Kamalbhai's Wadi in Dixal Village

Kamalbhai's wadi is part of DHRUVA's YIP. He belongs to the Kolcha tribe, officially classified as a primitive tribal group. His wadi also serves as a cashew collection centre. Kamalbhai first came in contact with DHRUVA officials at an awareness programme as early as 1995, at which time he was growing traditional crops like *nagli* (ragi)

---

[1] Personal communication with DHRUVA representatives.

and urad. What was particularly appealing to him was DHRUVA's claim that the wadi could generate enough income for them so as to stop distress migration.

Not everyone in the Dixal village had adopted the wadi concept. The landless (25–30 families) could not adopt it and another 15 to 16 families were uninterested in taking assistance. Of these, DHRUVA personnel asserted that some were incapable of managing a wadi because of their waywardness and drunkenness, others did not need assistance as they owned more than 5 acres of contiguous land and were involved in large-scale agriculture (eight families owned more than 10 acres, one family owned 40 acres!). Yet others were *satipatis* — a clan of people who declined any form of governmental assistance.

Kamalbhai's wadi was an old and established one. During the seven years of DHRUVA's support, his wadi had stable yields averaging 125 kg of cashew annually. After DHRUVA's withdrawal, there was a rapid decline in yield, with the average falling to 35 kg a year. Hence DHRUVA introduced the YIP in select wadis where they expected a dramatic improvement, which in turn would have a demonstration effect. The YIP was no more than implementation of proper plant practices including use of pesticides and fertilisers. Yields rose to around 200 kg annually, in Kamalbhai's wadi and other wadis in the programme, as was borne out by the collections at the cooperative, which rose to 90 T from a stagnant collection of around 30 T after DHRUVA's withdrawal. During the initial seven years of DHRUVA's involvement, the collection averaged around 50 T annually.

Kamalbhai had a large family of over a dozen people, comprising his wife, three unmarried daughters, two unmarried sons, a married son and daughter-in-law and their three children. His wife was a member of the Dixal cooperative. Their eldest son (married), Madanbhai, had a contract job with the state government's Water and Sanitation Management Organisation (WASMO). He was also an insurance agent and a member of the panchayat, and had been a barefoot accountant for the Ayojana Samiti in the past, for which his basic education till the senior secondary level (class 12) was an asset. He was the GVM secretary. Madanbhai also managed the cashew collection centre, for which he got a commission of Rs 2 per kg collected. Kamalbhai's younger son, who had completed his second year of graduation, worked in the family-owned and operated flour grinding machine, which yielded a profit of Rs 2,000 a month. The youngest son, who had completed class seven, worked on their fields and also did basic tailoring and repairing activities from his home. In addition to the 1.5 acres devoted to the wadi, Kamalbhai owned 3.5 acres of land and leased an additional 2 acres where he cultivated *nagli* (ragi), urad and paddy. They also earned between Rs 1,500 and Rs 2,000 a month from selling milk. Mangoes were sold as one lot (around 200 kg in 2011), while different household members sold small amounts of cashew at different times to the cooperative or at the weekly haat, based on their need for money to make other household purchases. Like Kishorebhai in Tutarkhed, Kamalbhai also had been selling saplings of mango prepared using grafting techniques and saplings for forest trees to line the wadis which used to give him an annual income between Rs 7,000 and Rs 8,000. This had been discontinued.

When we visited, the family was gearing up for Kamalbhai's eldest daughter's marriage. It was an inter-tribe marriage, which was becoming quite common. Kamalbhai's family members informed us that given the unbalanced sex ratio (fewer women) among the forward tribes, men from those tribes were willing to pay a 'bride price' for Kolcha women. The bride-to-be looked frail and undernourished like her nephews. This was in contrast to her more healthy-looking niece who was being educated at a residential school. A possible reason for this difference was the adequate and balanced nutrition provided by the tribal residential school as compared to what was cooked in Kamalbhai's home.

Kamalbhai was conscious of the fact that the wadi intervention had increased their knowledge about, and access to, different development schemes and opportunities. Not only did they get the wadis which increased their incomes, they also got access to drinking water, obtained funds for a sewing machine and were able to set up a shop. They also bought a cow at subsidised rates and set up a vermicomposting pit through WASMO. Moreover, the family had a Kisan Credit Card (KCC) in Kamalbhai's name which was obtained from the Sutarpada Baroda Gujarat Grameen Bank. His was one of the 12 fortunate families of a total of 112 families in Dixal to own a KCC. Of the 112 families in the village, only 60 owned land. He proudly claimed that he had been able to make a provision of between Rs 100,000 and

150,000 for his daughter's marriage, while in the past he could not think of spending any more than Rs 8,000 to Rs 10,000.

Kamalbhai, observed that contrary to his initial expectations, distress migration still occurred in the village. In years with poor cashew yields, a lot of the menfolk left for towns in search of work.

Samarsingi

Samarsingi was a Kokna and Warli dominated village. Owing to its hilly landscape, this tribal village was selected by DHRUVA for several interventions ranging from comprehensive soil treatment of the entire village for wadi development to credit extension for livestock and dairy. The villagers had been encouraged to participate in a joint forest management (JFM) process to conserve the local forest from which they got firewood for cooking purposes. We gathered from them that availability of water was a major concern. An attempt to dig a well had failed as the water table was very low in this area. At present, water resources were managed through creating and widening access to three natural springs and increasing storage capacity for the spring water. Around the village, diesel pumps and PVC pipes were ubiquitous, with four groups of farmers being given portable engines for irrigation as a part of the project.

This village was considered a model for livestock breeding and dairy, despite the chronic water shortage (see Box 10.2). Given the terrain, it was a challenge to retain any water as it just ran-off along the slope. This meant that for half the year the livestock were fed only on dry fodder which drastically reduced the productivity of the cows. Moreover, the dearth of water resulted in the biogas digesters, provided to 8–10 households in the village, running dry, leaving the villagers without any access to biogas as fuel for their kitchens.

The biggest change the intervention had brought about was a dramatic fall in migration from the village and an improvement in financial conditions. All 77 landholding families of the village were wadi owners, and in the last year three SHGs had been formed as a result of another initiative from DHRUVA. This was in addition to the six *sakhi mandals* already in place. Many of the SHGs actually kept their deposits at this dairy collection centre which functioned as an informal bank, as the nearest formal bank was 65 km away.

Box 10.2: Surrogate Sarpanch

We visited a milk collection centre in Samarsingi village. It was evening and there were many women who had gathered to sell milk and exchange notes on the happenings of the day. Compared to the traditionally dressed women with *ghunghat* (veil or head scarf to cover one's head and face) in the other villages in Gujarat that we had visited, the womenfolk here were dressed in 'urban night wear' with a dupatta, which could probably double up as a ghunghat if required. The women were proud to share with us that the 11-member Ayojana Samiti had two elected women representatives.

We were in the midst of an interesting conversation with the women when we noticed that everyone stood up in obeisance on seeing a gentleman who had just alighted from a rather heavy and shining motorcycle. There were hushed whispers that this was Jivyabhai Somabhai Mashe, the sarpanch of the village, whose panchayat had recently won an award as the best panchayat in the district. The authority of the sarpanch was evident — some people rushed to carry his bag, yet others pulled out a chair for him and cleaned it. Jivyabhai conveyed to us that he had just visited a nearby village and shared with us the various initiatives his panchayat had taken. He explained that most of the improvements were initiated by the common village folk themselves through a participatory process facilitated by DHRUVA. He also shared with us how, as sarpanch, he had no inhibitions about going directly to the then chief minister, Narendra Modi, demanding a 12 km long road to connect two hamlets in his village under the MGNREGA scheme, and believed that his exposure to DHRUVA had given him such self-confidence. When asked about his political ambitions, he responded that given a choice he would rather work as a contractor for DHRUVA than be involved in political activity.

Later, we were informed that Jivyabhai was a *sarpanch pati*, that is, the husband of the sarpanch, who was the lady in charge of the dairy collection centre who we had been in conversation with. Since the post of sarpanch in this panchayat was reserved for a woman, his wife was the notional sarpanch, although all the panchayat affairs were conducted by Jivyabhai. This was the norm in this part of the country and women, no matter how empowered, appeared to be at ease with this norm.

This village took pride in being thrifty; it was claimed that their stock of stored grain was enough to last them for five years running! When we visited, we were told that mango and cashew production was much lower than average for that season. However, the mood in the village was not one of alarm. To address the problem, the wadi owners had decided to increase the application of pesticides and cow dung to improve cashew yields for the future (see Plate 10.2).

Plate 10.2: Cashew Trees with Watershed Bunding Structures

Cooperatives

We visited four cooperatives that were part of the DHRUVA project design in order to understand their structure and work. During our visits we had an opportunity to sit through a complete meeting of the Tutarkhed cooperative steering committee. The committee members included representatives from the Ayojana Samitis, the master field guide, accountant, and three deputed personnel from DHRUVA, an auditor, and two representatives who managed five DHRUVA cooperatives each. The salaries of the last two representatives were borne by the cooperatives (a practice started from April 2011). Registered in 2001, the Tutarkhed cooperative had 2,000 members, each owning shares worth Rs 50. The cooperative had accumulated funds of over Rs 1.6 million over the past 10 years of operation. They had also received Rs 350,000 from DHRUVA as a fixed deposit to take care of initial working capital needs.

The greatest concern of the committee was the relatively low cashew collection rate that year. Part of the reason was, of course, the low yields, but the other and more disturbing concern was that farmers preferred selling the cashew to private buyers at the Dharampur market who often exploited them. The steering committee had met to decide on the price to be offered for raw cashew, based on the prevailing market rate, and settle on a price. They met every two weeks during the cashew collection season to ensure that pricing was determined dynamically based on changing market conditions. This pre-empted private traders from setting a marginally higher rate for cashews and diverting the village produce. Cashew procurement amounts had gone up as a result of the dynamic pricing and subsequent publicity of rates offered. Notwithstanding the low yields that year, abysmally low collection rates had the steering committee concerned about whether there was some systematic leakage of raw cashew. Some losses, because of village children stealing some produce and selling it locally, were acceptable. The steering committee then asked the master field guide to look into the crop production practices. The master field guide communicated that although there were enough people who had been trained in the standard prescribed procedures for cashew production and the YIP was in effect, it was a challenge to get wadi owners to buy inputs like pesticides and fertilisers as these inputs had been provided gratis in the first seven years of the wadi.

We also observed a standing committee meeting of representatives from all the cooperatives (including the DHRUVA representatives) at the Karjan Cooperative premises (see Plate 10.3). When we entered, the committee was in the process of finalising the contents of a handbill which was to be distributed in each village and which stated that the cooperatives were conducting a cashew collection drive. Also, it was decided that an announcement would be made using loudspeakers across the entire village a day before the scheduled village haat day, and the same publicity vehicle would collect cashews simultaneously. These measures were proposed as one of the member cooperatives had tried it successfully in their village. The dynamic price issue was also discussed. At that time, the cooperatives were offering a price of Rs 80 per kg of raw cashew against the prevailing rate of Rs 75 at the village haat. Despite this there was leakage, because the traders treated

Plate 10.3: Standing Committee Meeting of all Cooperative
Representatives at Karjan

cashew as ready money for villagers to buy their provisions across the
counter. Traders often exploited a villager's inability to count by paying him lower amounts. The payment would often be in terms of a
large number of low denomination currency notes. They also cheated
the villagers by using faulty weighing machines. At the meeting, a
decision was taken to call the local Member of Legislative Assembly
(MLA) to the next standing committee meeting to request him to
check malpractices by traders. We found that most of the arguments
provided for decision-making came from the DHRUVA representatives. It was their initiative in leading the discussions that enabled
the committee to arrive at a decision. Another observation was the
absence of women in the standing committee.

When asked about mango procurements, the committee members explained that there was little concern, as the cooperatives were
easily meeting their procurement targets. There were several long-
term contracts with bulk buyers like ITC (for organic mangoes at a

premium of 15 per cent over prevailing rates) in place. Some part of the produce was sent to Vasundhara cooperative for further processing and the rest sold to other big players and in local markets. Mango collection and selling was so lucrative that the cooperatives did not deduct the standard 10 per cent of weight (for weight loss due to moisture) when procuring the fruit, that is, they paid the 'farm-gate price'.

The Impact of Wadi

DHRUVA had commissioned several assessment studies by independent agencies for the wadi project (IRMA 2007; Shah 2005). These studies revealed that wadi income constituted about 40 per cent of total income. The average incomes reported in several villages were just 5 to 10 per cent above the poverty line. Clearly, even if the horticulture income remained stable, any major variations in non-wadi income (above 10 per cent) could bring the average income down to below the poverty line. Hence the stability of income above the poverty line was unlikely to be assured by wadi income alone.

One major objective of the diversification strategy was to deter migration from the village to other areas to augment incomes. While temporary migration for work by the wadi-owning households had declined, it was still positive. The percentage of households from which temporary migration took place had declined, but the average number of days a migrant left the village had actually gone up. It could be due to improved opportunities outside the village, or due to a decline in real wages that made migrants work a larger number of days to earn the same real income. In two of the three villages that we visited, DHRUVA had to return with a YIP because wadi yields had fallen substantially. Without DHRUVA's renewed interventions, migration was likely to have gone up.

In terms of the social impact of the wadi intervention, the biggest gain appeared to be the significant decline in alcohol consumption as the wadi project made it a necessary condition that people who volunteered for the wadi benefits would have to shun alcohol. A large number of people we talked to thought it important to empower women in the process of development. However, we learnt that not much was done in this regard. Women's SHGs had been formed but the numbers were well below the targets set. Only 16 per cent of Ayojana Samiti members were women.

The impact of the wadi on other productive activities was mixed. For instance, while the typical cropping pattern in agriculture was unchanged, there was an increase in the use of both vermicompost as well as chemical fertilisers. The rise in the use of chemical fertilisers and pesticides for the wadi trees ran counter to the spirit of sustainability and environmental conservation. Forestry trees were planted to reduce the dependence on forests for firewood and fuel and prevent cattle from entering the wadis for grazing. While everyone we talked to agreed that the dependence on forests had gone down, many were of the opinion that boundary trees were liquid assets that should be sold in the market, and hence should not be used for self-consumption. This implied that these people were getting their fuel and firewood from the forest. Since the wadis were protected from stray cattle grazing, the total land available for grazing had reduced, leading to a concern about over-intensive grazing on the village commons.

DHRUVA had introduced a four-point grading system of wadis according to their quality, determined by soil and water conditions in a particular garden, which in turn was determined, to some extent, by the quality of the effort put in. One report noted that the variation could be very large, from 15 kg of cashews to 235 kg of cashews in two wadis of similar size but different grades in the same village. In the Dharampur area, around 57 per cent of the wadis were graded in the bottom two categories by DHRUVA. Over and above the grading, there was a cut-off mark based on survival rates of mango and cashew. If less than 25 per cent of the trees survived in a wadi, it was deemed to have dropped out from the project. Hence no further benefit would be provided to the owner. The reasons for this low survival rate could range from poor natural conditions to lack of effort or sheer bad luck. It may be noted that wadis at Dharampur had greater chances of dropping out because of the lower survival rates.

The sophisticated organisational structure, which required the rural population to link with urban markets, probably needed a more commercial mindset which must have been difficult to inculcate. The wadi project was designed to strengthen backward and forward linkages. The challenge was to go beyond individual incentives and to encourage collective responsibilities for improved water and soil management for the entire village. There were efforts made in capacity building and training in new skills for the beneficiaries, and there were well thought out processes and structures in place for marketing of produce and integration of the value chain. The participants were exposed to modern agricultural techniques and practices and got a feel for how a modern marketing enterprise carried out its activities. This was reflected in the significant overshooting of expenditure (against the budgeted amount in the project) in capacity building and participation activities to create people's organisations like GVMs and the Ayojana Samitis.

The wadi project was conceived as an experiment to move tribal people from a situation characterised by 'self-defeatism, alcoholism and dependency' (Shah 2005: 98) into a more positive frame of mind which was characterised by BAIF's philosophy of '*Majoor moto, malik bano*' (become self-reliant rather than be dependent on someone for a livelihood). DHRUVA would be the mediator in this transition.

Dependence

The structure of the cooperatives and the various activities they indulged in made the entire organisational structure large and complex. Without this integration the incomes that could be earned by the wadi owners, left on their own, would be significantly lower and uncertain. A large structure also allowed other complementary activities including the provision of credit flows for production and consumption purposes. Decisions regarding the logistics of collection, of processing and pricing, and assessment of outcomes (like the complicated gradation and rating system of wadis) were almost entirely handled by the DHRUVA professionals. This structure, in our opinion, had become too large and perhaps too complex for the participants to be able to completely take over from DHRUVA. We found that even at the level of the individual wadi, the first effects of the withdrawal of DHRUVA led to a sharp decline in productivity. This in turn induced it to go in for another round of hand holding in the form of the YIP.

The project at its very inception was conceived by a foreign development bank (KfW of Germany) and the Government of India. The implementing agency was a big NGO and NABARD came in as a monitoring agency. All the details of the project had been developed without the participation of the the tribal people who were the beneficiaries. The two main products promoted, cashews and the particular variety of mango, were not indigenous to the region. The challenge was to make the beneficiaries buy-in to the project.

The process that we have described indicated the need to integrate productive activities into the market economy in a significant way. This, according to our understanding, was a novel feature of how modernity could reach out to the traditional sector and transform it to suit the needs of the market-oriented enterprise. The traditional sector was not changed into a full-fledged capitalist enterprise with wage labour and reproducible capital, but it was nevertheless drawn into the complex relationships that facilitate transactions in a market economy. The project emphasised the need for each landowner included in the wadi to think of themselves as entrepreneurs who, through participation in a wider market nexus, would be better off than their brethren in the village. Indeed, we came across an acknowledgement of the growth of the wadi walas who went on to make up a 'wadi class' emerging as a new set of privileged people within the village. The degree of complexity (accounts, pricing decisions, working capital management, quality controls in production, supply chain management, knowledge management, logistics, processing and marketing) that emerged was beyond the capability of the local people. Hence the role of DHRUVA became essential, and any attempt to disengage from the enterprise would be unsustainable (the lessons from the YIP were particularly revealing). The role of DHRUVA as a mediator had become an integral part of the structure to connect small farmers to the world of large markets.

11

Choosing to Change

Located in the middle of India, Chhattisgarh, recently carved out of Madhya Pradesh as a separate state, has one of the lowest population densities and highest forest covers in the country. Home to the largest proportion of tribal population, barring the hilly states of the north-east, it is a relatively less developed state with a Human Development Index (HDI) of 0.358, which is the lowest in India against a national average of 0.467 in 2011 (Planning Commission 2011). Scheduled Castes and Scheduled Tribes (SCs and STs) together constitute more than 50 per cent of the state's population. Of late, Chhattisgarh has been in the news because of the widespread Maoist insurgency there, which, many believe, began as a result of prolonged poverty and underdevelopment (Choudhary 2012). We made field visits to two villages in this state to study the implementation of a scheme called the Village Development Plan (VDP) (see Map 11.1).

The VDP was an initiative launched by the National Bank for Agriculture and Rural Development (NABARD) in 2007 to transform an underdeveloped village through people's participation and financial inclusion by integrating state and central government development initiatives within the village. The need for developmental initiatives would have to be articulated by the villagers themselves through a development plan, which in turn would be implemented and monitored by a democratically elected Village Development Committee (VDC). The core costs of implementing a VDP would not be met by NABARD. It would identify a nodal agency (usually a non-governmental organisation or NGO) to coordinate efforts to bring to the village existing government schemes based on the preferences of the local villagers. Financial outlay from NABARD would be minimal, with the nodal agency receiving some incentives for forming self-help groups (SHGs), Kisan Clubs and a sum of Rs 10,000 per annum

Map 11.1: Jashpur and Raigarh Districts in Chhattisgarh

Chhattisgarh

Jashpur

Raigarh

INDIA

for coordinating all efforts. One backward village was to be identified in each district for the VDP initiative.

To develop the village in an integrated manner, the nodal agency would have to create awareness, take leadership in building the VDC and other community-based organisations (CBOs) and introduce development schemes to the village. This agency also would have to build capacity of the villagers to prepare and implement a plan to improve livelihood opportunities. At the same time, this agency would have to ensure that the village ecosystem and natural resources were not damaged in the process of creation of physical infrastructure. Activities coordinated and supported under the VDP would include application of Participatory Rural Appraisal (PRA) techniques and formation of SHGs, Joint Liability Groups (JLGs) and farmers' clubs to encourage participation. Watershed development and other livelihood-based activities such as wadis (horticulture), skill enhancement and microenterprise development could also be part of the VDP. In addition, the VDP would entail assessment of credit needs, formulation of projects for rural and social development with the support of government-sponsored programmes.

The VDP, prepared through Participatory Rural Appraisal (PRA) techniques, would include developmental activities with credit support from banks or promotional support from NABARD or other government agencies. The VDC would monitor the programme on a routine basis. Further, a monitoring committee at the district level, including representatives from other stakeholders, would review progress on a quarterly basis. Key focus areas of the VDP included a family-centric approach to lending, 100 per cent financial inclusion and popularisation of the Kisan Credit Card (KCC). Hence, economic activities were to be taken up by people as individual enterprises facilitated by the availability of credit and market linkages. Infrastructure would be planned to support these individual enterprises.

We visited Kapartunga and Barpani in the Raigarh and Jashpur districts of Chhattisgarh in January 2011. These villages were adopted by NABARD for a VDP intervention in 2007. Kapartunga was located just 18 km from its block headquarters at Sarangarh (and 72 km from the district headquarters), and connected by metal road. Barpani, in the Jashpur district, lay almost 200 km away from Raigarh town and almost 500 km from the state capital; it had poor connectivity, and did not even have electricity till after 2007 as the transformer installed near the village was defunct. The nodal agency responsible for implementing VDP in Kapartunga was the Raigarh Sahyog Samiti (RSS), a local NGO headquartered at Raigarh. For Barpani, the corresponding organisation was an offshoot of the RSS, headquartered at Duldula town near the village.

Kapartunga

Kapartunga had 181 families with a population of around 781 people, with 397 females. Families were single units and not joint families. The village population was mixed; 29 people were from SCs, 326 were members of STs (predominantly Gond), 387 people were from Other Backward Classes and around 39 people belonged to the general category. Around 57 per cent of the villagers were literate, 75 per cent families lived below the poverty line, and one-third were landless. The villagers were dependent on the adjoining forests for firewood as well as *mahua*. Major crops grown were paddy, groundnut and vegetables. Other means of livelihood included small business and trades such as carpentry, masonry and ironmongery. In addition to being backward, this village was chosen because of its proximity and connectivity with Raigarh. This meant that if the VDP programme was successful then the village would be convenient to showcase as a model. RSS was of the opinion that the size of the village, 181 families, was ideal, not too large to be affected by the complications of village politics, and not too small for the impact not to be noticeable and replicable.

At Kapartunga, we were welcomed to the community hall by a well-to-do farmer named Gangadhar Patel (one of the many Patels in the welcoming committee) who delivered a formal welcome address. He rued the lack of cooperation and group work prior to 2007 before the advent of NABARD. In this village, the word 'NABARD' was used to refer to the NGO as Raigarh Sahyog Samiti was too long a name and its acronym, RSS, had political connotations (RSS is often used in reference to the Rashtriya Swayamsevak Sangh, a Hindu nationalist group with political connections). In 2007, the villagers were wary of outsiders; the general belief was that the outsider represented corporate interests and for every freebie they distributed they would take back double the amount. However 'NABARD' persisted, and its continuous encouragement ultimately yielded results.

Gangadhar reminisced that the relatively larger farmers who were net sellers of grain had to take their grain for selling to a government procurement centre located around 25 km away. The general waiting time in the centre was 15 days unless one could bribe the government official to jump the queue, the rate for which was Rs 10 per quintal. The alternative was to sell the grain to *bicholiyas* or intermediaries who would pay Rs 100–Rs 150 less per quintal than the government minimum support price. With respect to banking, the village had acquired a bad reputation as there were some loan defaulters in the past. Most of the villagers used to depend on the seth sahukars for their loans. Rates were Rs 60 for every Rs 100 loaned annually, and people preferred to go to moneylenders *outside* their village. Education was not given much priority either. Alcoholism was a huge problem.

According to the RSS, the greatest challenge was to get the attention of the villagers to listen to what they had to say. Conversations about development followed much later. The villagers had seen people from the government, recovery agents from the banks and even some politicians, but had not ever heard of NABARD or of any NGOs. Efforts were made at addressing groups of villagers and attempting to identify influential people from among them. From these, select people were co-opted into the RSS as employees. This sent a strong signal about the intent of the NGO as employment opportunities in the village were rare. The new employees also served as a bridge between the NGO and the villagers. In addition to a focus on financial inclusion, the RSS conducted targeted interventions to build their credibility. Ten below poverty line (BPL) households were selected and a rainwater harvesting structure coupled with a sanitary toilet system was set up for them by the RSS with funds from the Council for Advancement of People's Action and Rural Technology (CAPART). Villagers were trained on superior agricultural practices such as line cultivation (as against random sowing) and they claimed that yield per hectare had risen by over 30 per cent.

The VDP process started with the RSS conducting a PRA. This helped in identifying the concerns of the villagers and their priorities for change. Following this, common areas and physical spaces to locate or upgrade infrastructure were identified. The entire village was involved in drawing a resource map of the village with RSS's guidance. During this activity, consensus would be needed on many common services, which would serve as the cornerstone of micro-level planning for the village. The RSS claimed that women were equally involved in the PRA process. To encourage participation, focus group discussions were conducted by RSS in communities who would not come forward to represent their views in a larger group. It took around four months to build confidence and to start conversing about development in their village. Some of the not-so-usual needs voiced by the villagers included toilets, stop-dams and *nullahs*. Drinking water was a persistent demand made by all.

The first realisation from the PRA was that people in the village were averse to working together. The RSS struggled to form farmers clubs among the men and SHGs among women. Capacity building was a key activity. Health camps, seed distribution missions and other promotional campaigns were conducted as confidence builders. It took over two years for the villagers to get over their inhibitions and start making specific demands. Exposure visits played a major role in this as villagers were able to visualise how their village could change. They visited Sirpur, a nearby town and other wadis in the state to observe development projects. Interacting with other villagers and exchanging notes with them helped generate interest and confidence. The RSS acted as a liaising agent between government bodies and the villagers, ensuring that when government officials visited, the villagers were given a patient hearing. Over time, the villagers were able to articulate their problems directly in front of government officials. This was crucial since the official's time and ability to identify local needs were limited. The villagers were now able to demand the introduction of available schemes in their village, with the RSS facilitating their awareness.

A big achievement of the VDP was getting the government to open a grain procurement centre in 2010 in the village as a result of which sellers of grain would not have to travel far distances (see Plate 11.1). In addition, four permanent (clerical) jobs, and around 30 temporary jobs (for 25 days between November and February) had been created at this centre. Between November 2010 and January 2011, over Rs 4 million worth of grain had been procured from this village and 22 other villages in the vicinity. The procurement centre had been set up on common land, which had been privately occupied

Plate 11.1: The New Government Grain Procurement Centre at Kapartunga

in the past. The occupants had willingly given it up for the greater good of the village.

Attendance in schools had increased substantially and vacancies for teaching posts filled up. Till even two years back, the school had been running on contributions from individual members for teachers' salaries. With government support, the quality of schooling had improved. Through a state government scheme, girls in classes nine and 10 were given bicycles, and schooling till class 10 was assured. One tribal commented: 'The best thing about schools is that the brain gets sharper as a result'. In addition, an adivasi hostel had been sanctioned and was being built in some of the common land near the village school to house children from areas that were further away. The villagers were happy with this arrangement as with more children attending classes the school would be viable.

According to the villagers, the role of politics in development had changed over the years. In the past, politics deterred development, but at present people were beginning to leverage their respective leanings and political connections to bring in and hasten change. The elected panchayat of this village had not been very active in the past, with politicians shunning the village as being too insignificant a vote bank. Hence, when enough confidence had been generated in the RSS, it decided to ensure that energetic members were elected unopposed to the village panchayat. Though formally elected, the Kapartunga panchayat was effectively a selected one. We met 38-year-old Chanda Kumari, wife of Jagatram Patel, who was being referred to as the SP (sarpanch pati, or husband of the sarpanch). She was the sarpanch of the village (a seat reserved for women), yet when we interacted with her she was dull and listless and hardly spoke. There were whispers that she was mentally unwell, which is why it took a lot of persuasion on our part to be able to arrange a meeting with her. Husbands of the women in power in the panchayat appeared to be more vocal than their wives.

The current village panchayat had been active with schemes such as deepening of village waterbodies, governance of schools, construction of a *samudayik bhavan* (community hall), and making of roads. The villagers had also been involved, through the panchayat, for the clearing and levelling of land for common spaces for infrastructure such as building a rural mart. A health camp was conducted for the villagers a year ago at Sarangarh with the help of the Marwari Seva Samiti. With respect to health care, there were active and trained health workers (*meetaneen*) in the village for the past two years. Family planning was encouraged and the meetaneens were given incentives to ensure that child delivery took place in hospitals. The villagers expressed interest to have a primary health centre (PHC) located in the village as the nearest one was over 6 km away. Alcoholism had been brought under control, mainly through greater awareness about its health implications, with the villagers not brewing their own alcohol inside the village any more. Brewing mahua was a common practice in the past, as the village folk had plenty of free time because they were practicing mono-cropping. A government approved liquor shop, however, operated in the village.

The VDP brought to the village a visibility as a result of which other government line departments brought their schemes into the village. A Jan Samasya Nivaran Shivir was held in the village in 2010 — a big honour for this backward village. This meant that the District Collector (DC), along with all line department heads, was present at Kapartunga to meet all the villagers. The villagers had even approached the chief minister (CM) for help in upgrading the village secondary school to class 12. The villagers claimed that they engaged in a lot of open debate and discussions on development issues. Travel expenses incurred for meeting government officials for providing common assets and services were defrayed from a kitty made of voluntary donations.

With respect to banking, all villagers were linked to the bank either through their own bank accounts or through KCCs, or through SHG accounts. While the women were dependent on the menfolk for transport to the bank, in the bank they were quite comfortable filling the forms and completing formalities. It was preferred that the women operate the bank accounts as the banks were generally crowded and there were separate, shorter, queues for women. The *seth sahukars*, who also ran the *kirana* shops, were getting little or no moneylending business from the village and were now requesting the farmers' club members to assist them in getting a KCC so that they also had access to loans. After the VDP intervention, all farmers had become members of the Kisan Clubs.

A farmers' (Sahayak Azad Krishak Club) club had opened a fertiliser store in the village with Rs 10,000 of its own and a grant of Rs 40,000 from the government the previous year. The nearest fertiliser store, at Salar which was around 6 km away, charged higher rates than this club. Vermicomposting was also encouraged, but not practiced on a commercial scale with households generating just enough organic fertiliser for self-consumption. The Sahayak Azad Krishak Club had earned a good reputation and had been identified by the Regional Rural Bank as one of eight in the entire state to act as business facilitators for the villagers. This included opening new bank accounts (for which they got Rs 10 per account as incentive), loan mobilisation and recovery (for which they got 0.5 per cent of the loan), formation of JLGs (an incentive of Rs 1,500) and facilitating KCCs by providing them assistance in obtaining loans and making repayments. This club had helped the formation of two JLGs, where the individuals were involved in a bouquet of activities — from running a paan shop, a restaurant (referred to as a hotel which also served meals), a snack shop, to carpentry, cycle repair, and masonry. It had set up a *krishi yantra* bank for agricultural implements (see Plate 11.2). The implements, including seed drills, hoes, ploughs and handpumps, donated

Plate 11.2: List of Farm Implements and their Rental Rates at the Krishi Yantra Bank

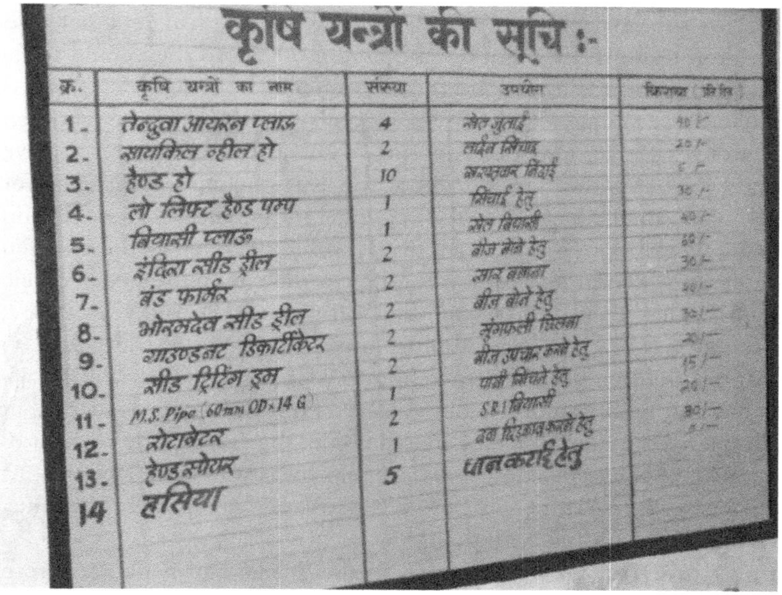

by NABARD, were loaned to any farmer at publicly displayed rates on a per day basis which were significantly lower than the market rates. Since there already were nine privately available tractors in the village, the Kisan Club was contemplating procuring a harvester as part of its agri-tool bank.

The state pisciculture department encouraged fish cultivation in common waterbodies through the SHGs. The agriculture department provided a 75 per cent subsidy for the procurement of pump sets. Sprinklers had been given to all farmers and foot-sprayers for pesticides made available at Rs 1,200 (as against Rs 3,000 in the market). To encourage entrepreneurship, NABARD had offered a grant of Rs 15,000 to set up a poultry unit. Only one villager, Arjun Patel, took advantage of this offer, and, starting out with 200 chicks, was successful in converting what was meant to be just a demonstration unit into a thriving commercial venture. He had obtained a return of Rs 50,000 in the first year. He was also in-charge of the midday meal programme in the village school.

Despite all this progress, aspirations for the next generation were clearly *naukri chakri karengey*, that is, they would be employed in a salaried job. Barsha Kumari, an illiterate farmer, had sent her two children to a private school in a different village so they could study and get government jobs. If not government, she would also be satisfied with corporate jobs. She was not concerned whether her children worked at Bhilai, Delhi or America — she just wanted them to have good jobs. Another farmer whose son was obtaining a diploma for practicing medicine wished for a hospital in the village where his son could work. Many villagers felt that it would be best if all the children could get government jobs according to their training in the village itself. Sridhar Patel, whose son was a software engineer in New Jersey, strongly felt that job opportunities must be created in the village so that the children need not leave home. When asked what would happen if the RSS withdrew, the villagers expressed deep concern, but also were confident that they would not let the village slide backwards because of the *samudayik jagrukta* (collective awareness) attained. As evidence, they shared with us an ambitious dairy project that they were now discussing with the RSS.

It was evident that all families in the village had benefitted from the VDP scheme, measured in terms of physical assets or increase in incomes. The families that benefited the most were the ones with relatively more land. One such success story was the case of Siddhartha Jaiswal, a progressive farmer with over 15 acres of land, who had taken up cultivation of tissue culture bananas, promoted under VDP activities. As a result of banana cultivation, his earning trebled from the time when he would cultivate rice. With respect to multi-cropping, he, like many other farmers, had planted haldi or turmeric and *arbi* (a tuber) in the shade as well as legumes and mustard as a safety net in case the rice crop failed. He employed agricultural labour in the field, as he was busy with administrative activities of the panchayat and his Kisan Club. Moreover, a tube well on his land served as the main water source for a large fraction of the village population. At the other end of the income spectrum, Muralimanohar, a landless villager, worked as a *raajmistry* (mason), whom the RSS had trained as a specialist in making rainwater harvesting structures, septic tanks and biogas harvesting units. He was happier than before as he had more work on his hands now. His choice of profession was different from his parents, both of whom were tattoo artists. The villagers were hopeful that his wife would pick up the art of tattooing from her in-laws to keep the tradition of tattooing alive.

The RSS claimed that the VDP had been able to mobilise around Rs 10 million as development expenses for Kapartunga between 2007 and 2010. Most of the villagers were insured, a positive fallout of the RSS being a registered life insurance agent. Moreover, Kapartunga had become the nerve centre of another wadi project involving 21 villages around it and of a watershed scheme for two adjoining villages. This meant that the RSS and NABARD would continue to assist the villagers of Kapartunga for another five to seven years.

Barpani

Although development agents are accustomed to some resistance when intervening for the first time in a new village, the experience at Barpani was particularly challenging. The villagers accused the NGO of being from a corporate house. They alleged that the NGO was promoting plantations only as a means to grab land, and that they had evidence that this was indeed the case in an adjoining district. The accusations were specific and the villagers even named the village in which this had happened. The truth was that while the villagers had accurate information with respect to the corporate acquisition, the NGO was never involved. The NGO was involved in another village with a similar name. To gain confidence, the NGO immediately organised a visit of the people who had made the allegations to the village in which they were accused of land grabbing to convince them that they had no such interests. If the villagers' suspicion was not challenging enough, the attitude of the collector was. He could not understand the concept of convergence in a VDP; if the people wanted a wadi, then it was NABARD's job to provide one — he did not see the role of the district administration. Much later, when the collector was called to inaugurate some of the innovations at Barpani, he was annoyed that the villagers were doing so well despite the apathy of the government. He commented that they might as well build a road to the village using *shramdaan* (voluntary labour) instead of approaching him for assistance!

When we visited the village and were taken to the church for a meeting, we were impressed with this very tight, disciplined and

cohesive group of men and women who almost automatically seg-
regated themselves by gender on two sides of the church. Sushant
Minch of the Surajmukhi Sanstha (sunflower SHG) described how
in 2007 social workers from the NGO and NABARD had created
awareness about what they could do once they were linked with a
bank and started availing of government schemes. It took three to four
visits by the NGO before the villagers even started listening. The villagers initially thought that bank linkage meant they would be asked
to pay money; opening a bank account would mean losing their land
as the bank would lay claim on it. Any outsider was believed to be
a bank recovery agent. Sushant asserted that the nurturing of a culture to cooperate and work together was perhaps the greatest benefit
of the VDP. This assertion of Sushant's was revealing as roads and
electricity were two major visible changes brought about by the VDP.
Kisan Club members shared their work in the field, with each landowner paying the other for services rendered. By working in turns on
each others' farms, they ensured an equitable pooling of labour. On
an average, most people here had 5 to 6 acres of land, but almost half
the land was *banjar* (wasteland). The crops planted include *nigoo* (small
sunflower), other oilseeds and pulses. These were being encouraged as
plantation in the wastelands as part of a watershed project. Cooperation was so strong that the villagers facilitated the provision of electricity in their village by transporting the transformer from Pathalgaon, a
nearby town, to their village with the help of contributions — Rs 50
per family. They shared the costs of setting up poles and drawing
electric lines. Even the village health centre that was supposed to be
run by the government was maintained and staffed by community
efforts.

The villagers appeared to have no expectations from the panchayat
system. While there were at least two panchayat members among
the villagers we met, they had been unable to contribute to the governance of the villages that they were supposed to serve. This was
because the panchayat *sachiv* (secretary) was frequently replaced, as
the incumbent would almost always be suspended on grounds of
corruption.

The villagers appeared to be very excited about the various changes
that had taken place. This was palpable from their positive attitude
and optimism. Women were no longer shy to speak to strangers.

Moreover, women shared their problems with each other and tried to solve them on a collective basis. The women believed that the NGO's role in the village was all-encompassing. In the past, it was customary to deliver babies in the home, resulting in mortality during childbirth. The meetaneen system coupled with immediate disbursement of a monetary incentive when a mother was brought to the local hospital for delivery had arrested this. The NGO had set up a health centre, a crèche (*baalwaan*), and also provided direct employment to four girls from the village. Indirect employment was also being generated through a watershed project that had just commenced. Nutrition levels in the village had increased as the children had tasty and more nutritious food in the baalwaan and demanded similar food at home.

The NGO was also instrumental in getting the Additional Chief Secretary of the state to come to the village and listen to the demands of the villagers. This civil servant was originally from the same region and belonged to the same tribe. His visit resulted in positive outcomes for the village, namely road connectivity and electricity. The NGO also empowered the women's SHGs through awareness drives, which resulted in a sharp decline in human trafficking, which was rampant in the past. However, one of the very first concerns raised by the women, the need for water, had not been fully met yet.

The NGO had introduced several other livelihood opportunities such as lac making, beekeeping, pisciculture, multi-cropping, tailoring, pickle making, candle making (for local consumption), and baking (a community oven was being made when we visited) (see Plate 11.3). A case of moving up the value chain was evident in the activity of *chiraunji* (an Indian spice) de-skinning, because of the value addition in the process. Raw chiraunji sold at Rs 25–Rs 30 per kg compared to the processed version which sold at Rs 300–Rs 350 per kg. The villagers had procured a machine for processing the chiraunji. Some of the village youth had been trained as drivers, but they now realised that they needed to be trained as mechanics. Despite these new opportunities, most of the women did not want their children to return to the village; many had sons and daughters studying in tribal boarding schools away from the village and they hoped they would find salaried jobs in the cities and towns. Young men seemed to be curiously missing. When coming away we heard that one or two young

Plate 11.3: Tailoring Enterprise at Barpani

men would disappear for 10–15 days and come back with a lot of money to spend. Stories went around that they were being trained by the Maoists.

In the past, due to impoverished conditions, this village had witnessed severe distress migration and alcohol and drug addictions. Often children went to school with only a drink of mahua (a local intoxicant) given to them by their parents since there was no food. The mahua would provide some calories to sustain them. It was not surprising to see the disproportionately high number of widows (30 to 40) in the village because their husbands had died due to alcoholism and drug abuse. At present, the sale of alcohol had virtually stopped in the village except during the festival season. The villagers asserted that it was not the NGO's constant sermonising that had brought this change. Rather it was the threat made by the Maoists to administer 52 beatings to anyone who returned to the village in a drunken state that had helped rid the entire village of alcohol addiction. Around 15 to 20 men from this village had gone as far as Punjab for employment as migrants almost two decades ago. At that time they would earn Rs 100 a day for their (agricultural) labour exclusive of food.

They had now returned, as had some retirees who were employed in the armed forces. The men reiterated that their primary concern was the availability of water, to which no solution had yet been found. They articulated the urgent need for a bore well.

In addition to the VDP, NABARD was implementing a watershed programme in this village. The secretary of the watershed was Sebastian Minch, who was also the preacher of the church. He discussed how the villagers had realised their plight long ago but they were unable to bring about change till the NGO stepped in and started assisting them. With respect to the watershed, with only preparatory work done, the water table had already risen by a perceptible 3 ft to 4 ft. The Kisan Club had adopted new cropping practices, which had resulted in a fourfold increase of yield. An additional 60 acres of wasteland had been brought under cultivation, where both organic (vermicompost) and chemical fertilisers were used.

We asked the villagers what their dreams were for the village in the near future. They responded that they would like a motorcycle and television in every house and a passenger car service operated by the Kisan Club to Jharkhand (a neighbouring state, whose capital was the nearest big city for the village) at least twice (preferably thrice) daily. Also high on their wish list were a tailoring and ready-made garments store in the village, cultivating wheat as a crop, like in Punjab, and floriculture. Although there were five community toilets at the time of our visit, the villagers wanted individual toilets for each household. They also wanted an *angrezi* (English medium) school in the village as the government school was not good enough.

When asked what if NABARD disengaged from the programme, the overall response was positive — the villagers believed that development would continue. There were some others who were not as optimistic — some felt that handling the government agencies (*shashakgan*) independent of the NGO would be a challenge as the government bodies might not give enough attention to the villagers and projects would get delayed indefinitely.

Seeking Development: Whose Voice and to What Effect?

The VDP would require the identification of a poorly motivated backward village to transform it. The NGO's primary role was to encourage the people to 'seek' development from a basket of available schemes. It was like a greenfield project where the challenge could be large, but once the initial breakthrough was made, delivery could be easy and uncomplicated. This required a lot of tenacity and an ability to relate to the needs of the locals, for which an NGO with local roots would have a great deal of advantage. In addition to linking the villagers to banks for financial inclusion, the NGO would facilitate the implementation of schemes of the government by working closely with its line departments. No new schemes were to be conceived, but a convergence or integration of all available schemes would be attempted.

Clearly the concept of a VDP was a reflection of the failure of government processes to reach the neediest people. In both the villages, one common response was that the neglect was due to the fact that the village and its adjoining hamlets never had a member of the legislative assembly or parliament elected from amongst them. The people's expectation that local needs were to be met by local representatives alone was a telling indictment of Indian democracy where people's representatives focused on the immediate interests of a narrow segment of their constituency. Getting things done from state agencies required personal connections and efforts. The Additional Chief Secretary and the DC's stories (they were both ready to act since they hailed from the same region) were instances of local identity-based politics.

The VDP was based on a village level integrated plan in which the villagers decided *themselves* the projects they thought would be most beneficial to them. In this sense the plan was about the villagers choosing the changes they desired in an entirely bottom-up manner. Thus the outcome of the VDP would be unique to each village, catering to their specific needs and aspirations. There were two implications of this design. First, in the absence of any development intervention, motivating people to come together could be difficult. People could be moved to act if they perceived individual (or family) gains. It would be much more difficult to move people if the gains were collective, benefitting all the villagers. Second, in the absence of strong and functional PRIs, it was most likely that the relatively well-to-do villagers, who were either landed or educated or both, would take the lead and the initiative in prioritising the village's needs.

Hence, with individual schemes and private interests the development interventions chosen could have an element of bias in favour of the local 'rich and powerful'. These people themselves could be very poor even by the entire district's benchmark, but they were relatively better off in the microcosm of the village. Correcting the element of bias in the plan would have to come from suggestions made by the NGO, who would have to play an active role. For instance, this correction could entail designing exclusive schemes for people below the poverty line or introducing schemes to create public assets like roads and rural haats.

Most government schemes that were implemented under the VDP were for individuals who would have to possess some assets or financial resources to avail them. For instance, schemes that offered subsidies on purchase of pump sets or digging of a borewell would not even be applicable to landless farmers. Schemes that benefitted common property resources, such as forestland, waterbodies and the village commons, were few and far between. This is not to argue that collective action was not encouraged. SHGs were promoted to encourage banking habits and members trained to tap supplementary livelihood opportunities. The SHGs were instrumental in forming the basis for the JLGs and Kisan Clubs. In all these collective fora, the final channelising of resources was aimed at the individual, and the benefits need not have been distributed evenly amongst all members.

In both villages, the articulate natural leaders were well-off by local standards. The Patels in Kapartunga had 10 or more acres of irrigated land (in a rain-fed agricultural belt where having any land, let alone irrigated land, was a privilege) and theirs were the most active faces of the village. The landless and the uneducated adults were the silent crowd that moved along with us to 'make up the numbers'. In the much poorer village of Barpani, the leaders were men who had seen the world: the preacher, the ex-military men, and the workers who had once gone to Punjab as migrants and had seen prosperous agriculture. The woman who was the most articulate leader was again from a household that had more than 5 acres of land. In this village where only one farmer was landless, the distribution of landholdings was not as uneven as in Kapartunga. This might account for the greater levels of camaraderie that we observed in Barpani.

The impact of the VDP was unfolding over time. In Kapartunga, the NGO took over two years to make a breakthrough to get people together to meet and discuss the needs of the village. The village moneylender had refused to cooperate and still did not come to meetings. But the overwhelming majority of villagers now thought that there were some benefits from participating. There were a lot of expectations amongst the villagers in Kapartunga about impending benefits from the VDP. The national TV channel had recorded their success story, a government grain procurement centre was set up in the village and Kapartunga was playing the leader's role in a watershed project between its two adjoining villages, and a wadi (private orchards) project involving 21 villages in the neighbourhood. All this was pretty heady stuff. Yet the observable outcomes were not as dramatic. The initial trees given for the kitchen gardens had died, and the initial income rise in the village in 2008 had been deeply eroded by a bad harvest in 2010.

In Barpani, the energy level seemed to be remarkably high. People were upbeat about their prospects of the good life. A smaller and poorer village than Kapartunga, it was culturally more homogeneous with 56 out of 61 households belonging to the Christian faith. The landholding pattern was more even, the cultural ties stronger, and the willingness to learn deeper in this village. We did not observe a great deal of change. But for the people in Barpani, the road connecting their village to the state highway (some 7 km or 8 km) and the arrival of electricity was like a long-standing dream come true. However this dream was realised by a bit of luck because the Additional Chief Secretary at that time originally hailed from the same tribe. The villagers were proud of the reduction in the costly dependence on hooch (local mahua and *handia*). Most people felt that change was possible and had just begun; they had dreams of moving from cycles to motorcycles, to even having a passenger vehicle. It was still early days, but in this village the pathway to change was likely to be more collective and participatory in nature.

Conclusions

Despite the encouragement of collective effort and organisation in the VDP, the benefits were parcelled out as individual gains and hence may have aggravated local inequalities. Expectations were dramatically changing for all, yet the observable changes were incremental. Indeed, the government schemes were designed to provide only incremental gains to the beneficiaries. There were new aspirations about their children, hoping they would achieve something that their parents had not been able to, and their dreams lay in urban spaces, often geographically far away. Distress migration had declined but children were moving out for education. Gender empowerment was ambiguous (see Box 11.1). The wide prevalence of SHGs had undoubtedly brought women to the forefront, but effectively power continued to be wielded by the men. The term SP, and our experience with Kapartunga's sarpanch, indicated that empowerment in Chhattisgarh was more formal than substantial. However, it was a beginning and by the time the young girls of the village grew up things could be different. The tired faces of many of the older women appeared to be scanning the horizon to see if change was discernible in the future. At least their menfolk would not sell their daughters to buy liquor (see Box 11.2).

Box 11.1: The Unimportance of Being a Woman

Sharada Devi, with about 2 acres of rain-fed land, runs a kirana shop. Her husband is a practicing 'doctor' (without a formal degree) and a member of the Kisan Club. The locals say that for the family there never is enough money; why else would Sharada's husband permit her to run a shop, mingling with all kinds of strangers! None of her children have any interest in farming, as they 'cannot waste time in the farms while they are busy getting an education'. Of the 12 people in her SHG, nine have land and three have 'less' land — the ones with less land work in the landed neighbour's plot in exchange for half the produce. During the harvest, labour is hard to get and the harvesting process is time-consuming and expensive. Hence the SHG prefers renting a harvester at Rs 1,000–Rs 1,500 for the job. The RSS had provided all the SHGs a set of saplings to grow around their plots of cultivable land. When asked about these saplings, she first claimed that they were still in sapling form and then confessed that most of what they had planted died due to lack of water and human care, and grazing by goats.

Sharada shared with us how when the RSS first came to the village, the NGO workers met the '*ghar ke mukhia*' (head of the household) multiple times but there was no real interaction with the women. We learnt that women talk to outsiders only after permission from the mukhia and this was true even for her interaction with us. In her mid-30s, Sharada wisely claimed that the most important contribution of RSS was to bring the women together to form SHGs and control alcoholism. To deter alcoholism, the Gram Vikas Samiti levied fines on consuming alcohol in the daytime. She was quite worried that if the RSS disengaged from the village then the menfolk might slide back into old ways. If she had a choice, Sharada said she would like to travel out of the village and meet new people and learn new things. When we asked her about the next major development initiative in the village, namely the wadi, her reply was apathetic. She candidly claimed that all such decisions were taken by influential menfolk, and she did not understand their games of power and politics.

Box 11.2: Transformation of an Addict

Sushant Minch, who was coordinating our discussions at Barpani church, asked a gentleman named Hemantraj to share with us his past and how the NGO's intervention had changed his life.

Hemantraj left Barpani village to join the Border Security Force (BSF) in the early 1990s. However, he was soon discharged due to health reasons; he suffered from irrational fears. He returned to the village and became an alcoholic, while indulging in tobacco and *ganja* (cannabis) as well. The change brought about by the NGO had helped him tremendously in a personal capacity. He had stopped drinking, smoking and consuming drugs. He explained to us with a missionary zeal that three bans should come into effect immediately in the village — *charaibandi, nashabandi* and *jangalkatabandi* (ban on free grazing, addiction and felling trees). He now worked on his own land and also as a labourer on the watershed project. Though the productivity of his land had increased he still emphasised the need for assured supplies of adequate water. He realised the benefits of planting fruit trees and had protected his plantation using tyres as fencing. He told us that he had learnt many things from his visit to the orange plantations in Nagpur, which was organised by the NGO. He had learnt from experience that for any development activity there was a need for clear land records and explicit permission from the owners to avoid complications and delays.

He had six children of whom five were girls. He shared with all of us that he had actually sold two of his daughters for money during the days when he was an alcoholic. From his matter-of-fact tone and the villagers' responses we gathered that this was not an uncommon practice in the region. Of the remaining three, one was in Mumbai on her own volition (presumably working as a sex worker), one was in Jashpur studying in a hostel where she got a stipend, and the other stayed with him. His only son was in class seven and he hoped he would grow up to serve the country, maybe in the BSF as his father had done.

12

Women, Water and Green Energy

Our case study of a tribal area in the East Godavari district of Andhra Pradesh (AP) was about the creation of a common property resource (CPR) that was not entirely natural, and yet was derived from natural resources. The project was novel in many other ways too. The fruits of successful collective action would not result in any direct improvement of personal incomes (except for three or four individuals who would be employed directly for project management). Gains from the project would be for the community as a whole, and used exclusively for the accumulation of other commonly owned assets. The overall supervision of the project would be left to local women.

The project was the construction of a set of mini hydel power plants (MHPPs) along the Yelleru River with public funds. The critical resource for the project was the Yelleru River as a natural capital asset and its ecosystem. The project, on completion, would generate and sell electricity to the grid. The net surplus (after meeting all costs and charges) would be available to the villagers, from which they could create common resources like schools, hospitals and roads in the village and its neighbourhood. This was a novel experiment in 'build and transfer-to-operate'. The power plants, once completed, would be operated and maintained by a committee formed by the local villagers, consisting almost entirely of people drawn from the community. The leadership of the management committee would have to be drawn only from women members chosen by the villagers themselves. The financing of the project came from the Rural Infrastructure Development Fund (RIDF) of the Government of India.

The purpose of RIDF is to promote innovation in the rural and agricultural sector and to ensure that good infrastructure projects are not stalled because of a lack of funds. The specific projects to be funded are decided keeping in mind the sectoral priorities of the government, and the new projects recommended by the different departments of the state governments. The projects chosen are typically very small ticket projects but with a large impact. For instance, the building of a concrete bridge across a small *nullah* (stream) could improve road connectivity for a large number of people. RIDF is a demand-driven non-concessional scheme where finances are provided in the form of loans from NABARD to the state government which implements the project through local government institutions and line departments, or through public-private partnerships (PPPs). NABARD has no role in implementing or monitoring the RIDF projects; this is the responsibility of the state government.

An MHPP produces electricity (usually above 1,000 MW at peak capacity) by using the energy from the flowing water of a river. The electricity generated is typically fed to the power grid for distribution. The power can also be locally consumed if there is adequate neighbourhood demand. The plant is supposed to function as a run-of-river system where water passing through the generator is directed back to the stream without the need of a reservoir. Maintenance costs are lower and longevity higher compared to larger hydels.

However, concerns about such projects persist. Mere availability of water flows is not enough to set up a hydel project. The choice of location has to be optimised across several parameters. The electrical potential of small streams, the distance of the plant site from the stream and from the location where the energy is to be consumed, and the costs of components such as batteries and inverters have to be taken into account. It is not up-scalable, and during dry months with weaker flows of water, power generation may be seriously hindered. Since one MHPP is unlikely to have any serious impact on the local ecology, a river or stream is usually harnessed for more than one plant. If too many such plants are set up, however, the stress can become substantial. Further, there have been instances where the lure of private profits led to forests being cleared to set up plant sites near natural streams (Ganeriwal and Bharadwaj 2011). Finally, the lifetime of an MHPP is around 10 to 12 years, by which time the flow of the river and the local ecology gets altered even without the usual problems associated with the construction of a reservoir.

Institutional Arrangements

This particular project emerged from the union government's thrust on increasing power generation from green sources. The Non-conventional Energy Development Corporation of Andhra Pradesh Limited (NEDCAP) had been set up as the nodal agency for promoting and managing green energy by the AP government. Given the restrictions on transfer of land in tribal areas and the potential of generating green energy from such relatively sparsely populated regions, the state had incorporated a separate agency, the Andhra Pradesh Tribal Power Company Limited (APTRIPCO), to explore the feasibility of harnessing green energy from these areas. Much like any private promoter, the APTRIPCO had to get its projects sanctioned by NEDCAP and link up with the state-owned power transmission company, Andhra Pradesh Power Transmission Company (APTRANSCO), to connect and sell power to the state energy grid. APTRIPCO's shares were owned by the various Integrated Tribal Development Agency (ITDAs) and Andhra Pradesh Scheduled Tribes Cooperative Finance Corporation Limited (TRICOR) in Hyderabad. It had a mandate to establish mini hydel power plants by involving local tribal women's organisations, and ensure that the entire profits from such projects would accrue to the tribals for developing the local areas. This was in consonance with ITDA's objective of socio-economic development of tribal communities through income-generating schemes, infrastructure development and protection of tribal communities from exploitation. This project had APTRIPCO and ITDA as two important stakeholders.

Genesis

The topography of East Godavari makes it ideal for locating sites for hydroelectric power generation (see Map 12.1). In this context a private company had surveyed the region, and identified the river Yelleru as a potential water body to tap for hydroelectric power. They surveyed the annual water flow and water discharges and mapped rainfall patterns. Based on their results they submitted a project plan to NEDCAP for approval. NEDCAP, however, could not approve the project as it involved some land acquisition to set up the power plant and divert the river. This land was in tribal settlements, and hence private

Map 12.1: East Godavari District in Andhra Pradesh

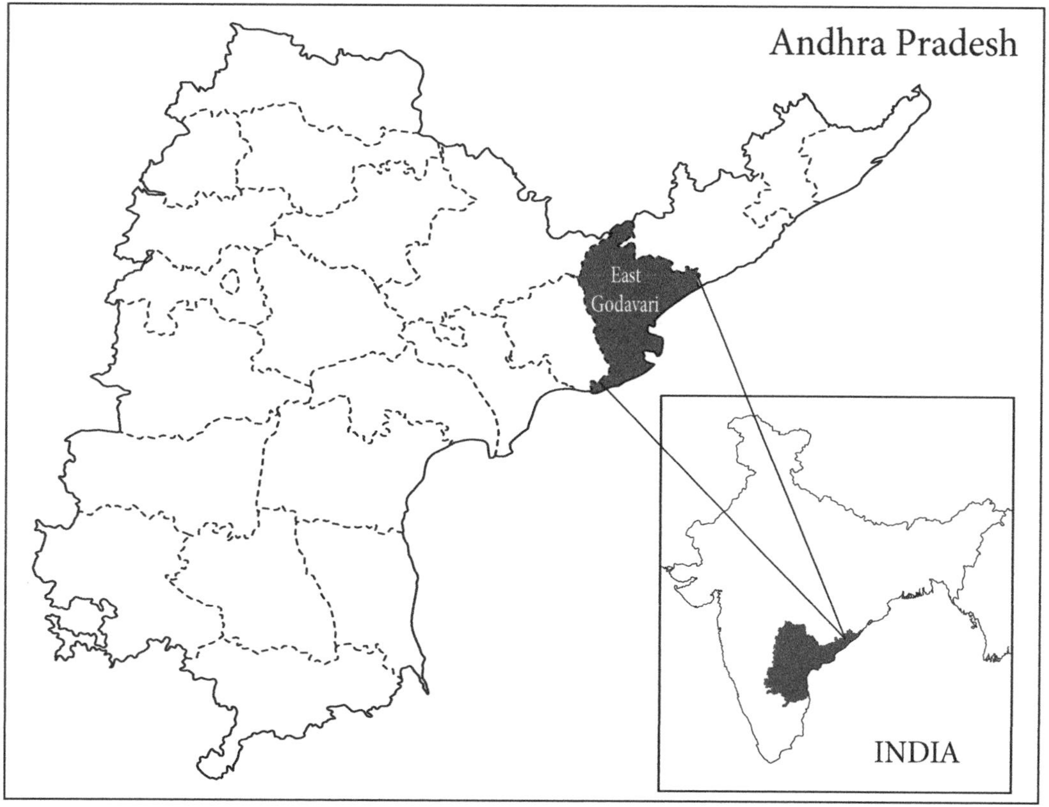

operators could not be given permission to acquire the land. However, the efforts of the private company were not in vain. Prerana Devi, the commissioner of ITDA at that time, was approached by NEDCAP, and she decided to take up the project through APTRIPCO. Clearly this was a project where participation was sought from above; it was not an instance of participation generated by people demanding intervention.

By around 2005, based on the initial surveys and assessments already conducted, APTRIPCO chose three sites on the Yelleru River, where a slight diversion of the river water could be used to generate power. The nearest town for all these sites, Addateegala, was small and sparsely populated; the tehsil itself had a population of around 40,000. The three sites chosen were located in Vetamamidi, Mitlapalem and Pinjarikonda villages. The projects were funded through the RIDF and from a subsidy scheme of the Ministry of New and Renewable Energy (MNRE).

Vetamamidi

The Eastern Ghats were gently rolling hills in the distance when one approached Vetamamidi. The November sky was blue with the ripe paddy swaying in the light breeze, ready for harvesting. A drive of a kilometre or so on a turn-off from the main road led us to the power plant. The plant gate had a large yellow board that marked the project site, where the plant capacity was listed as 1,200 KW. The funding details were also painted on; it gave the project cost as Rs 60 million, of which Rs 29 million was from RIDF, and the residual Rs 31 million was a subsidy from MNRE. Over the years there had been a 25 per cent cost escalation of the project from Rs 60 million to around Rs 80 million. The area was green and lush, and the rocky undulating terrain reminded us of the presence of thickly wooded hills not far away.

A group of five or six people received us at the gate. The officer of the National Bank for Agriculture and Rural Development (NABARD) who was with us pointed out that the plant had been constructed on what was earlier a nursery plantation of ITDA. The plant was situated on 11 acres of land, of which 8 acres of hilly terrain had been acquired from the state government, 2 acres from ITDA, and the remaining 1 acre from private sources. The last acre was bought from two landowners. One landowner, who gave 0.2 acres, was compensated for only the value of the land at around Rs 35,000 per acre since the land had been lying fallow anyway. The other person, who sold 0.8 acres, was compensated for the land value as well as for the 13 cashew plants he had planted on that land. The project began in 2005 and the plant had begun to produce electricity from April 2011.

We were shown around the plant by an engineer from APTRIPCO and Parvati, a young lady electrical engineer recruited for the plant (see Box 12.1). The president and secretary of the management

Box 12.1: The Rookie Engineer Takes Charge

Parvati, a fresh electrical engineering graduate from a local college, has been appointed as assistant manager at the Vetamamidi MHPP. Hailing from the Kondareddy tribe, Parvati comes from a village within the same ITDA region as Vetamamidi. Her education was taken care of by ITDA, and she got this job by responding to a newspaper advertisement in her last year at college. She comes from a farming family, with two older brothers, one volunteering at an upper primary school and the other a computer operator at a government office. Her younger sister is pursuing nursing, while an older sister helps at home. Joining as assistant manager at the Vetamamidi plant has been an interesting experience for her. From taking up residence at a small house at Addateegala town, to trying to get older people in the plant to listen to her, she has been facing a variety of challenges. Moreover, the work and operations at the plant are quite different from what she learnt in her academic course work and she is still learning and trying to adapt.

Her responsibilities include supervising operations and staff. According to her the staff members are poorly trained. She is also responsible for social mobilisation of the VMC, so they are prepared to take over the project on completion. She gets exasperated with the staff who do not pay heed to her and the attendants who are always looking for overtime and extra pay. Nevertheless, she is relieved to have a job (although her salary is a meagre Rs 9,000 per month) which offers so much responsibility and opportunities to learn. For now all she can think of for the future is this plant reaching full capacity, and she is looking forward to the equipment vendors and contractor coming to Vetamamidi in the next month or two to set right some of the deficiencies in the equipment. Her focus on her job is remarkable as is her eagerness to learn.

committee that were supposed to take full responsibility of the plant in less than a year's time were also there (see Plate 12.1). A local youth of the village, recruited as a non-technical employee of the plant, made up the team that showed us around. The engineer from APTRIPCO did most of the talking when the equipment was being shown to us (see Plate 12.2). The plant was operating at 600 KVA and the low utilisation was allegedly due to a combination of different factors. The first factor was the lower than normal flow of water attributed to low rainfall in the just concluded monsoon season. Second, the quality of the civil construction was poor and work on some of the channels was incomplete. There were water leaks all around reducing the pressure of an already lower than normal flow. The poor construction quality was evident from the leaks and puddles of water in the room housing the turbine underneath the control room. Third, the operators of the power plant (mainly some contract workers employed by APTRIPCO) along with Parvati who has just graduated from college were inexperienced and slow to respond to problems. Overload alarms kept going off in the control room.

Plate 12.1: The Future Operators of the Hydel Power Plant at Vetamamidi

Plate 12.2: Turbine Room under the Control Room at the Hydel Power Station

The site where the river was diverted was around half a kilometre upstream from the power plant. Here some of the civil construction work was yet to be completed. While the project had been operational for less than a year, one could see the formation of sandbanks on the riverbed where its flow had been diverted to go to the power plant. We were surprised to hear that this was not a source of ecological concern to the engineer at APTRIPCO, who confidently reiterated that such a minor diversion of water would not change the pattern of the river's flow.

According to the management committee members who accompanied us on the tour, the plant had come up largely because of the enthusiasm of Prerana Devi. She used to visit the village often, and was able to convince the villagers that supporting this project would give them self-confidence, as she believed they could manage a complicated thing like a power plant by themselves. It would also give them access to revenue flows which would help create valuable village infrastructure. There were a lot of factors that made the project appealing to the villagers. No investment would be needed from the village. Moreover, the availability of water in the village would not be affected, and very little land would be required. They formally gave their consent to the project in a meeting of the *gram sabha*. Since the ITDA administration and APTRIPCO were known entities, there were no serious reservations about outcomes and consequences. In addition to the villagers' consensus, a more formal tripartite memorandum of understanding (MoU) was signed between the APTRIPCO, ITDA and a committee chosen by the villagers through the meeting of the gram sabha regarding responsibility and revenue sharing.

The understanding was that APTRIPCO would supervise the construction and initial operations of the plant and ultimately (after one full year of running the completed project) hand over the plant to the Village Management Committee (VMC) for sustained operation and maintenance. The VMC would represent two beneficiary villages, Vetamamidi and Panukurathipalem comprising 178 households (733 people). Though nothing was explicitly mentioned in the MoU, we were given to understand that the ITDA wanted the composition of the VMC to be 80 per cent women, with the key positions held by them. The gender of the previous commissioner of ITDA might have been the source of the emphasis on women being brought to the fore and encouraged to take long-term responsibility of maintaining the common assets to be created. The persons who would be displaced from their land would be accommodated in the VMC. The actual handover of the project from APTRIPCO to VMC would take place under the supervision of the ITDA. In addition to project supervision, APTRIPCO would be responsible for training local tribal youth and members of the VMC on maintenance and management aspects of the project. The contractor appointed by APTRIPCO would be responsible for commissioning commercial operations and for maintenance of the project for one year from the date of commissioning. The contractor would also be responsible for imparting hands-on training to the project employees.

The MoU was supposed to document carefully the cost and revenue sharing model for the project. Unfortunately, the MoU was not available with the APTRIPCO engineer or with the VMC. However, the engineer and the members of the VMC separately told us what the revenue sharing formula was. They matched perfectly. To start with, regardless of the revenues generated, 4 per cent of the project cost, estimated as operation and maintenance, insurance and working capital costs, had to be set aside. Actual costs incurred in handholding, subject to a maximum of 0.5 per cent of the project cost was earmarked as annual fees to APTRIPCO for services rendered until the entire RIDF loan component was repaid. After the repayment the VMC had the option of continuing with APTRIPCO under the same conditions if it so desired. Once revenues start flowing, an amount up to Rs 3 million annually could be utilised for repaying the RIDF loan through APTRIPCO. About 1 per cent of the project cost was to be apportioned as an emergency fund to meet operational exigencies. From the remaining revenue, 50 per cent was to be directly utilised by the gram sabhas of Vetamamidi and Panukurathipalem villages for development activities, mainly the creation of common assets for the villages. Around 25 per cent of the remaining revenue was to be utilised by the local ITDA for development activities in the Addateegala area, and the residual 25 per cent would be devoted to developing renewable sources of energy which could benefit the tribal people within the local ITDA region of Rampa Chodavaram.

This was a complicated calculation. With a little prompting from each other the VMC members recited these relative shares. We asked the committee members about the revenue and net revenue prospects. They were not sure and gave us the percentage share of gross revenue that the committee would have power over to use in building assets in the village. We pointed out that even if the tariff offered by the grid for green energy was fixed, the amount of power they could supply would be variable, depending on the plant efficiency and the amount of water available. Thus they could plan only on the basis of some expected amount. They stared at us blankly, not comprehending any part of our argument.

We were keen to have an idea of the net surplus that the VMC could earn for using for village development activities (see Table 12.1). The net surplus would depend upon the power generation capacity utilised. This would be an outcome of managerial and technical efficiency along with the levels of water flow in the river. We did not have any data on power tariffs, nor could the APTRIPCO engineer help us; we decided to look at some alternative scenarios assuming different levels of overall efficiency (both technical effort and environmental parameters). We simulated three alternative states of affairs,

Table 12.1: Revenue Generated from MHPP at Vetamamidi and its Distribution

	Shares	Best Case	Average Case	Worst Case
		(in Rs million)		
Units	–	4,800,000	2,592,000	1,152,000
Revenue	100%	19.2	10.37	4.61
O&M costs	3.2	3.2	3.2	3.2
APTRIPCO annual fee (max)	4	0.4	0.4	0.4
Loan repayment	3	3.0	3.0	0.21
Emergency fund	0.8	0.8	0.8	0.8
Remaining revenue	26%	11.8	2.97	0
Distribution of Remaining Revenue				
Village common asset fund	13%	5.9	1.48	0
Local ITDA (common asset)	6.5%	2.95	0.74	0
Local ITDA (green energy)	6.5%	2.95	0.74	0

Note: Assumptions:

Green power feed in tariff assumed as Rs 4 per unit.

Best Case: 1,000 KW generated on average for 10 months in a year, with the plant operating 16 hours per day.

Average case: 800 KW generated on average for nine months in a year, with the plant operating 12 hours per day.

Worst Case: 600 KW generated on average for eight months in a year, with the plant operating eight hours per day.

with the assumption that revenue per unit of power sold to the grid was Rs 4. The tariff charged by the grid to the transmission companies for green energy was of the order of Rs 6 per unit. Hence we took a conservative estimate of Rs 4 per unit that the grid would pay to the generating unit.

We looked at a 'best' situation where we assumed that the plant could generate 1,000 KW for 10 months for 16 hours a day, although the rated capacity of the plant was 1,200 KW. The net surplus that the VMC could earn in such a situation would be Rs 5.9 million. Rs 2.95 million would be used by ITDA, as per the MoU, to develop the ITDA area and another Rs 2.95 million to promote renewable energy sources. The sum of Rs 5.9 million in a year could be considered a healthy amount to build a portfolio of assets in the village that would promote the capabilities of the villagers in terms of health and education and accessibility. An average level of utilisation — assuming 800 KW of generation for nine months at the rate of 12 hours per day would reduce the net surplus available to the village to only Rs 1.48 million. The ITDA would get a similar amount. This sharp decline was the result of the fixed maintenance costs and loan repayment built into the project finances. The third scenario was simulated on the assumption that the plant would only be able to generate 600 KW for eight months at eight hours per day. Indeed, when we visited the plant, the condition of the equipment, the technical expertise of the personnel supervising operations, and the state of the river allowed only 600 KW to be generated and the plant had just begun to move to a second shift. Under this worst-case outcome, the net surplus available to the VMC would actually turn negative. Since that is not physically possible, we assumed that revenue would be zero, and not all costs and commitments could be met. If the entire loan was not repaid, but all other costs and fees were met, the repayment amount for the RIDF loan would be a mere Rs 0.21 million instead of Rs 3 million. So unless the project was run at a high degree of capacity utilisation and technical efficiency (over which the villagers had some control) the sudden drop in net surplus would imply that the benefits flowing from this project would be effectively zero. The vagaries of the monsoons that might affect the water flow and pressure would make the net surplus estimates highly uncertain too. Variations in utilisation rates and hence net surplus would be high.

The VMC comprised 19 members of which four men and three women were from Panukurathipalem village and five men and seven women were from Vetamamidi village. The gender ratio was not the expected 80:20 in favour of women. The office holders, namely the president, Manasa, secretary, Vijaya, and treasurer, Preksha, were all women though. Five of the male members in the VMC formed the operation and maintenance team of the project and earned salaries. The VMC included representatives of the two families from whom land had been acquired. While there was a provision through which 10 per cent of the committee (two members) could be changed through consensus or elections by the gram sabha every two years, it had not been exercised so far.

Although it had been a couple of months since the power generated was linked to APTRANSCO's grid at Addateegala, generation had not stabilised and the billing of units was still in progress. Hence there were no revenue inflows into the project, and the operating costs of the plant were still being met by APTRIPCO. The divisional engineer deputed by APTRIPCO to the project was actively involved in supervising the day-to-day progress of the plant as this was the only one in the series of three MHPPs that had seen the light of day. Successful handover of this plant to the VMC would be a feather in his cap. He had been involved with this plant since May 2009. According to the divisional engineer, APTRIPCO itself was in disarray with many of its senior officers resigning due to unmanageable delays in project execution. He believed that his hard work and patience could lead to a more rapid career progression given the number of vacant top-level positions. Towards this objective, he even claimed to have spent up to Rs 0.3 million from his personal funds to assist the contractors so as to ensure that the projects were completed. He empathised with the contractor's reluctance to complete the projects as they were allotted the projects on the basis of estimates made in 2005, and given cost escalations over the last few years it was not economically viable for the contractors to honour their commitments. This was part of the reason why in Vetamamidi, although the contractor's work was incomplete, the contractor had not been fired and the project team was being patient.

The VMC members had been involved in the supervision of construction work. Committee members took turns supervising so as to ensure that quality was not compromised during construction, without jeopardising their domestic commitments. The enthusiasm and sincerity of the VMC, as they described the construction phase, made up for their lack of knowledge. During construction, it was not unusual for a committee member to call an APTRIPCO official to ask what brand of cement was to be used or the exact proportion of sand, stone chips and cement to make concrete. To get the contractor's attention and ensure that he complied with APTRIPCO standards, the VMC often had to resort to measures such as stopping work or threatening to disengage the contractor.

There were situations where, to ensure that the local APTRIPCO official was not in connivance with the contractor, the VMC confirmed the contractor's deviation from the work plan in writing with the local APTRIPCO official and sent it over to APTRIPCO's office at Hyderabad for validation. APTRIPCO officials, however, personally supervised critical construction and erection works at the water intake point and at the plant site. While the villagers working at the civil construction site got daily wages between Rs 60 and Rs 80 (compared to the rural employment guarantee scheme rate of Rs 140), supervision was entirely voluntary, with the VMC volunteering because they felt that the creation of this public good would mean an improvement in the living conditions of the village in the long term, and because it would earn them more respect from the villagers. Thus the construction phase of the project had been directly beneficial to the villagers of Vetamamidi and Panukurathipalem. Other than that, the villagers were yet to see any other benefits from the project. For the few who were directly employed, earnings were not very high, with salaries ranging around Rs 3,500 a month for unskilled labour.

They did realise that revenues would flow to the village for development activities only if the revenue earned was over and above operating costs and loan-servicing amounts. However, as noted earlier, the VMC did not fully appreciate the nature of uncertainty and the numbers involved, and the need to operate the plant consistently at very high levels of capacity utilisation. Without a full understanding of the kind of outcomes possible, and the sharp decline of the net surplus (falling even to zero) with relatively small changes in the rate of capacity utilisation, the incentive for individual sacrifice (effort) for reaping collective benefits (common assets created) could be destroyed.

Perhaps the greatest benefit of this project was the increase in self-confidence and awareness of the womenfolk in the village (see Box 12.2). In 2005, when ITDA and APTRIPCO approached the villagers with the proposal, the womenfolk had little to ask about or say as they did not feel that they had a voice. Important questions about how the project would affect the village were not raised by them. The design of the MoU to involve more women in the VMC had the desired outcome of empowering and emboldening the women. They were proud of the assertive role they had played in the supervision of the civil construction works, more so in light of the fact that construction work had been stalled at the other two MHPP sites.

Box 12.2: Small Steps to Big Aspirations

Manasa Amma, president of the VMC of Vetamamidi, is the wife of a landless labourer and mother of two daughters. They have taken 5 acres of land on lease and cultivate paddy there. Her husband lives in Addateegala and drives a goods vehicle. ITDA takes care of the educational expenses of both children. The interaction with APTRIPCO helped Manasa Amma realise that her primary education (she was a class eight dropout) was not good enough to get ahead in life and she pursued her secondary education through distance learning, graduating class 10 last year. Now she is looking for opportunities to pursue a college degree using a similar mode.

She was elected into the VMC by the gram sabha, and in turn the VMC elected her as the president, as they believed (in Manasa Amma's words) that she was capable and aware and had proved her ability before on numerous occasions. She comes across as an intelligent and ambitious person and was elected to the mandal elections (comprising three panchayats) on a Congress ticket; her position as president of the VMC worked in her favour. She believes she has it in her to become an MLA from her constituency, but would contest only if she is given a ticket from leading parties (which in her opinion include the Congress, Bharatiya Janata Party [BJP], Telugu Desam Party [TDP] and the Communist Party of India [CPI]).

She would like to help create an irrigation project for Vetamamidi by diverting water from an existing storage reservoir located a few kilometres downhill from the village. She knows that the topography does not lend itself to such a diversion and the costs of the project could exceed Rs 10 million but believes this to be the only way to eradicate hunger from the village. On the personal front, she believes that VMC members should get some financial benefits from the MHPP project, and she would like to use that money to buy pesticides, which amount to Rs 2,000 a year. If the benefit was paid as a lump-sum amount, she would like to utilise it to set up a store 'like a shopping mall' or augment the Rs 60,000 she is eligible to receive under the Indira Awas Yojana (IAY) to make a new home. Her ultimate objective is to ensure that her children have a good life and whatever the MHPP can do to facilitate that is welcome.

In addition, the training they had obtained from APTRIPCO on how power generation took place gave them confidence.

However, the women were still shaky on operating and managing the power plant once APTRIPCO handed it over. For example, Preksha, their treasurer, who had had formal education only till middle school (class eight), had no idea of how to maintain or keep books of accounts since she had not been exposed to these aspects. All the accounting was currently being done centrally by APTRIPCO. She, however, was confident of operating the bank account of the VMC, which had the president and secretary as the other signatories. Moreover, the VMC was aware that based on the MoU they would have APTRIPCO support and involvement till the RIDF loan was repaid.

The employment potential of the project was limited. There was no binding obligation to employ villagers other than the ones who were displaced from their land. Nevertheless, some of the village youth who were obtaining vocational training as technicians were hopeful of employment in the MHPP. The state environment committee had once visited Vetamamidi and, in recognition of their extraordinary success, announced a reward of Rs 1.5 million to the managing committee. However, the money was not forthcoming as it would get activated only if all three power projects along the Yelleru River were completed. When chatting at a local 'tiffin' shop, we realised that in sharp contrast to the awareness and energy exhibited by the members of the VMC, the villagers who did not belong to the VMC had little information about the project or its progress. They were under the impression that, once operational, the plant would provide free power to the villagers. They were hopeful that as APTRIPCO disengaged more employment opportunities would be available for the village folk. Unfortunately, both their expectations about free energy and new jobs were hopelessly inaccurate.

Mitlapalem and Pinjarikonda

At Mitlapalem, the construction site (the power generation station was not completed yet) was far from the metalled road, over uneven terrain. The undulations on the path, sudden curves and a road full of stone, gravel and rocky outgrowths made the ride to Mitlapalem unbearably bumpy. The driver of our four-wheel drive was reluctant to risk his vehicle on this road and had to be coaxed to take us as close as possible to the site. We found a few pieces of rusted equipment, including the turbine blades, scattered at the site where the plant was to come up. Upstream, where the river water was to be diverted, the view of the setting sun over the Yelleru was captivating. A closer inspection revealed that only a small part of the civil construction was over — the diverting weir was half-made and we could see the beginnings of the concrete channel for the diversion canal. Nature had taken over — there were saplings and trees growing out of the cracks in the concrete, giving the place a feeling of historic ruins.

As we entered the centre of the tiny village, a lamp post with a red cement base which had CPI-ML (Communist Party of India – Marxist Leninist) painted on it caught our attention. Hailing from the historic Koidara tribe, made famous by freedom fighter Sriramraju, the villagers at Mitlapalem wore a forlorn look when asked about the progress of their MHPP. The villagers we spoke to were despondent; they had been hoping for some intervention from the ITDA to help resolve their standoff with the truant contractor but no help was forthcoming. In this village, almost 12.4 acres of the 14.2 acres required for the MHPP had been acquired from private landholders. Persuaded by APTRIPCO officials, they had sold their land willingly, quite happy with the lump sum payment they received. As land donors, they harboured an expectation of an increase in esteem among fellow villagers once the MHPP was up and running. Some of the landowners hoped that in the future APTRIPCO would compensate them with some land, but that was not to be. Erstwhile landowners like Srikanth and Srinath who used to cultivate cotton, tapioca, paddy or cashew on their lands earlier had now become daily labourers, and they regretted that they did not save more from the compensation they had received. In retrospect they felt that the compensation amount of Rs 35,000 per acre was low since losing the land implied that they lost an income of around Rs 15,000 to Rs 20,000 per acre per year. Nevertheless, if and when the hydel plant saw the light of day and revenues started flowing from its operations, the creation of social assets would make their loss easier to bear since the village as a whole would benefit for generations to come.

Only seven of 19 members of the managing committee were women, both because fewer women from this village had showed interest and also because one representative (usually male) from each of the families that had lost land had to be accommodated in the committee. The five major posts of president, vice president, secretary, joint secretary and treasurer were however held by women. Work on the MHPP in this village had been stalled for a long time. There had been no government intervention in the village since 2005–6.

The committee members appeared crestfallen and in despair. Their incomes had fallen, since their landholding had been reduced, and yet the project was at a standstill. When we arrived in the village, many of the committee members were of the opinion that we had come from the state capital to see if the subsidies for agriculture and procurement prices for produce could be revised. When they realised that we were not representing the state government, their interest waned, but their helplessness about getting the project going once again came through quite intensely. The despondency of the president of the VMC was patently evident. It was as if she had given up, and was a trifle disturbed that she was letting the village down. She was soft-spoken and somewhat diffident. Did she have a Plan B? She would not go to the court of law so as not to repeat the Pinjarikonda story (where legal problems had arisen). Was she taking pains to negotiate with the truant contractor? No, the negotiations had to be handled by APTRIPCO; the VMC was not good at these kinds of things, was her reply.

The contractor had stopped work at this site citing problems of inaccessibility and cost escalations from the time the contract had been awarded. This was the same contractor as that in Vetamamidi. To resume work, the villagers had even offered that the contractor and workers could stay in the village itself. The managing committee was concerned about terminating the contract as they had seen the situation in Pinjarikonda, the third site, where, because of termination of contract, the contractor had filed a case and the project was on hold because of litigation issues. ITDA, who, as per the MoU, was supposed to step in to handle situations such as work stoppages, had let them down. The ITDA was so preoccupied with arbitrating land disputes that it did not have time to find out more about the conflict brewing at the Mitlapalem MHPP. In fact, ITDA involvement and frequency of official visits to the village had been steadily declining. After the hands-on involvement of Prerana Devi, there were some routine visits by her successors and just one visit to Addateegala town by the current commissioner. The managing committee was at a loss to handle the current impasse, and was unsure whether APTRIPCO's advice to write a complaint to ITDA would help in any way. The engineer explained that APTRIPCO's inability to influence the contractor was because the tenders of the Mitlapalem MHPP had to be issued for the third time before any contractor participated in the bid. We rued the irony of the situation: the RIDF was set up to provide funds to complete stalled government projects, and instead here was an instance of another stalled project!

The situation at Pinjarikonda was even more distressing. Young villagers around the area had little idea of the location of the project site. Others unexcitedly gave us directions to the place where the power generating site was to be set up. After a rough ride for almost 3 km on harsh rocky paths, we came across an old rusted turbine lying in the middle of an overgrown piece of land which appeared to have been converted into a level field sometime in the past. There was an iron signboard where some yellow paint could be seen, probably marking the site. There were no other signs of the hydel project. The large turbine lying there was a monument to how development interventions can be wasted. The project had come to a standstill in 2008, when the village committee in its wisdom had decided to terminate the contractor's services because of the poor progress he had made since 2005. The contractor had gone to court challenging his termination and had obtained a stay order. Since the matter was sub judice, no work could now be done on the site. Meanwhile, the turbine lay there, gathering dust and slowly disintegrating into scrap under the vagaries of the weather.

Concluding Remarks

Self-interest may not be the only force that drives people (Dasgupta 2001; Sen 1977). Dasgupta (2010) discusses motives like mutual affection, pro-social inclinations and creation of trust and credibility as possible motives why people undertake collective action. There could be ethical reasons too as to why people cooperate. In the case of the villages we describe in this chapter, personal interest could not have been the driving force, because there were no individual incomes that resulted from a successful completion of the project, except for three or four salaried beneficiaries. While the benefits were collective, and could not be apportioned to individuals, the costs were personal. There were opportunity costs in terms of time foregone in working on one's own fields or working as day labourers. It was like a 'voluntary tax' paid for the well-being of the community, even beyond the boundaries of their own village.

In this case, too, as in the previous chapters, the creation of a network for collective action was at the heart of the functioning of a temporary organisation, the VMC. The network, between the village community and the representatives chosen, the APTRIPCO employees in the project, the private contractor, and the powerful ITDA officials, did not evolve as per the wishes of the community, but was imposed on them by the MoU. People who voluntarily joined the network (not the officials of agencies like APTRIPCO and ITDA) did so because they had shared beliefs about the importance of the subsequent accumulation of common assets like hospitals, schools, roads, and street lights. It was a form of civic engagement through interpersonal networks. However, there could be repercussions on the governance of the project, which would be determined by the relative competencies of these volunteers. Perhaps, this is what explained the relative success of Vetamamidi over Mitlapalem and Pinjarikonda.

The project design was identical, and the sizes and socio–economic profiles of the three villages were very similar. In Vetamamidi, the plant was complete and power generation (albeit at a low level of capacity utilisation) had begun. In Mitlapalem, the civil works were about three-fourths completed, after which the contractor had stopped work and had refused to come to the site. In Pinjarikonda, work was at a standstill. It was the same contractor appointed in all the three villages, all in the same vicinity. Was the leadership of the VMC a determining factor for the observed differences?

In Vetamamidi, the leadership of the VMC was very strong. The office-bearers had relentlessly pursued the contractor and the engineers of APTRIPCO to complete the works. The optimism of the president, an eighth class dropout, was almost contagious. The VMC members would constantly be questioning Parvati, the engineer, about the running of the plant and seeking explanations when anything went wrong. This was not like a boss supervising a subordinate, but rather a co-worker trying to learn about a colleague's job. The project cost had ballooned from Rs 60 million to Rs 80 million. The management committee mentioned that while they were not fully aware as to all the reasons behind the escalation, they were very conscious that one reason could have been their insistence on high quality materials for the civil works.

As part of his defence for abandoning the projects, the contractor had officially cited the lack of proper access to the project site in Mitlapalem and Pinjarikonda. Transporting heavy equipment was a challenge in contrast to transporting them to Vetamamidi. However, the contractor must have known about the terrain of the sites when he accepted the job. APTRIPCO officials claimed helplessness; but shared that a number of requests had been made to the contractor to resume work. Obviously, if and when work resumed there would be further cost escalations.

It is important to note two institutional implications of this project failure. The first relates to the way the job contract was drawn up. The APTRIPCO engineer at the sites had not seen the contract and was unclear about the penalties for the failure to deliver by the contractor. He was not even sure about the responsibilities arising out of complementary commitments of the ITDA (like the building of roads to the project sites if necessary). The contract was at the APTRIPCO head office. We followed up on the issue with the ITDA commissioner-in-charge of the project area. She was unaware of the impasse, and claimed that land-related disputes took up all her time. Her office was also not able to produce a copy of the contract. No one seemed to be too concerned about the formal structure of the agreement with the contractor. The second issue was the effect legal institutions could have on people involved in participatory development. The court, like the faraway state government, was a distant nebulous but powerful force that could intervene and upset their lives in unanticipated ways with often irreversible negative consequences.

The project was brought to the village from outside by development agencies and policy planners. It was adopted by local villagers and a form of participation was imposed by its design where the incentives transcended individual benefits. A diverse set of outcomes were observed in the way that local participants emerged from their participatory role with different experiences. These experiences ranged from the need to learn new things like accounting or the insight that a sacrifice for the community's benefit was a rewarding moment of self-realisation, to the agony of failure and a sense of impotence against bigger powers of the contractor and the courts of law. A mix of leadership styles and institutional failures combined to create the outcomes we witnessed. Collective action and the creation of a temporary organisation is itself problematic; the intent to act collectively towards a common cause may not be a guarantee of success.

13

Sometime in the Future, in Someplace Else
Another Development

The idea of transformation, as has been discussed in Chapter 1, is about the advent of capitalism and the emergence of capitalist structures in every sector of the economy. In the absence of such a complete transformation, change could be partial, leading to hybrid structures; or change could be of a purely incremental and quantitative nature. The interventions discussed so far were market-friendly changes designed to bring about full-fledged transformation. Ideally, the design of these interventions would focus on creation of access to markets, adequate infrastructure and human capabilities. These interventions would have to be acceptable to the people who would be affected by them. They would have to take ownership of the interventions to ensure that the flow of benefits was sustained. However, we found several deviations from an ideal intervention, some of them glaring, others more subtle. The implications of these deviations for the bigger picture of change are what we term 'Another Development'.

Field Realities

All the studies we undertook had some of the characteristic features of market-friendly development. They focused on creating market access, especially access to credit markets; creating infrastructure, especially natural assets; and developing human capabilities, especially through capacity building and empowerment of women. These features would be expected to contribute towards transformation. However, we were unable to discern any unambiguous transformative trends that were emerging in the rural sector.

ACCESS TO MARKETS

Access to land markets is critically important as land is the most important asset in the rural sector. In none of the projects did we find any impact on these markets. Given the distribution of land and its current usage, some alterations were evident. These included planting of fruit trees, lining the plots with trees for fuelwood and growing fodder for cattle (Chapters 3, 5, 9, and 10). The interventions did not necessitate or lead to any buying or selling of land. We found that land markets continued to remain thin and illiquid. Those who did not own land were unable to directly access many of the benefits accruing from the interventions.

The ownership and operational holding patterns of agricultural land are notoriously uneven in India. Ownership determines one's access to credit markets as land can be an important collateral. The size of operational holdings determines the scale of operations and hence influences the ability of a supplier to access product markets. Indeed, many small farmers are actually net buyers of foodgrains and vegetables. There are regulatory restrictions also on ownership, tenancy and transferability of agricultural land as an asset (Chapter 12). Putting land to the most efficient use is claimed to be the hallmark of a market-based allocation mechanism. Yet the interventions did not bring about any significant changes in the pattern of land use.

Given the nature of the land market, access to credit markets would obviously be difficult and restricted. There were attempts made to encourage the habit of financial savings in a formal way by keeping records of all transactions (deposits and withdrawals) through the institution of the SHGs. The SHGs played an important role in addressing the imperfections of the credit market. They built the social capital or capacity of trust and reliability amongst the members, usually women. While the drive towards financial inclusion was noticeably strong, we found that bank linkages were more formal than substantial. Much depended on the attitude exhibited by bank officials towards the rural customers as well as the degree of self-assurance and confidence demonstrated by the members of self-help groups (SHGs). In Chittoor (Chapter 9), for example, villagers talked of the inconvenience and humiliation of visiting a bank where they would have to wait in long queues and be jostled from one counter to another because they were not very knowledgeable and their transaction amounts were small.

Often, the physical distance of the bank and road connectivity proved to be deterrents to deepening bank linkages. The nearest bank for the village of Tutarkhed (Chapter 10) was 65 km away at Dharampur town, and in villages in Udaipur (Chapter 5) the nearest banks were over 25 km away, with poor connecting roads. Most of the SHGs we spoke to were not even thinking about using banks as an important resource for entrepreneurial ventures or for increasing their scale of activities. In Kerala (Chapter 7), despite having taken small loans from the bank and repaid them in time, one Joint Liability Group (JLG) was wary of applying for a larger loan as it believed it did not have adequate margin money and was contemplating going back to the local moneylenders.

Yet we found most of the SHGs extremely energetic in mobilising small savings, keeping books and records, and providing small loans for family exigencies or for very small livelihood ventures such as buying seeds. Thus they were simulating banks in their own microcosm, without any of these transactions being part of the formal banking system.

Impact on product markets was weak and these markets appeared incomplete and thin. In Gujarat (Chapter 10), we found that the participants often went to local markets to barter a portion of their cashew produce for regular needs such as cooking oil, salt and spices. Yet the Gujarat project was one instance where there was a perceptible impact on the market for cashews and mangoes as their collection was centralised over a large geographical region and distribution channels were spread across the country.

Besides the usual flows of foodgrains and vegetables, we did find a new emphasis on fruits and dairy products. However, the latter hardly constituted a quantity or variety that could indicate an emergent break from the past in the product mix of agriculture. Similarly, we observed several consumer items like toiletries, ready-to-eat snacks and savouries typically consumed by urban populations being stocked in the rural *kirana* stores, but the quantum of transaction was insignificant, as indicated by the low inventory maintained and the infrequency of visits to the wholesalers.

Given the nature of the land, credit and product markets, it was not surprising that the rural labour markets and capital markets were also underdeveloped. There was no discernible flow of investible resources into the rural areas, other than the investments brought in by the projects themselves in the name of development. There was no significant flow of labour to the modern sector either, except for some distress migration, which continued despite the interventions trying to contain this trend. We were surprised to see the SHGs talking of investing in harvesters and tractors for farming even though there was a large labour surplus. In the absence of adequate private demand for wage labour, the government stepped in to fill this gap with the Mahatma Gandhi National Rural Employment Guarantee Act (MGNREGA) which aimed at enhancing the livelihood security of people through guaranteed wage employment for 100 days of unskilled manual work. Many of the landowners thought the MGNREGA scheme not only provided higher wages, but also involved lesser effort as there was hardly any supervision. They tended to blame the MGNREGA scheme for distorting the labour market and raising wages to the extent that it was uneconomical for them to employ labour on their land. Rather than progress towards wage labour, we observed members of SHGs working on each other's fields and reducing the use of wage labour wherever possible.

Participation in Markets

Market transactions require certain resources to be available to the participants. If these are not available, one method of ensuring access would be to create a critical mass of people to pool their individually inadequate resources. From the perspective of banks, the experience of 'financial inclusion' through SHGs provides the critical minimum resources required to access credit markets. Such access did not, however, bring about a significant impact on local skill formation or the growth of local industry. Hence the transformative impact of this innovation was minimal. Indeed, one might argue that it helped to reinforce the poverty trap (Bateman 2010) without allowing it to become worse and socially more volatile.

Against the collective risk in obtaining a loan as an SHG, individual activities were undertaken with the borrowed resources. In Nidhal (Chapter 3), a group of five farmers had pooled their land (35 acres) to take a loan to share (commonly own) a borewell. The liability of repaying the debt was equally shared but the benefit from the borewell was not equal for all. It would be based on the output from the commercial crops grown on individual land. The activities were traditional and small scale with production essentially for the local markets. As an instance, the farmers' club in Raigarh (Chapter 11) — had facilitated two JLGs, where the individuals were involved in a bouquet of activities — *Pan thelakiya* (pan shop), 'hotel' (snack shop), *badhaigiri* (carpentry), cycle repair, and *raajmistry* (masonry). As a result, only marginal increments were possible to each family's income stream. This kind of risk-taking was inefficient. In an overwhelmingly large number of cases, SHG participants indicated that joint work was best avoided since it led to disagreements and conflicts within the group. It was only in the case of the fishermen in Kerala (Chapter 7) that we found that activities undertaken by JLGs were collective in nature. This was germane to fishing as an activity since fishermen go out in a group, and newer and more powerful boats meant more people could go out at a time.

A noticeable feature of the design of the micro-level interventions was that they targeted people with land. Those without land were included only residually to allow them opportunities to work in peripheral activities. In Gujarat and Maharashtra (Chapters 3 and 10), one had to own land to have a *wadi*. We saw the emergence of a new class of farmers called the *wadi walas* in Gujarat who were able to benefit more from the interventions. In Andhra Pradesh (Chapter 9) we found that access to credit to buy cattle was possible only if one owned land for fodder cultivation.

The landless could be included in activities that were much less valuable in terms of income. The relatively higher income-generating activities (in the range of Rs 2,000–Rs 4,000 per month) would be the ones where the possession of land was a prerequisite, while the lower range activities (between Rs 400 and Rs 1,500 per month) would be the ones that would be available for adoption by the landless. Clearly, even where all households in a village or a block of villages were included in the benefits from the intervention, the degree of inequality in the local economy was bound to increase. We saw how the economic conditions of the landless Ramoshis in Nidhal (Chapter 3) were in complete contrast to the rest of the villagers, despite their having put in maximum effort for constructing the watershed from which the benefits flowed. The ecotourism experiment in Sikkim (Chapter 8) clearly favoured those households who had a relatively good quality dwelling close to a metalled road, leading to the Lepchas from Lingee feeling left out.

MOBILITY OF RESOURCES ACROSS MARKETS

An indicator of the strength of a market economy is the ease with which productive resources such as capital and labour can move across activities and markets in response to changing economic opportunities. Many interventions attempted to diversify the activities a poor farmer was involved in. We observed that the different activities introduced invariably generated incremental incomes that at best ranged from around Rs 400 to around Rs 4,000 per household per month. In Bhalki (Chapter 4), the villagers experimented with growing corn and medicinal plants. They were cheated in the markets of Kolkata by individuals who reneged on their promises to buy back corn produce after selling them the seeds and they had nowhere else to go with their produce which was left to rot.

We did not find evidence of new opportunities for sustainable livelihoods actually replacing any primary income-generating activity like agriculture. These were always supplementary. They did offer some possibility of smoothening out income fluctuations from agriculture through diversification of activities, but they could hardly be transformational in their impact. The only instances we found where some concerted effort was made to coordinate these activities and organise them into a larger scale so as to cater to markets outside the locality was in Gujarat (Chapter 10) where BAIF was able to create an extensive organisation of cooperatives. However, the structure of the cooperative was beginning to weaken as BAIF began to withdraw. Individual farmers were found to be unable to look after their cashew and mango trees, so much so that BAIF had to begin a fresh phase of handholding. This observation left us with questions about the long-term sustainability of these livelihood diversifications.

INFRASTRUCTURE

As noted earlier, without different types of infrastructure in place, markets would not be able to function well. The interventions attempted to create social infrastructure through the promotion of SHGs, farmers' clubs and JLGs. In addition to the pure economic purpose of financial inclusion, these had a key role to play in reinforcing social networks and building confidence, nurturing a spirit of teamwork, sharing ideas, and pooling resources. We found that the women SHGs used their weekly meeting to exchange views on larger social issues. Group members got together to support each other, helping tide over exigencies in their everyday lives.

This kind of social infrastructure was not exactly the kind that would emerge from the functioning of institutions based on representation such as the panchayat. The panchayat provides a platform for the common person to raise larger political issues. With the SHGs such issues were discussed only within the group and each SHG could have a very different opinion, which was never shared or discussed in an open forum. In almost all instances (except perhaps in Bhalki, Chapter 4) the interventions were in areas where the Panchayati Raj Institutions (PRIs) were inactive, unenergetic and somewhat docile. This view of the PRIs was corroborated by local residents when asked about governance in the village.

In contrast to building social infrastructure the challenges in building physical infrastructure are few. People usually articulate their need for physical infrastructure, such as roads or electricity, and the resources to build them are often made available through the intervention itself. Further, the creation of these assets is a yardstick by which success in implementing the project is measured. This was also corroborated in our observations. However, maintenance of these assets after completion of the intervention could be a matter of concern, as we observed in Bhalki (Chapter 4) and in Vetamamidi (Chapter 12).

Financial inclusion was a focal point of the interventions. There was considerable momentum as far as the creation of SHGs, JLGs and farmers' clubs were concerned. There was also a noticeable degree of comfort the members had in making financial transactions. This same level of comfort was missing when it came to interaction with commercial or cooperative banks. We did notice that the SHGs preferred to run an almost parallel banking system with the resources they mobilised. In Udaipur (Chapter 5), an SHG was able to quickly tell us the amount of cash it had in hand but could not tell us the state of their bank account and details of savings they were undertaking, and to what purpose. In Sikkim (Chapter 8), people were loath to take loans as they preferred grants. In Kerala (Chapter 7), a JLG felt it did not have enough margin money to take a loan.

The focus of the interventions had some component which addressed the creation or preservation of natural assets like trees and forests or water. These resources, by their very nature, are held as common property, though some can be held as private property too. For instance, forests are community property while an orchard can be privately held. There were instances where we found that there was an encouragement to have privately acquired natural assets. In Chittoor (Chapter 9), we observed that there was a business model to own cattle, grow fodder and also use the excreta of the cattle to have biogas plants as a fuel source for personal cooking. While this was certainly a new 'integration' of resources, the individual biogas plants were not often feasible because of the inadequacy of the cow dung that could be collected. Having a community owned biogas plant would have been much more efficient.

In many cases the commons were partitioned to give individuals usufruct rights, as in grazing pastures. These were instances of a partial privatisation process with presumably a more efficient use of the resource, but there were concerns that we heard about the long-term consequences of population growth that would put greater pressure on these resources. In Bhalki (Chapter 4), where social plantations were attempted as part of the watershed development project using both private as well as public land, there were a host of problems that arose as absentee landlords asserted their individual property rights. In Alappuzha (Chapter 7) the overuse of the commons, that is, the Arabian Sea, was leading to a decline in the total catch for all the fishermen, especially the poorer ones who had no alternative but to fish closer to the shore.

We found that natural capital was always valued for being instrumental in supplementing incomes. The intrinsic value of natural assets as part of ecosystems and biodiversity never came up as a matter of concern (Chapter 8). The instrumental value is important as the return on ecological capital, but an exclusive emphasis on this could lead to a variety of intense and inevitable conflicts. Some examples of these conflicts were too much drawing of groundwater, continued use of chemical fertilisers and pesticides, hills being dynamited for granite quarrying, and the dust from the quarries damaging the top soil of the fertile land. There was no well thought out plan for maintaining the pristine beauty of the region in Sikkim (Chapter 8), despite the natural capital being the main resource for ecotourism. In Vetamamidi (Chapter 12), sandbanks were already evident where the local river had been diverted to generate green power for the grid. Actually, as is well recorded, communities have traditional ways of protecting natural capital in focusing on their intrinsic worth over and above the instrumental value (Ostrom 1992). We did not find any non-market method of negotiation or sharing of natural resources being promoted or encouraged except for the *charagah samitis* in Udaipur (Chapter 5). Even there, the exact mechanism for protecting the commons was not developed, though there were indications that it would have to be a collective community decision.

Human Capabilities

Creating a diverse set of livelihood opportunities entails, amongst other things, the creation of human capabilities so that people can avail of these opportunities as they emerge. Capabilities can be of different types and of different degrees of complexity (Sen 1985). In the context of development interventions, we were obviously on the lookout for the quality of health and education services available in the villages. Public health services related to maternity and childbirth, sanitation facilities and improved consciousness of hygiene contributed to a healthier population. Adult education to promote literacy and the ability to access government services like banking, and vocational training enabled people to take advantage of economic opportunities.

In our travels and discussions with the villagers, we were surprised to note that there were very few demands for better health services articulated by them, although some complained about the distance of the primary health-care centre from the village. We did not find (except in one instance in Nidhal, Chapter 3) that the improvements in sanitation and public hygiene were agenda items in the people's charter for change. Also, we did not observe any involvement of the people in the provision of better health services except in the village of Kapartunga (Chapter 11). Our experience with education was markedly different. The consciousness of the need for education was very high and people were concerned about the primary schooling of their children and the quality of the schools as well. However, there was little interest of the villagers for their own education and learning to improve their lot. Some efforts at adult education for illiterate women, in the

Bhalki village (Chapter 4), came to naught after a promising start because of trivial issues such as the lack of lanterns for the night school.

Vocational training was a key feature of every intervention as part of their capacity building budget. The approval of project design was contingent on a demonstration of some capacity building for the beneficiaries. As a result, we found evidence of training activities such as making soft toys, making jewellery with beads, embroidery, tailoring, candle making, bee keeping, and *lac* making. However, the economic consequence of these activities were extremely limited, and we found little planning behind the choice of skill development in a particular location. For instance, after 25 women were trained in a specific skill, such as tailoring, only one or two of them ventured to take it up as a supplementary source of income. There were some exceptions, however. Training activities in Sikkim (Chapter 8), such as imparting spoken English skills and culinary expertise, would have a direct and positive impact on their ecotourism venture. In Kapartunga (Chapter 11) training was imparted to a mason on more specialised activities such as making rainwater harvesting structures for the village.

People's Participation and Empowerment

We found that attempts to promote participation in the interventions revolved around the issue of private material benefits, rather than on improvements in social well-being. In this sense, participation was an apolitical process, focused only on the ultimate private economic gain. This kind of participation would be unlikely to enhance the ability of beneficiaries to control and question processes and outcomes in the larger sociopolitical context. Vetamamidi (Chapter 12) was an exception where the core outcome of the design was the creation of common property resources. Even there, however, sufficient thought on the sociopolitical implications of the project appeared to be missing.

Yet, given the priority assigned to participation in development interventions, it has been treated in mechanical and superficial ways. The community of beneficiaries was treated as being homogenous in social and political characteristics though not necessarily in economic status. Even in Nidhal (Chapter 3), where people's participation indicated a very positive collective energy, there were the Ramoshis who were marginalised. Despite the good intentions of MASS (Chittoor, Chapter 9) in trying to improve the lot of the Yanadis, they did little to integrate them into the mainstream, staying away from them after sundown because they were deemed to be culturally different.

A mechanical approach to participation implied a number of interesting things. First, the formal part of participatory processes, such as keeping of minutes, creating appropriate organograms and representative committee structures, and producing data in a prescribed format, all gained greater importance when compared to the ability of beneficiaries to take decisions. We saw the enthusiasm the members of the SHGs demonstrated in signing the minutes of meetings, yet when asked about their expectations from the intervention, they were mostly silent. Everybody seemed to have bought into the project in terms of increased incomes yet no one reflected deeper into the longer term implications of participation such as improved health and education. It was only in very rare situations (Nidhal, Chapter 3) that people were looking at outcomes transcending the immediate future of the project.

Second, the time bound nature of project and target management phases acted as a deterrent to the slow and tortuous processes of including marginalised people and ensuring that they felt comfortable to raise questions on their own. David Mosse commented that:

> Success depended crucially upon the timely implementation of measurable quantities of high quality development schemes that would hold the attention of outside observers, political bosses and paymasters (and continue to secure 'participation' from villagers). But the timely delivery of programme outputs — the construction of kilometers of soil conservation structures, planting of trees, deepening of wells, purchase of pumps, or the supply of input credit — had become far too important to be left to participatory (i.e. farmer-managed) processes. (2011: 192)

In Udaipur (Chapter 5), the blank faces of the 'participants' clearly demonstrated their complete lack of engagement with the interventions, yet the project would be called a success by all the conventionally used parameters of evaluation. In Chhattisgarh (Chapter 11), we came across the term SP, which surprisingly did not mean Superintendent of Police but was a short form for sarpanch *pati*. Reservation implied the sarpanch had to be a woman but the actual decision-making power rested with the SP. This was one of the many instances demonstrating how women's participation was more on paper than in practice. While initiatives were being taken to reduce the drudgery for women, their burden increased from many other aspects of the project related to livelihood diversification. This was true across projects in Udaipur, Chhattisgarh, Gujarat, and Andhra Pradesh (Chapters 5, 9, 10, and 11). Was the stress on formal participation likely to become the 'new tyranny of development' (Williams 2011: 239)?

Real participation allows people to experience social networks, make political claims and join struggles for power and control. In Chhattisgarh (Chapter 11), when a block development officer asked a sarpanch for a bribe for implementing a government scheme in the village, the sarpanch refused to do so, citing that the National Bank for Agriculture and Rural Development (NABARD) also undertook developmental activities but never asked for bribes. However, participation by the beneficiaries of the projects did not give them confidence to articulate their thoughts on changing their immediate lot. In Bhalki (Chapter 4), the committee was concerned about their inability to sustain the benefits from the project. In other situations the beneficiaries could not think beyond the direct opportunities provided by the intervention. In Kerala (Chapter 7), a group of fishermen who wanted to get out of the grip of the local *therakan* succeeded, but only to find that the leader of the group was considering becoming a moneylender himself as it was the best economic opportunity available.

As the development facilitator disengaged, we observed a gradual collapse of the entire intervention process (Chapters 4, 10). This indicated an undue dependence on the facilitator. It appeared that to sustain the formalities of participation and prop up the rural economy, a new kind of mediator in the form of a development facilitator was becoming essential.

The explicit goal of empowering women led to resources for development of individual households being channelled through them. Many women we spoke to were articulate and involved in the temporary organisation, often in leadership roles. Despite these empowered women being 'showcased' as successes of the intervention, we observed that few had emerged from the shadow of male dominance — their menfolk were always at hand when we interviewed the women. There was a sense of tolerance towards women doing work other than household chores, simply because they were acting as a conduit for accessing financial resources as development assistance.

The villagers when questioned about their children's future indicated, without fail, that they would like to see the next generation settled elsewhere, anywhere, but not in their village. When asked about the most preferred job for their children, the concern for job security trumped other concerns of the remuneration package. The preference was quite evidently in favour of government jobs in big urban towns. One of the ladies we spoke to in Sikkim (Chapter 8) aptly remarked: 'If only I were born a few years later'. There were some instances, however, where some individuals had indeed been able to move beyond the confines of their immediate concerns and craft their own future. We saw glimpses of this in Jyoti of Himachal Pradesh and Yansempa of Arunachal Pradesh (Chapter 6), where they empowered themselves to become confident entrepreneurs with focused business goals and ambitions.

The Big Picture

What was the impact of these deviations on the bigger picture of development? Was there a growing network of markets and an increasing number of participants? Were market linkages or human capabilities moving towards a qualitative transformation beyond the quantitative increments in transactions and incomes? We expected that some indication of this transformation, even if in a nascent form, would be discerned from the following three outcomes. First, access to markets should have increased significantly. Second, the institution of wage labour should have become more prevalent. Third, there should have been more inter-sectoral mobility of resources, particularly investments coming in from the modern sector, disrupting the traditional structure of the rural economy.

While access to markets had improved, it was neither inclusive nor penetrative. There was clearly a bias in favour of the landed farmers and the critical endowment needed for market access was not there for all. There was physical infrastructure being created but it catered to local needs rather than opening up the rural areas to connect to modern economic spaces. While health services seemed to be a neglected element, the importance of education in the minds of the participants and the expansion of primary education were noticeable. The importance of wage labour in rural economic activities continued to be limited. In fact, we found that rural wage rates were increasing mainly due to the presence of the government intervention of MGNREGA, and employers were trying to substitute wage labour with the use of more mechanical equipment. MGNREGA itself is indicative of the underdevelopment of the labour market and the inadequacy of rural infrastructure. Inter-sectoral mobility of resources was poor and was not contributing to changes in technology or scales of production. From the rural sector, food products were being supplied to the modern sector and consumer goods were flowing in to avail of increasing incomes. Though strongly discouraged, distress migration was the only noteworthy indication of labour mobility to the modern sector. There was no discernible flow of investible resources into the rural areas. Despite efforts to link the villages with the rest of India through markets, we observed that the beneficiaries were not capable of leveraging the linkages to change their lives independently.

Micro-interventions were designed to act as a catalyst for transformation since, left to its own devices, the process of capitalist economic growth was not enough to pull the rural sector out of its traditional mould. However, there was no convincing evidence of a transformative process being triggered by the micro-interventions. It would, therefore, be difficult to conclude that these interventions were powerful enough to break up or disrupt the traditional economy, forge enduring links with the modern sector and ultimately become indistinguishable from it.

If transformation were not discernible, could it imply a situation where this transformation was merely delayed and had the potential to occur later? One indication of this possibility would be in the coexistence of traditional economic activities with modern organisations, technologies and institutions. These were absent in the rural areas. One exception was in Gujarat (Chapter 10), where BAIF was able to set up a modern organisation using state-of-the-art technology of food processing, creating a branded portfolio of products and taking it to an all-India market. However, the economic structure was based on traditional small peasant farming, which was turning out to be unsustainable without the support of BAIF.

Instead of finding a seamless and growing connectivity with market networks, we found a sector that appeared to be increasingly bounded as far as the movement towards modernity was concerned. It was a system from which exit was difficult. The macro picture that emerged were islands of exclusive rural hamlets, supported through the largesse of the government or other philanthropic sources. Yet, an unimpeded view of the unattainable modern sector was available for all. There were concerted efforts to stop or contain distress migration by providing improved sources of livelihood and marginally better amenities. *Including* more people in this type of development simultaneously implied *excluding* them from most of the fruits of modern economic growth. We characterise this feature of the development interventions, however well meaning it may be, as one of inclusive exclusion. For those without a meaningful exit option, the benefits of modernisation were not within reach, and they represented what Bauman (2004) refers to as the unusable wastes of modernity.

We have argued that the traditional sector was neither being transformed nor was there a growing presence of modern institutions that had the potential to disrupt the traditional structures. Could it be possible then that there was *change* going on but *transformation* was impossible?

The creation of a diversified set of livelihood activities was providing only incremental incomes for the participants. When practised by small and marginal landholders the ability to scale up these essentially private activities was severely limited. Moreover, financial assistance came primarily as loans supplemented to some extent by resources generated by the savings of the SHGs. The kind of capacity creation activities were all geared to meeting local demand and requirements. With increased horticulture and cattle rearing, the local consumption of such goods had also increased. So it was as if a system was emerging where the increased incomes generated in the sector would be spent mainly on food, local products and a few urban consumer goods. Links through the exchange of commodities did exist, but they were quite tenuous.

One possible conclusion could be that the interventions were merely about minor changes in a closed and contained rural economy with very little penetrative links with the modern sector.

Another Development

This is not to suggest that the modern–urban and the rural–traditional are rigidly separated. Just as exchange possibilities existed in terms of movements of goods and services, the possibility of exit, however small, also existed. Some people of the next generation were going out for higher education and non-rural jobs. In Chhattisgarh and Andhra Pradesh (Chapters 9, 11), we met farmers whose sons were software engineers in the United States of America (USA). In Kerala (Chapter 7), a young person from a fishing village was going to a marine engineering college and was trained in Visakhapatnam and Mumbai. None of the fishermen wanted their children to take up their profession, and would be very happy to see them in jobs anywhere else in India. In Sikkim (Chapter 8), the villagers felt that ecotourism would provide exposure to their children on what the outside world was like. This would influence them to stay in school to learn good English that, in turn, would enable them to get a job in faraway cities just like the tourists who visited them.

From all our conversations, we were left with the powerful impression that people strongly believed that there was a better life outside the confines of their village. They were unable to indicate what the constituents of the better life exactly were, except for describing the image of city life that they saw on their television screens and the opportunities to work in urban environments, especially in government jobs. It was also clear to them that their ability to acquire adequate resources for their own exit were severely limited. Hence, they desired their children to attain what they were unlikely to achieve in their own lifetimes. They just wanted their children to exit the rural sector and it was in this sense that urban–modern spaces, though seemingly formless, was the desirable 'Other'. The better life was much more than mere changes in income and wealth. In Nidhal (Chapter 3), where a lot of villagers had actually settled outside the rural sector, a desired objective of transformation was to change their own village into an urban space to formally get it classified as a town.

One feature of the quality of life for their children that people repeatedly articulated was the importance of having a government job anywhere in urban India. In Rajasthan (Chapter 5), an illiterate farmer was sending her two children to a private school in a different village so they could study and get government jobs. This was perhaps a reflection of their own uncertain existence, where the concerns for stability of earnings trumped other considerations when choosing what they thought was best for their offspring.

There was some evidence of qualitative transformation in the rare instance as well. Villages in Chhattisgarh (Chapter 11) had come a long way from the time when children went to school with only a drink of *mahua* (a local intoxicant) since there was no food. The possibility of a disruptive change persisted in Gujarat (Chapter 10) as the modern Valsad Agricultural Producers Company Limited (VAPCOL) slowly pene-trated individual farmlands through the farmers' cooperatives, moving from barter to monetary exchange to branded goods for national markets.

There were instances, too, where the power of human agency was evident, both at the individual and collective levels. We saw in Himachal Pradesh and Arunachal Pradesh (Chapter 6) the success stories of individuals with an aspiration to change their immediate lot, their ambitions evolving not from listening to stories or looking at role models but through their own experiences. Their success was bringing about a quiet revolution in the lives of many other women in the states. In Bardhaman (Chapter 4), though the sustainability of the watershed was in doubt, the learning from this experience gave the Village Watershed Committee (VWC) members enough courage and confidence to reach out to other villages and offer their consulting services for similar projects. In East Godavari (Chapter 12) we found local people directly involved with the mini hydel project, engaging with ideas of looking for opportunities beyond the project at hand such as large irrigation projects. Some of them also realised that to make these possibilities come true participation in politics was a pre-requisite and they nurtured their own political ambitions.

This belief mixed with desire could be interpreted as a very nascent form of agency. Its transformative power was absent because there was neither a destination nor a road map of change although the movement away from the here and now was deemed necessary. One could think about agency in both individual as well as collec-tive ways. Differences in power, access to resources and social con-texts could yield wide variations in the incidence of agency, though it could be universally present in some form. According to Sewell: 'Agency ... characterizes all persons. But the agency exercised by persons is collective in both its sources and its mode of exercise. Personal agency is, therefore, laden with collectively produced differences of power and implicated in collective struggles and resistances' (1922: 22). It varies in form and extent as well and is not distributed homogeneously in a given pool of people.

> It is equally important, however, to insist that the agency exercised by different persons is far from uniform, that agency differs enormously in both kind and extent. What kinds of desires people can have, what intentions they can form, and what sorts of creative transpositions they can carry out vary dramatically from one social world to another depending on the nature of the particular structures that inform those social worlds . . . . Occupancy of different social positions — as defined, for example, by gender, wealth, social prestige, class, ethnicity, occupation, generation, sexual preference or education — gives people knowledge of different schemas and access to different kinds and amounts of resources and hence different possibilities for transformative actions. (ibid.: 21–22)

It is this presence of human agency that does not entirely negate the possibility of transformative change. The ability of people to dream of alternatives, however vague, and even if for future generations only, is important. We observed that inadequate empowerment to change the present did not deter desires to at least see (if not create) a new future. The nature and direction of changes brought about by this nascent human agency was not easy to discern in the rural sector. Yet there was some change, and this story of change could be described as *another development* because it was distinct from the pattern of change in the urban-modern world. For the people residing in the villages, *another development* was something nebulous to be found in someplace else at some other time.

Looking into the Future

The outcomes of *another development* are not easy to predict. Multiple patterns of change could lead to multiple sets of outcomes in different locations.

Change could emerge as a consequence of the accumulation of frustrated expectations. Increasing income inequality both within the sector and across sectors could provide a trigger for unattained ambitions to become fuel for discord. The reach of the electronic media through the ubiquitous dish antennas allowed everyone to imagine life outside the rural confines. This could serve as the opium for the masses (Marx 2009) in the short run, lulling them into inaction. This imagined life could also become the source of discontent in the event of repeated unavailability of transformation opportunities and the greater consciousness of human agency. In many of our field visits we found evidence of Maoist activities, yet the local populace did not seem perturbed by their proximity or presence. The alarm and concern shown by the media and government about the Maoist insurgence was not echoed, even remotely, when we spoke to people in Chhattisgarh and Andhra Pradesh, both in East Godavari and Chittoor (Chapters 9, 11 and 13). Rather, it could be that the Maoists talked of different possibilities and they could be viewed by the local people as harbingers of revolutionary change.

Another possible outcome could be a collapse of the natural eco-system which supports the entire spectrum of rural livelihood opportunities. While we saw a conscious attempt to preserve the natural environment by promoting its instrumental value and creating natural assets to provide an income stream, several contradictions were evident. While trees were being planted to recharge the groundwater, subsidies were being availed of to sink bore wells for extracting the water. The lack of water was a recurrent theme in all the places we visited. Tree plantation, for horticulture and timber, was encouraged, yet little thought seems to have gone into the long-term impact of such monoculture. New species of cows and goats were introduced to increase yields but we saw no concern with regard to their effect on the biodiversity of the region. Even decisions such as restricting ruminants to stall feeding or providing them dry feed with additional nutrients and not allowing them to graze to 'protect' the commons could have long ranging implications for the animals as well as for the lands in which they hitherto grazed. There were several examples where the common land was increasingly evolving into restricted land, accessible to a select few, which could lead to over exploitation.

We also saw the likelihood of a completely different outcome where the repeated experiments with *participatory* development, however superficial or mechanical they may have been, would eventually lead to new voices and new questions being raised. That would lead to a more substantial democratic engagement with other kinds of stake-holders of development interventions. A new kind of politics could emerge. The relationship of human beings with nature also could evolve to restore the balance between its intrinsic and instrumental worth. It would be a different empowerment of a deeper kind that could herald changes at the grass-roots level, where transformation would emerge from within.

Bibliography

Alsop, R., Bertelsen, M. F. and J. Holland. 2006. 'Empowerment in Practice: From Analysis to Implementation', World Bank-free PDF. http://siteresources. worldbank.org/INTEMPOWERMENT/Resources/Empowerment_in_ Practice.pdf (accessed on 6 February 2014).

Amin, Samir. 1976. *Unequal Development*. London: Monthly Review Press.

Angeles, Leonara. 2011. 'Participatory Development', in T. Forsyth (ed.), *Encyclopedia of International Development*, pp. 506–11. London and New York: Routledge.

Appadurai, A. 2004. 'The Capacity to Aspire: Culture and the Terms of Recognition', in V. Rao and M. Walton (eds), *Culture and Public Action*, pp. 59–84. Stanford: Stanford University Press.

Baocchi, G. 2011. 'Talking Politics in Participatory Governance', in Andrea Cornwall (ed.), *The Participation Reader*, pp. 306–21. London: Zed Books.

Baran Paul, A. and E. J. Hobsbawm. 1961. 'The Stages of Economic Growth', *Kyklos*, 14(2): 234–42.

Bardhan, Pranab. 1988. 'Alternative Approaches to Development Economics', in Chenery Hollis and T. N. Srinivasan (eds), *Handbook of Development Economics*, Vol. 1, pp. 39–71. Oxford: Elsevier.

Bateman, M. 2010. *Why Doesn't Microfinance Work? The Destructive Rise of Local Neoliberalism*. New York: Zed Books.

Bauman, Zygmunt. 2004. *Wasted Lives: Modernity and It Outcasts*. Cambridge: Polity.

———. 2013. *Society Under Siege*. Cambridge: Polity.

Bebbington, Anthony. 1999. 'Capitals and Capabilities: A Framework for Analyzing Peasant Viability, Rural Livelihoods and Poverty', *World Development*, 27(12): 2021–44.

Brewer, Anthony. 1980. *Marxist Theories of Imperialism: A Critical Survey*. London: Routledge & Kegan Paul.

Chambers, R. 1997. *Whose Reality Counts? Putting the First Last*. London: Intermediate Technology Publications.

———. 2011. 'Managing Local Participation: Rhetoric and Reality', in Andrea Cornwall (ed.), *The Participation Reader*, pp. 165–71. London: Zed Books.

Chambers, R. and G. Conway. 1992. 'Sustainable Rural Livelihoods: Practical Concepts for the 21st Century', IDS Discussion Paper 296. http://opendocs. ids.ac.uk/opendocs/bitstream/handle/123456789/775/Dp296.pdf (accessed on 5 February 2014).

Chatterjee, Partha. 2008. 'Democracy and Economic Transformation in India', *Economic & Political Weekly*, 43(16): 53–62.

Choudhary, S. 2012. *Let's Call Him Vasu: With the Maoists in Chhattisgarh*. New Delhi: Penguin Books.

Das, Keshab. 2011. 'Rural Industrialization in India: Enhancing Reach and Returns', in *Micro and Small Enterprises in India: The Era of Reforms*, pp. 208–24. New Delhi: Routledge.

Dasgupta, P. 2001. *Human Well-being and the Natural Environment*. New Delhi: Oxford University Press.

———. 2010. 'Nature and the Economy', in *Selected Papers of Partha Dasgupta*, Vol. 2, pp. 444–68. Oxford: Oxford University Press.

Datta, S. and V. Sharma (eds). 2009. *State of India's Livelihoods: The 4P Report*. New Delhi: Access Development Services.

Di Vincenzo, F. and D. Mascia. 2012. 'Social Capital in Project-based Organizations: Its Role, Structure, and Impact on Project Performance', *International Journal of Project Management*, 30(1): 5–14.

Dietrich, Perttu, Mikko H. Lehtonen and Päivi Lehtonen. 2007. 'A Contextual Model for Researching Temporary Organizations', Paper submitted to the 19th Nordic Academy of Management Conference (NFF), 9–11 August, 2007, Bergen, Norway. http://www.nhh.no/Files/Filer/institutter/for/ conferences/nff/papers/lehtonen-m.pdf (accessed on 5 February 2014).

Dreze, J. and A. Sen. 1995. *India Economic Development and Social Opportunity*. New Delhi: Oxford University Press.

———. 2002. *India Development and Participation*. New Delhi: Oxford University Press.

ECOSS. 2007. Ecotourism and Conservation Society of Sikkim Newsletter, October 2006 – March 2007. http://www.stanford.edu/class/msande75si/ ecoss3.pdf (accessed on 6 February 2014).

Eisenhardt, K. M. and M. E. Graebner. 2007. 'Theory Building from Cases: Opportunities and Challenges', *Academy of Management Journal*, 50(1): 25–32.

Escobar, Arturo. 1997. 'Anthropology and Development', *International Social Science Journal*, 49(154): 497–515.

Ferguson, J. 1994. *The Anti-Politics Machine "Development," Depoliticization, and Bureaucratic Power in Lesotho*. Minneapolis: University of Minnesota Press.

Foucault, Michel. 1980. *Power/Knowledge: Selected Interviews and Other Writings 1972–1977*, edited by Colin Gordon. New York: Pantheon Books.

Frank, A. G. 1978. *Dependent Accumulation and Underdevelopment*. London: Macmillan.

Frankel, Francine R. 1971. *India's Green Revolution: Economic Gains and Political Costs*. Princeton: Princeton University Press.

Furtado, C. 1973. 'Elements of a Theory of Underdevelopment — The Under-developed Structures', in Henry Bernstein (ed.), *Underdevelopment and Development: The Third World Today*, Harmondsworth: Penguin.

Ganeriwal, Ramesh and Atul Bharadwaj. 2011. 'Small Projects, Big Impacts: Micro and Mini Hydel Projects of Himachal Pradesh Dams', *Rivers and People*. http://www.sandrp.in/drp/April%20May%202011.pdf (accessed on 12 February 2014).

Giddens, Anthony. 1971. *Capitalism and Modern Social Theory: An Analysis of the Writings of Marx, Durkheim and Max Weber*. Cambridge: Cambridge University Press.

Glaser, Barney G. and Anselm L. Strauss. 1967. *The Discovery of Grounded Theory: Strategies for Qualitative Research*. Chicago: Aldine Publishing Company.

Grabher, G. 2002. 'Cool Projects, Boring Institutions: Temporary Collaboration in Social Context', *Regional Studies*, 36(3): 205–14.

Graebner, M. E. 2009. 'Caveat Venditor: Trust Asymmetries in Acquisitions of Entrepreneurial Firms', *Academy of Management Journal*, 52(3): 435–72.

Gramsci, Antonio. 1971. *Selections from the Prison Notebooks*. Translated and edited by Quintin Hoare and Geoffrey Nowell Smith. New York: International Publishers.

Grillo, R. D. and R. L. Stirrat (eds). 1997. *Discourses of Development: Anthropological Perspectives*. Oxford: Berg.

Harikumar, G. and G. Rajendran. 2007. 'An Over View of Kerala Fisheries with Particular Emphasis on Aquaculture', *IFP Souvenir*, pp. 39–58, National Institute of Fisheries Post Harvest Technology and Training. http://ifpkochi.nic.in/IFPS2.pdf (accessed on 6 February 2014).

Harris-White, Barbara. 1999. 'State, Market, Collective and Household Sector in India's Social Sector', in Barbara Harris-White and S. Subramanian (eds), *Illfare in India: Essays on India's Social Sector in Honour of S. Guhan*, pp. 303–28. New Delhi: Sage Publications.

Harris-White, Barbara and S. Subramanian (ed.). 1999. *Illfare in India: Essays on India's Social Sector in Honour of S. Guhan*. New Delhi: Sage Publications.

Healy, Hali, Joan Martínez-Alier, Leah Temper, Mariana Walter, and Julien-François Gerber. 2013. *Ecological Economics from the Ground Up*. London: Routledge.

ENVIS Sikkim Centre. 2014. http://ces.iisc.ernet.in/hpg/envis/envis_centres/homepages/sikkim.htm (accessed on 11 February 2014).

IDFC Rural Development Network. 2013. *India Rural Development Report 2012|13*. New Delhi: Orient Blackswan.

Indira Gandhi National Centre for the Arts (IGNCA). 1999. 'Art and Crafts of North East'. http://ignca.nic.in/craft201.htm (accessed on 6 February 2014).

Institute of Rural Management Anand (IRMA). 2007. *Adivasi Development Programme: Valsad and Dang District Gujarat Evaluation III*, Unpublished report submitted to NABARD, Mumbai.

Johnson, Craig. 2009. *Arresting Development: The Power of Knowledge for Social Change*. London and New York: Routledge.

Joshi, V. and I. M. D. Little. 1994. *India Macroeconomics and Political Economy 1964–1991*. Delhi: Oxford University Press.

Kay, J. 1975. *Development and Underdevelopment: A Marxist Analysis*. London: ELBS and Macmillan.

Leal, P. A. 2011. 'Participation: The Ascendancy of a Buzzword in the Neo-liberal Era', in Andrea Cornwall (ed.), *The Participation Reader*, pp. 70–84. London: Zed Books.

Lewis, W. A. 1954. 'Economic Development with Unlimited Supplies of Labour', *The Manchester School of Economic and Social Studies*, 22(2): 139–91.

———. 1979. 'The Dual Economy Revisited', *The Manchester School of Economic and Social Studies*, 47(3): 211–29.

———. 1988. 'The Roots of Development Theory', in Chenery Hollis and T. N. Srinivasan (eds), *Handbook of Development Economics*, Vol. 1, pp. 27–37. Oxford: Elsevier.

Lipton, Michael. 1977. *Why Poor People Stay Poor: A Study of Urban Bias in World Development*. London: Temple Smith.

Lundin, Rolf A. and Anders Söderholm. 1995. 'A Theory of the Temporary Organization', *Scandinavian Journal of Management*, 11(4): 437–55.

Lyotard, Jean-Francois. 1984. *The Postmodern Condition: A Report on Knowledge*, trans. Geoff Bennington and Brian Mssumi. Manchester: Manchester University Press.

Marx, Karl. 1965. *Pre-capitalist Economic Formations*, 2nd ed., edited by E. J. Hobsbawn. London: Lawrence and Wishart.

———. 1973. *Grundrisse*. New York: Vintage.

———. 1998. 'The German Ideology', in *Literary Theory: An Anthology*, 2nd ed., pp. 653–58. Oxford: Blackwell.

Marx, Karl. 2009. 'A Contribution to the Critique of Hegel's Philosophy of Right: Introduction', in Joseph O'Malley (ed.) and Annette Jolin and Joseph O'Malley (trans.), *Critique of Hegel's Philosophy of Right*. Cambridge: Cambridge University Press.

Meillassoux, Claude. 1983. 'The Economic Bases of Demographic Reproduction: From the Domestic Mode of Production to Wage-earning', *The Journal of Peasant Studies*, 11(1): 50–61.

Midgley, J. 2011. 'Community Participation: History, Concepts and Controversies', in Andrea Cornwall (ed.), *The Participation Reader*, pp. 172–81. London: Zed Books.

Mohan, G. 2011. 'Participatory Development', in R. Potter and V. Desai (eds), *The Companion to Development Studies*, 2nd ed., pp. 45–50. London: Hodder Education.

Mohan, Rakesh. 2008. 'Growth Record of the Indian Economy, 1950–2008: A Story of Sustained Savings and Investment', *Economic and Political Weekly*, 42(19): 61–71.

Mohanty, M. 1995. 'On the Concept of "Empowerment"', *Economic and Political Weekly*, 30(24): 1434–36.

Mohanty, R. 2011. 'The Politics of Domesticating Participation in Rural India', in Andrea Cornwall (ed.), *The Participation Reader*, pp. 265–80. London: Zed Books.

Moore, Barrington Jr. 1966. *The Social Origins of Dictatorship and Democracy*. Boston: Beacon Press.

Mosse, D. 2011. 'The Making and Marketing of Participatory Development', in Andrea Cornwall (ed.), *The Participation Reader*, pp. 182–202. London: Zed Books.

Narayan, D. and E. Glinskaya. 2007. *Ending Poverty in South Asia: Ideas that Work*. Washington, DC: World Bank.

Narayan, Deepa, Robert Chambers, Meera K. Shah, and Patti Petesch. 2000. *Voices of the Poor: Crying Out for Change*. New York: Oxford University Press for the World Bank.

National Bank for Agriculture and Rural Development (NABARD). 2014. https://www.nabard.org/english/mission.aspx (accessed on 3 February 2014).

———. 2014a. https://www.nabard.org/english/UPNRM4.aspx (accessed on 3 September 2014).

National Rainfed Area Authority (NRAA). 2013. CEO's Message. http://nraa.gov.in/ (accessed on 6 February 2014).

O'Connor, J. 1998. *Natural Causes: Essays in Ecological Marxism*. New York: The Guildford Press.

Ostrom, E. 1992. 'Community and the Endogenous Solution of Commons Problems', *Journal of Theoretical Politics*, 4(3): 343–51.

Parpart, Jane. 2011. 'Rethinking Gender and Empowerment', in V. Desai and R. B. Potter, *The Companion to Development Studies*, 2nd ed. London: Hodder Education.

Planning Commission. 2011. *India Human Development Report 2011: Towards Social Inclusion*. New Delhi: Oxford University Press.

Polanyi, Karl. 1944. *The Great Transformation*. Boston: Beacon Press.

Rawls, John. 1971. *A Theory of Justice*. Harvard: The Belknap Press of Harvard University Press.

Sanyal, K. 2007. *Rethinking Capitalist Development: Primitive Accumulation, Governmentality and Post-colonial Capitalism*. New Delhi: Routledge.

Scoones, Ian. 1998. 'Sustainable Rural Livelihoods: A Framework for Analysis', IDS Working Paper, No. 72, Institute of Development Studies, Sussex.

———. 2010. 'Livelihoods, Perspectives and Rural Development', in S. M. Borras Jr (ed.), *Crtitical Perspectives in Rural Development Studies*, pp. 159–84. Oxon: Routledge.

Sen, Amartya. 1977. 'Rational Fools: A Critique of the Behavioral Foundations of Economic Theory', *Philosophy & Public Affairs*, 6(4): 317–44.

———. 1985. *Commodities and Capabilities*. Amsterdam: North-Holland.

———. 1988. 'The Concept of Development', in Hollis Chenery and T. N. Srinivasan (eds), *Handbook of Development Economics*, 1st ed., Vol. I, pp. 9–26. with Amsterdam: North-Holland.

———. 1999. *Development as Freedom*. New Delhi: Oxford University Press.

———. 2003. *Rationality and Freedom*. New Delhi: Oxford University Press.

———. 2006. *Identity and Violence the Illusion of Destiny*. London: Allen Lane.

Sewell, William H. Jr. 1992. 'A Theory of Structure: Duality, Agency and Transformation', *American Journal of Sociology*, 98(1): 1–29.

Shah, Dilip. 2005. 'Sustainable Tribal Development Model Case of WADI', Department of Economic Analysis and Research Occasional Paper-43, NABARD, Mumbai.

Sheppard, Eric, Philip W. Porter, David R. Faust, and Richa Nagar. 2009. *A World of Difference:Encountering and Contesting Development*. New York: The Guilford Press.

Skinner, Quentin (ed.). 1985. *The Return of Grand Theory in the Human Sciences*. Cambridge: Cambridge University Press.

Streeten, P. and Lipton, M. 1968. *The Crisis of Indian Planning, Economic Policy in the 1960s*. London: Oxford University Press.

Taylor, J. 1979. *From Modernization to Mode of Production*. London: Macmillan.

The Times of India. 2013. 'Sikkim has Maximum Unemployed; Chhattisgarh Lowest'. http://articles.timesofindia.indiatimes.com/2013-09-19/india/ 42216929_1_unemployment-rate-sikkim-labour-bureau (accessed on 11 February 2014).

Turner, J. Rodney and Ralf Müller. 2003. 'On the Nature of the Project as a Temporary Organization', *International Journal of Project Management*, 21(1): 1–8.

Udaipur Times. 2011. http://www.udaipurtimes.com/mines-close-starving-workers-protest/, 5 September (accessed on 6 February 2014).

Wallerstein, Immanuel. 1979. *The Capitalist World Economy*. Cambridge: Cambridge University Press.

Warren, Bill. 1980. *Imperialism: Pioneer of Capitalism*. London: Verso.

Waters, Malcolm. 1999. *Modernity Critical Concepts in Sociology*. London and New York: Routledge.

White, S. 2011. 'Depoliticising Development: The Uses and Abuses of Participation', in Andrea Cornwall (ed.), *The Participation Reader*, pp. 57–69. London: Zed Books.

Williams, G. 2011. 'Towards a Repoliticisation of Participatory Development: Political Capabilities and Spaces of Empowerment', in Andrea Cornwall (ed.), *The Participation Reader*. London: Zed Books.

WWF. 2014. Khangchendzonga Landscape. http://www.wwfindia.org/about_ wwf/critical_regions/khangchendzonga/ (accessed on 17 February 2014).

Yin, R. K. (ed.). 2003. *Case Study Research: Designs and Methods*, 3rd ed.. Thousand Oaks, CA: Sage Publications.

About the Authors

Runa Sarkar is Associate Professor of Economics, Indian Institute of Management Calcutta. Prior to this, she taught at Indian Institute of Technology Kanpur. A chemical engineer from Birla Institute of Technology and Science Pilani, she pursued her Masters in environmental engineering at the University of North Carolina at Chapel Hill, USA. After a five year stint as an environmental consultant with a subsidiary of Tata Steel, she graduated from the Fellow Program at the Indian Institute of Management Calcutta. Her interests lie in exploring corporate sustainability. She has been closely involved in European Union and World Bank projects on the application of social informatics in agriculture and is currently on the board of two companies of the BASIX group.

Anup Sinha is Professor of Economics, Indian Institute of Management Calcutta. He was educated at Presidency College and University of Rochester. He did his doctoral work at the University of Southern California. He has taught at the Centre for Economic Studies, Presidency College and held visiting appointments in a number of institutions in India and abroad. His academic interests and publications are in the areas of sustainable development, ethics, and macroeconomics. He was Dean, Indian Institute of Management Calcutta and has also served as a non-executive Director on the Board of National Bank for Agriculture and Rural Development.

Index

accumulation economy 12–14

Adivasi 70, 72, 78, 79

Arun Kutir Udyog Cooperative Society (AKUCS) 117

animal husbandry 80, 83, 86, 98–99, 111, 173, 175

Apatani 117, 119

Andhra Pradesh Tribal Power Company Limited (APTRIPCO) 238, 240–46, 252

Ayojan Samiti 194–99, 203, 212

azolla 175, 177

BAIF 84, 92, 192, 212

belief, belief systems 1, 4, 22, 63, 108, 217, 255, 273

bicholiyas 218

biodiversity 127, 147, 201, 264, 275

biogas 80, 91, 114, 177, 182, 205, 224, 264

'blocked dialectic' 11–12

business model 98, 104, 111, 124, 153, 160, 167, 172, 264

cage cultivation 141–43

capacity creation 6, 271

capital accumulation 5, 9, 11, 14, 25

capitalism 5–13, 257

carrying capacity 145

caste 24, 53, 63, 67, 77, 79, 82, 141, 158, 179–80, 186, 214

change: quantitative 6, 257; transformative 31, 274; incremental 26, 233, 257; structural 10, 18

Chenchu 173

civil society 13

class 1, 8, 19, 24, 33, 44, 72, 82, 158, 176, 179, 190, 213, 217, 261, 274

coercion 11–12, 14

collective action 32, 43, 61, 63, 67, 71, 79, 145, 231, 236, 254, 256

common property resources 12, 27, 141, 143, 189, 231, 236, 266

commons 19, 26, 38, 85, 87, 90, 129, 176, 187, 190, 211, 231, 264–65, 275

community 21, 23–24, 27, 38, 45, 58, 63, 79, 82, 102, 158, 195, 216, 265

conservation 27–28, 37, 55, 87, 149, 167, 170, 176, 190, 194, 211, 267

convergence 33, 171, 175–76, 225, 230

cooperatives 51, 79, 119–23, 171, 195–96, 198–99, 207–10, 262, 273

core-periphery 5–6, 9–10, 15

Council for Advancement of People's Action and Rural Technology (CAPART) 218

credit 17, 28, 96, 103, 129, 176, 195, 212, 216, 257–61, 267

culture 1, 21, 32, 148–49, 159, 167, 167

deprivation 13, 16–17

development: bottom-up approach 170, 230; top down approach 17, 84, 99, 170

development agency 28, 171

development as transformation 1–5, 15, 18, 30, 257

development interventions 19, 22, 25, 27, 102, 126, 230–31, 265–66, 271, 276

development strategy 16–18

development: taxonomy 5–6

distress migration 87, 185, 188, 203, 205, 228, 233, 260, 270, 271

distribution 2, 3, 8, 25, 27, 104, 146, 163, 189, 246

diversification of livelihoods 19, 24–25, 38, 80, 127, 143, 145, 148, 210, 262, 268

District Rural Development Authority (DRDA) 173, 183, 188

ecology 32–33, 237
economic Growth 2, 16, 270–71
ecosystem services 26
ecotourism 32, 104, 148–52, 261, 265–66, 272
Ecotourism and Conservation Society of Sikkim (ECOSS) 148
ecotourist 151, 154, 165
empowerment 18, 31, 102–03, 105–06, 124–25, 138, 164, 194, 233, 257, 274, 276
entitlement 27
entrepreneur 71, 103–04, 106, 111, 121, 124, 138, 160, 194, 213, 269
entrepreneurship 103–04, 223
environment 19, 24, 26–27, 32, 51, 53, 104, 117, 148, 161, 184, 189, 272, 275
environmental assets 12
Erugula 173

feudal 4, 8
financial inclusion 17, 39, 52, 90, 175, 214, 216, 218, 230, 258, 260, 262–63
fishing 24, 70, 103, 127, 129–44, 261, 272
Foundation for Ecological Security (FES) 84

Gameti 85
Gandhi Smaraka Grama Seva Kendram (GSGSK) 131
Garasiya 85
generations 3, 27, 54, 97, 168, 180, 183, 187, 224, 269, 272, 274
governance 11, 13, 84, 87, 91, 143, 160, 221, 226, 255, 263
Gram Vikas Mandal (GVM) 195, 197
Green Revolution 16, 61

hegemony 11–12, 14
horticulture 33, 71, 178, 210, 271

human agency 9, 12–15, 26–27, 31, 273–75
human capabilities 17, 257, 265, 269
hybrid structures 4, 15, 257

identity 77, 230
Indira Awas Yojana 250
Indo-German Watershed Development Programme (IGWDP) 37, 41, 80
industrialisation 2
inequality 25, 60, 79, 145, 172, 232, 261, 274
infrastructure 16–17, 28, 98, 126, 143, 163, 175, 216, 218, 221, 243, 257, 262–65, 270
instrumental value of nature 26, 162, 264–65, 275–76
Integrated Child Development Services (ICDS) 108–09
intervention: micro 18, 27, 30, 189, 270
intrinsic value of nature 162, 264–65, 276
investment 4, 6, 16–17, 141, 167, 175, 243, 260, 269
Integrated Tribal Development Area (ITDA) 238

Joint Forest Management (JFM) 38, 82, 205
Joint Liability Groups (JLG) 77, 114, 132, 175, 216, 259

Kisan Credit Card (KCC) 204, 216, 222
KfW (German Development Bank) 31, 37, 80, 83, 212
Kisan Club 109, 114, 214, 222–24, 226, 229, 231
Koidara 252
Kokna 192, 205
Kolcha 192, 202, 204

landless 55, 68, 163, 175–76, 178, 180–81, 183–86, 190, 198–99, 203, 224, 231, 261
Lepchas 157, 159, 166-7, 262
liberties 1–2

license raj 16
livelihoods 12–14, 17, 19, 23, 27–30, 63, 80, 87, 95, 97, 117, 127, 130, 143, 145, 157, 175–76
livelihoods: alternative opportunities 78, 83, 159, 189, 262
livelihoods Approach 20, 24–25
livestock 24, 33, 36–38, 127, 182, 205

Mahajan 74
market: access 14, 17, 25, 33, 70–71, 79, 104–05, 141, 171, 189, 257–58, 260
market:linkage 49, 71, 74, 211, 216, 269, 271
market friendly interventions 257
,market-friendly approach 17, 257
merchant 51, 68, 120
merchant capital 10
microenterprise 17, 24–25, 103, 105, 195, 216
microfinance 28, 63, 68–69, 132
migration 27, 43, 45, 54, 57, 59, 69, 86, 148, 159, 205, 210
migration: distress 57, 87, 185, 188, 203, 205, 228, 233, 260, 270–71; temporary 41, 58, 97, 210
mini hydel power plants (MHPPs) 236, 238, 273
mining 95
Mitra Association for Social Service (MASS) 176–80
Mahatma Gandhi National Rural Employment Guarantee Act (MGNREGA) 55–56, 67, 74, 85, 91, 97, 206, 260, 270
modern sector 4,7, 27, 260, 269, 270–71
modernity 5, 7, 11, 13–14, 32, 165, 213, 271
moneylenders 32, 52–53, 67, 74, 129, 131–32, 134, 144, 218, 259

natural assets 26, 68, 78–79, 148, 167, 170–71, 188, 257, 264, 275
natural capital 26, 33, 65, 72, 148, 190, 236, 264–65

natural resources 4, 11, 27, 33, 127, 149, 175, 188–90, 194, 216, 236, 265
need economy 12–14
networks 21, 32, 71, 102, 117, 173, 255, 263, 268, 271
non-capital 6, 13
Non-conventional Energy Development Corporation of Andhra Pradesh Limited (NEDCAP) 178, 238

Panchayati Raj Institutions (PRIs) 105, 216, 263
participation 20, 23, 31, 37, 60, 82, 102, 106, 140, 170–72, 191, 213–14, 240, 256, 266–69
participatory development 22–24, 256, 275
participatory management 84
Participatory Rural Appraisal (PRA) 216
passive revolution 11
peasant farming 129, 270
persuasion 11–12, 14
Project Management Unit (PMU) 31, 83–85
policies 3, 17, 143
politics 23, 31, 53–54, 61, 68, 72, 77, 79
portfolio diversification 99, 129
portfolio of activities 14, 24
portfolio of assets 19, 246
poverty 9, 13–14, 16–17, 19, 23, 25, 55, 87, 105, 192, 194, 214, 260
power 8–9, 11–12, 23, 31–32, 60, 103, 116, 124, 130, 221, 233–34, 256, 267–68, 273–74
Pradhan Mantri Gram Sadak Yojana (PMGSY) 66
pre-capital 4–6, 8–12, 14
processes of change 1
production: forces of 7–8; relations of 7–8; scale 194
property 4, 12, 19, 25, 27, 85, 99, 132, 134, 141, 143–45, 162, 171, 189, 200, 262

quality of life 54, 76, 97, 175, 180, 272
quarrying 171, 184, 264

Rai 152–53, 167
Raigarh Sahyog Samiti 217
Ramoshis 57–8, 60, 261, 266
rights 1–4, 27, 85, 132–33, 145, 176, 189, 264
rural infrastructure 28, 185, 236, 270
Rural Infrastructure Development Fund (RIDF) 185, 236
Rural Innovation Fund (RIF) 109

safety net 26, 127, 224
savings 39, 52–53, 77, 92, 103, 134, 196, 258–59
self-help groups (SHG) 39, 52–53, 80, 103, 105–06, 112, 115, 139, 175, 199, 231, 258–63
self-reliance 31, 61, 125, 189
seth sahukars/ sahukars 218, 222
social capital 21, 29, 32, 258
stakeholders 29, 68, 83, 171–72, 195, 216, 238, 276
state 3, 4, 7, 10–11, 13, 16–18, 23, 27, 31–32
subsistence farming 3
Sugali 173
sustainable development 20
sustainable income flows 14
sustainable livelihoods 14, 27, 127, 262

technology 2–4, 6–7, 10, 12, 17, 23, 67, 129, 270
temporary organization 18, 20–24, 79, 83, 98, 255–56, 268
Therakan 132–35, 268
tokenism 23–24
trader 50, 208–09
traditional sector 4–7, 10–11, 213, 269, 271
transformation 1–15, 26, 172, 257, 262, 269–73, 275–76

transition 5, 7, 11–13, 31, 212
Tribal Development Project (TDP) 176, 192, 194

underdevelopment 5–6, 9–10, 14, 214, 270
United Nations Development Programme (UNDP) 13
unemployment 6, 14, 16, 147, 179
uneven development 10
United Nations Educational, Scientific and Cultural Organization (UNESCO) 148
Umbrella Project for Natural Resource Management (UPNRM) 175–76, 178
usufruct rights 85, 189, 264

valuation of natural assets 162, 190
Valsad Agricultural Producers Company Limited (VAPCOL) 196–98, 273
Village Development Plan (VDP) 171, 214, 216–21
vermicompost 67, 115, 177–78, 181–82, 186–87, 204, 211, 222, 229
Village Watershed Committee (VWC) 38–39, 44, 47, 49–51, 54–55, 57, 59, 64, 68–79, 83, 88, 91, 273
vulnerability 26, 55, 192

wadi 192, 194–95
Warli 192, 205
watershed 36–39
well-being 27, 30–31, 37, 122, 171, 254, 266
weltanschauung 4,8
World Bank 13

Yanadi 173, 176, 180, 184–86, 190–91, 266

Zawar Mines 94–97

For Product Safety Concerns and Information please contact our EU
representative GPSR@taylorandfrancis.com Taylor & Francis Verlag GmbH,
Kaufingerstraße 24, 80331 München, Germany

Printed and bound by CPI Group (UK) Ltd, Croydon, CR0 4YY
08/05/2025
01864335-0001